TABLE OF CONTENTS

ISSUE 9..3
ISSUE 10..68
ISSUE 11..134
ISSUE 12..200

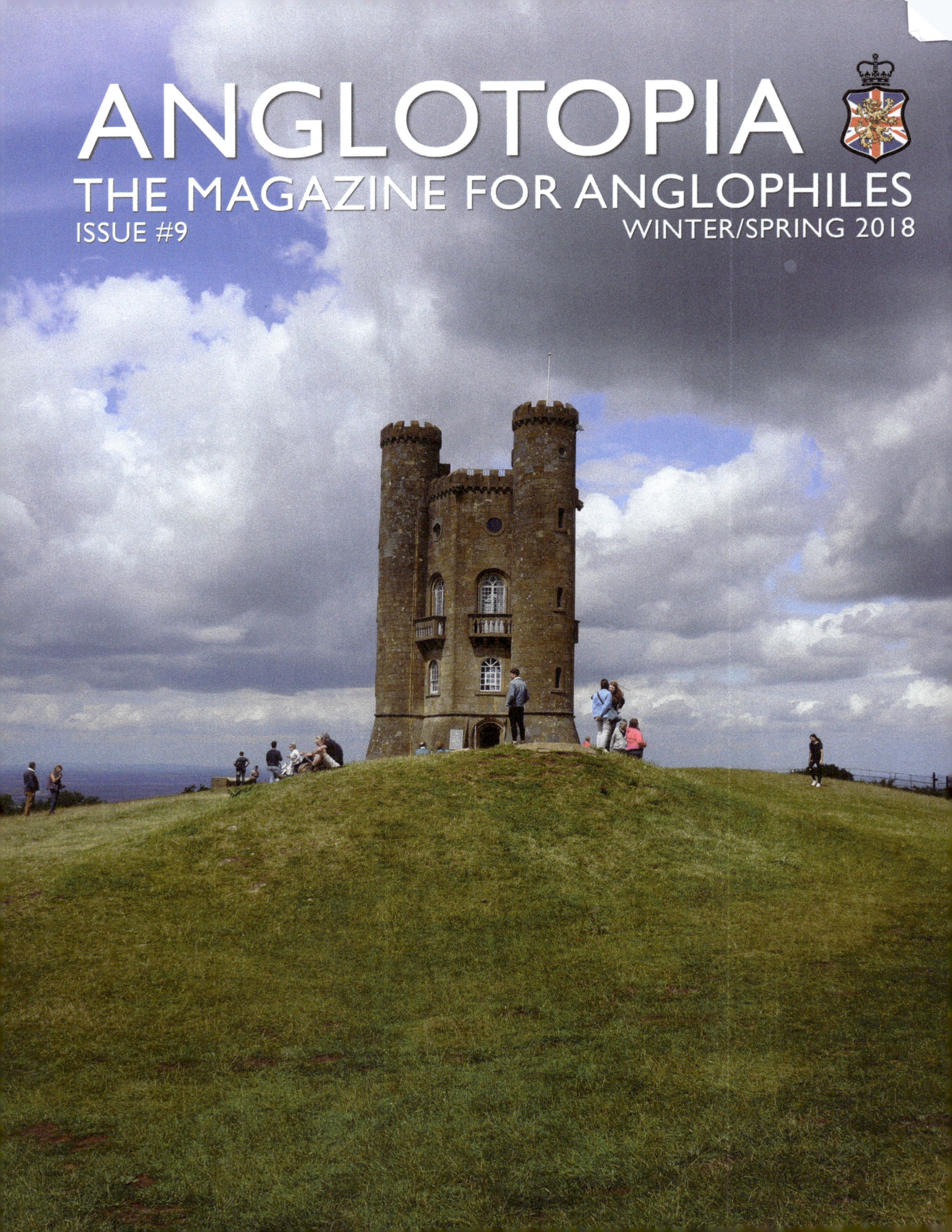

Letter from the Editors

Welcome to the third year of the Anglotopia Print Magazine. It's been a challenging and interesting experience so far, and we're looking forward to another great year of publishing long-form writing about Britain.

There will be a few incremental changes this year. We plan to introduce some new writers and features to the magazine. But the biggest change is in the design of the magazine itself. We have decided to opt for a consistent style inside and out using the Gill Sans font, a very British font that you will find all over Britain - on signs and in the media. We've also changed the copy font to Times New Roman, which was invented by the *Times of London* and became one of the most versatile fonts in the world. On the front cover, you can see our brand new logo/crest that was designed by Malcolm Watson.

We have several exciting adventures planned this year. First up - Jonathan will be going to Windsor to cover Harry's Wedding to American Meghan Markle. Royal Weddings are always exciting and rare events.

Later this year, both of us will be doing something very special; we'll be driving from Land's End in Cornwall all the way through England and Scotland to John O'Groats. It's going to be an incredible adventure, and we can't wait to share it with everyone who follows Anglotopia.

And finally, something we've been planning since the beginning of Anglotopia in 2017. In November, we're going to go on our first guided Anglotopia tour. We've partnered with Reformation Tours to offer a special Mayflower themed tour, taking in important sites related to the Mayflower Pilgrims. Details are on our website!

Cheers,
Jonathan & Jackie
Publishers
Anglotopia

Table of Contents

Living the Oxford Dream..................2
Brit Book Corner..............................12
Then & Now....................................14
The Royal Horticultural Society......16
Lost in the Pond.............................20
Britain's Iconic Bridges...................22
Great Britons: William Beveridge...32
This English Life.............................36
Great British Questions..................39
Great British Icons: Concorde........40
George IV.......................................49
Auntie Beeb: A History of the BBC..52
British Icons: Rolls-Royce..............60
Slang Page: Railways.....................64

About the Magazine

The Anglotopia Magazine is published quarterly by Anglotopia LLC, a USA registered Corporation. All contents copyrighted and may not be reproduced without permission.

Letters to the Editors may be addressed to:

Anglotopia LLC
1101 Cumberland Crossing #120
Valparaiso, IN 46383
USA

Photos: Cover: Broadway Tower Cotswolds, This Page: Dorset Coast. Back Cover: Castle Combe Wiltshire, Inside Back Cover: New Billboard in Piccadilly Circus

Printed in PRC

LIVING THE OXFORD DREAM
ONE REMARKABLE WEEK AS AN OXFORD STUDENT

By Jonathan Thomas

It was but a brief moment of my trip but a major event in someone else's life. Someone who had spent three years in Oxford, away from their family, in some cases in a completely different country, studying at the world's most prestigious university. It was surely not without its challenges. It was Diploma Day. Diploma Day is when the actual pieces of paper student spend three years at Oxford working towards are handed out. There's a ton of Oxford pomp and circumstance to this. Families come from all over the world. Each College has its own day, and I was staying at Worcester College. On Diploma Day the place was swarmed with students dressed in their formal Oxford gowns and their families dressed in formal clothes. It was quite a sight to see. And it got me thinking. It made me jealous. These students had accomplished something amazing, a degree from Oxford and now was their day to celebrate. And celebrate they did. They earned it. I was just an interloper, nibbling at the fringes of being an Oxford student.

Oxford changes in the summer. The students leave, and the tourists descend upon the city. It becomes a different place. I've visited Oxford during Term Time, and it's a quiet, studious time with students rushing about to their tutors or living their lives amongst the dreaming spires of Oxford. In the summer, they're gone save for the occasional return for their diploma day. What kinds of people visit Oxford in July? Tourists do. But not just tourists. It's a chance for students from all over the world to come to Oxford and get the Oxford Experience so they can see if it's the place for them when it's time to attend university. The colleges are filled with under-18s - many away from home for the first time.

But they're also filled with older travelers. I should know, I was one of them. People come from all over the world to soak up some of the Oxford magic and enrich themselves, culturally and academically. I was invited as a guest of the English-Speaking Union USA, an important organization that fosters understanding of the English language, its history, and its future throughout America. One of their outreach programs is the TLab which offers teachers and now interested travelers an opportunity to live in Oxford and study. I attended as part of the Future of English program. I would spend one week staying

Worcester College

at Worcester College, attending lectures in the morning and then exploring the city with guided tours in the afternoon.

When I arrived in Oxford, the first order of business was to check-in and get my rooms. I took the bus from Heathrow directly to Oxford, it took about 45 minutes. Though, how long it actually was, I'm not so sure as I fell asleep on the way. I tried like hell to sleep on the overnight flight over but for the life of me, could not fall asleep. Five minutes on a bus to Oxford and I was out like a light! The bus deposited me at the Gloucester Green bus station, a newer bit of Oxford home to the local market, a movie theatre some shops and a lot of places to eat. Thanks to hours spent pouring over maps of Oxford before the trip, I knew the exact route to walk, and within minutes, I was at Worcester College.

Worcester College was established in 1714, and it's a 'newer' college compared to many of Oxford's colleges that existed for hundreds of years more. This is reflected in the architecture which is not medieval but more Georgian, Palladian and later styles. The college is known for having the largest gardens in Oxford, and once you're inside the walls of the college, the sounds of bustling Oxford fade away, and you're in a cloistered and quiet environment the feels like paradise for learning. Some notable alumni of Worcester College include Rupert Murdoch, former "Doctor Who" showrunner Russell T Davies and US Supreme Court Justice Elena Kagan.

The University of Oxford is college based. When you apply to the university, you also apply to a college. Your college is your base while you study at Oxford. It becomes your surrogate home. It's where you study one on one with your Tutor, where you stay, where you eat and where you do your schoolwork. Lectures are run at the University level, so you attend those outside your college. Meals are served in the dining hall every day for students and visiting fellows. The menu changes and there is quite a bit of variety. Your 'loyalty' is to your college not to the university itself, and college pride runs very strong. Each college is financially independent and runs its own affairs (and has their own criteria for who they let in). Some colleges are richer than other - St John's is reportedly the richest of the colleges as they own land throughout southern England which makes them a lot of money. Exams are run at the University level and conducted

My favorite picture from Oxford

at the end of Term time. The year is divided into three 8-week terms: Michaelmas (October-December), Hilary (January to March) and Trinity (April to June). Most US universities have two terms (or semesters). Consequently, you can finish an Oxford degree in 3 years instead of 4 like at a US university.

When I arrived at the college, I was greeted by the porters at the Porters' lodge. The porters control access to the colleges - most are only open to the public a few hours a day so as visitors don't disturb the students. The porters are also responsible for caring for the students - arranging anything they need while they're students. During my stay, I found the porters to be very knowledgeable and helpful, even to 'pretend' students like me. In addition to the porters, there are the scouts. The scouts clean your rooms and keep the college tidy. Back in the day, scouts used to have a personal relationship with you. I'm not sure if that's the case anymore, my scouts were more like maids and I rarely ever saw them. They did keep my rooms clean and tidy, however!

My vision of Oxford was heavily influenced by TV and literature. *Brideshead Revisited* is my favorite work of British literature and also my favorite British drama. Charles Ryder describes Oxford so perfectly, that I've been dreaming of his vision of Oxford since I read it. "Oxford, in those days, was still a city of aquatint. In her spacious and quiet streets men walked and spoke as they had done in Newman's day; her autumnal mists, her grey springtime, and the rare glory of her summer days - such as that day - when the chestnut was in flower and the bells rang out high and clear over her gables and cupolas, exhaled the soft airs of centuries of youth. It was this cloistral hush which gave our laughter its resonance, and carried it still, joyously, over the intervening clamour."

Did my time in Oxford match this fantasy? Mostly. As it was the summer, there weren't many students about. But there were hordes of tourists. And not the good, thoughtful kind. Massive groups of tourists, with loudspeakers to scream their trivia at them as they clogged the streets and all around irritated locals and tourists who are more sensitive to their surroundings. I do realize it's a bit rich to criticize tourists in Oxford when I was one myself, but there's a right way to do it, and there was a lot of the wrong way on display while I was there.

The best parts of the day were after 5 p.m. when the tour buses had departed, and Oxford was left to those who were actually staying there. It was a much quieter and studious place. And since the sun doesn't go down to almost 10 p.m. in July, there was plenty of time to see the city in a late afternoon golden glow that did indeed match the description of Charles Ryder in Brideshead.

During my ESU-sponsored stay, every day was the same. I woke up around 7 or 8 am., and either did breakfast in the dining hall wit.h the other students, or I ate breakfast in my room. After that, it was time for lectures at 9 a.m. There were two lectures each morning, with a short tea break in between. After the lecture, it was lunchtime. Sometimes I'd go to lunch with a classmate (shy me made several new friends), or I'd plan to go to lunch myself. The afternoon was usually given away to a guided tour - of Keble College, Oxford itself, The Ashmolean Museum or The Bodleian Library. After that, we were on our own to explore Oxford. Full dinner was provided in the evenings, but it was optional - I opted for it a couple of times but chose to have dinner out to get the most out of Oxford.

I won't summarise each individual lecture in this article, I've already done that in detail in my trip diaries on Anglotopia.net. I will talk about my favorite lecture - about the difference between American and British English. The subject is particularly fascinating to me as the author of a British slang dictionary. It's amazing how much difference there is in a language that's essentially the same. The lecturer was very thorough and went into detail on my English is so different in Americavs. the UK (we have Noah Webster to thank for lots of the changes).

One night, I was bored after eating dinner and still had plenty of the day left, so I decided to go for an amble through Oxford, taking random streets to see where I ended up. This is my favorite part of travel, discovering something new that wasn't planned. I found the Oxford Castle, took my favorite picture from the trip at Nuffield College, explored the shops and all around soaked up the atmosphere of Oxford in the summer after the tourists had left. It was glorious. As I was in Oxford by myself, there was a lot of time to think and do some self-care. I was there to work, but I certainly got a lot out of the experience personally. I'm a huge admirer of architecture and Oxford is full of

Clockwise from top left: Trinity College, Pitt Rivers Museum, Natural History Museum, Tolkien's Grave

beautiful architecture from medieval buildings to new ones. It's interesting to see them living side by side. One of the oldest buildings in Oxford is now a currency exchange and a Pret a Manger. Not something the original builders of the building could have imagined. The original Norman castle is surrounded by a shop selling everything from travel gear to books. Plop a Norman down on St Aldate's, and I'm sure he would not recognise the place despite Oxford's seemingly timelessness. It was not always so.

I'm a huge fan of writer Bill Bryson - an American who's settled in England and written several books about life in the UK. Before I travel anywhere big, I like to see what he's written about the place. In "Notes from a Small Island" in 1995, he wasn't so nice about Oxford. "I have the greatest respect for the university and its 800 years of tireless intellectual toil, but I must confess that I'm not entirely clear what it's for, now that Britain no longer needs colonial administrators who can quip in Latin. My gripe with Oxford has nothing to do with fund-raising or how it educates its scholars. My gripe with Oxford is that so much of it is so ugly." I could easily see why he would think so in the 90s; there were many regrettable architectural decisions made in Oxford during the latter half of the 20th Century. If you need proof, simply watch old "Inspector Morse" episodes.

Bryson was much nicer about Oxford in his latest book, *The Road to Little Dribbling*. "Oxford is a victim of its own attractiveness. More people want to live there than it can comfortably accommodate, and you can't blame them. Traffic aside, I am prepared to nominate Oxford as the most improved city in Britain. In "Notes from a Small Island", I was hard on the dear old place, not because it was especially bad but because it wasn't good enough. My feeling is that certain places that are beautiful and historic… have a particular duty to remain so, and Oxford for quite some time didn't seem to understand that. Well, how that has changed." I agree with him. Oxford is a delight now, and it was a joy to visit and study, even if for a week.

Since I had the time after my lectures, I was determined to visit as many of Oxford's museums as possible. The place is positively packed with them. They're world-class, just like the museums in London and it's a shame that many people don't

Blackwell's Bookshop

think of Oxford for its museums. But a place that has been educating people for almost a thousand years is bound to acquire a few good museums. My favorite was the Natural History Museum. This glorious Victorian structure is a temple to natural history and has some amazing fossilised animals and dinosaurs (don't miss the dodo!). But by far the biggest treat is located through a hallway at the back of the Natural History Museum, The Pitt-Rivers museum. This place is hard to quantify. It's a massive gathering of cultural artifacts all over the world - an ethnographic survey of human cultural history. There are artifacts from all corners of the globe, and all of them are given the way weight an important they deserve.

There's some rather macabre item on display such as some real human shrunken heads. But there are also some amazing items on display from samurai armor to North American native artifacts. The sheer number of items in the collection is mind-boggling - hundreds of thousands of items have been saved, but only a few are on display at any given time. What you see in the grand Victorian central Hall is a sliver of a massive collection of cultural importance. If we were to save anything of humanity in the face of the apocalypse, we should save this entire museum. I will visit this place every time I visit Oxford from now on. There will be something new to see every time. There's just so much that you can never say you've seen it all. The Ashmolean is also worth your visit. My friend Bryson has this to say about the place, "The Ashmolean, for instance. What a wonderful institution, the oldest public museum on Planet Earth and certainly one of the finest." The best part about Oxford's Museums? They're all free.

No trip to Oxford is complete without a stop at Blackwell's, the renowned bookstore on Broad street that has become an Oxford institution. It's basically the bookstore of your dreams. Five levels of new books plus one level of select used books. They've expanded into a music shop (frequented by a certain Inspector Morse) and an art shop. Blackwell's is a huge operation - with branches all over the UK (and even within Oxford), but their main store on Broad Street is the spiritual home of the bookstore founded in 1879 by Benjamin Henry Blackwell. The Norrington Room, in the basement, dug out of the grounds beneath the store is home to the largest amount of bookshelf space in the

The Trout Inn

world - with more than 100,000 titles along 3 miles of shelves. If the helpful staff can't help you find a book, that book does not exist. I'm not capable of exerting self-control in Blackwells. Thankfully, they will affordably ship your books home to the USA (mine arrived there shortly after I did).

What's so great about Oxford is that it's a compact city. If you're staying in the city center, you can walk pretty much everywhere. There's so much to see you will not have a shortage of places to visit. A highlight of my time in Oxford was actually when I left the city center for the day. I took a taxi up to Wolvercote Cemetery to pay my respects to JRR Tolkien, writer of "The Lord of the Rings"and "The Hobbit." He's buried there with his wife in a shared grave, and it's become a bit of a shrine to Hobbitheads. After that, I walked along the main roads towards Godstow, a lovely old medieval settlement home to two major attractions: The Trout Inn and Godstow Abbey. The Inn is a classic English pub made famous by Philip Pullman and Inspector Morse. Godstow Abbey is a ruined monastery that's free and open to explore. This was a great way to end my trip in Oxford and oh so relaxing to enjoy a hearty pub meal beside the Thames at The Trout Inn.

When you spend a week in a place, you begin to get the rhythm and feel of the place. It begins to feel like home. Every day there was a treasure. From the lectures to walking in the college grounds, to exploring a new bits of Oxford I'd not seen before. Oxford was amazing. I've come to the conclusion that I want to spend a week in Oxford every summer for the rest of my life. I think my very soul will need it. I should see about getting a Doctor's prescription. Living amongst the dreaming spires is a treat that I recommend to anyone who loves learning and soaking up history and architecture. Oxford is the place for you. And there's so much there that you'll spend a lifetime finding something new every time. I only saw, but a sliver of life at Oxford and I will spend a lifetime trying to see the rest.

If you would like to experience what I did, contact the English-Speaking Union TLab who run education tours of Oxford and other places in the UK. http://www.esuus.org/

Top 25 Things to See and Do in Oxford

1. Tour an Oxford College (any will do but Trinity and Worcester are great)
2. Blackwell's Bookshop (Best bookshop you'll ever visit)
3. Eagle and Child Pub (Tolkien and Lewis drank here)
4. Go for a Random Stroll
5. Natural History Museum
6. Pitt Rivers Museum (You MUST visit this museum above all others)
7. Science Museum
8. Ashmolean Museum
9. Attend Concert at Music Hall
10. Climb St Mary's Tower (It's a bit claustrophobic, but the views are worth it!)
11. Attend a Church Service
12. Visit Waterstones
13. Oxford Covered Market
14. Ben's Cookies
15. Eat at Nando's
16. Botanic Gardens
17. Rent a Punt
18. Oxford Castle
19. Port Meadow
20. Godstow Abbey
21. The Trout Inn
22. Wolvercote Cemetery (Tolkien's Grave)
23. Gloucester Green Market
24. Carfax Tower
25. Westgate Shopping Centre

BRIT BOOK CORNER

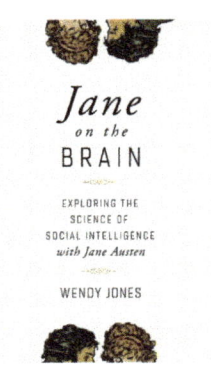

JANE ON THE BRAIN BY WENDY JONES

This book explores what gives Jane Austen's work that certain "spark" that delights readers young and old. Wendy Jones, an Austen scholar and practicing therapist dig in deep into Austen's work. She explores what made Austen's characters feel so real to her readers. Jones, goes on to investigate how we, the reader empathise, and rejoice for Austen's characters in a way that unique to her. This was a fantastic read, not only to learn about the richness of Jane Austen's characters but also how those character capture our imaginations and hearts. This book is a beautiful fusion of literary analysis and modern phycology; it looks at why Austen's characters have been so well loved, and continue to be today. Pegasus $27.95

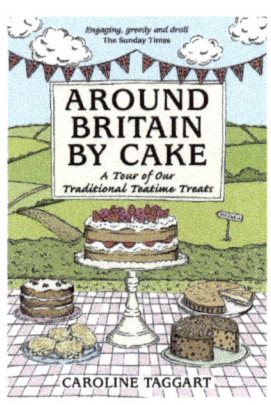

Around Britain by Cake by Caroline Taggart

"Around Britain by Cake " takes a charming look at some of the most beloved treats from Britain. The book is broken down by regional favorites from Cornwall to Scotland. As someone who is getting to know British baked goods, this was an excellent primer. The book includes brief history's of many of Britain's favorite tea time cakes as well as recopies. There are a wide variety of cakes featured in this charming little book. I highly recommend this book for the baker in your life. AA Publishing $14.95

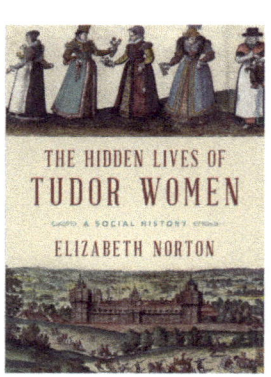

The Hidden Lives of Tudor Women: A Social History By Elizabeth Norton

When I think of women of the Tudor age, I think women in white ruffled collars adorned with jewelry but, I also think of those who were not as well off. I have often wondered what the life of a Tudor woman would've been like. Elizabeth Norton's "The Hidden Lives of Tudor Women" is a vivid depiction of what it would have been like to live as a woman during this historically significant time. She chronicles the stages of life from birth to old age, across many social statuses. Each chapter is broken down by "age" as she calls it. I also really enjoyed the selection of color pictures in the book. I could not put it down. This book was well written and fascinating to read. Pegasus Books $28.95

Splendours of the Subcontinent: A Prince's Tour of India 1875-6, By Kajal Meghani

Meghani's book "Splendours of the Subcontinent" is a feast for the eyes from start to finish. The book chronicles the gifts King Edward VII received when he took an eight-month tour through the Indian subcontinent in 1875. He met with more than ninety rulers through what is now modern-day India, Sri Lanka, Pakistan, and Nepal. Each ruler bestowed a gift to the traveling King. This trip helped solidify the relationship between the Indian Subcontinent and Britain. The book is well organised and broken down into chapters by objects such as jewelry, courtly objects and so on. There are also beautiful drawings and paintings in this book. I was utterly fascinated by the exquisite craftsmanship of the items when mass production was not readily available in the Subcontinent. Many of the treasures in this book have never been published before. The book accompany's an exhibition that will be shown at The Queen's Galleries at The Palace of Holyroodhouse and Buckingham Palace. The University of Chicago Press $39.95

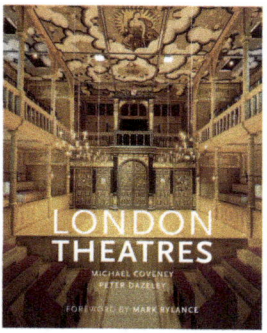

London Theatres By Michael Coveney and Peter Dazeley

London is known worldwide for many things, the home to Big Ben, where Buckingham Palace is located and Theater. I would argue that London is the world center when it comes to theater. Michael Coveney and Peter Dazeley's is a beautiful pictorial journey of the playhouses of London, from the grandest to the meekest. The book is well organized and a pure joy to look through and read. Each theater that is showcased in the book has a small essay that gives the history and some of the significant events that have happened there over its lifetime. While the writing is excellent, the pictures in this book are the real showstoppers, if you will pardon the pun. They are composed beautifully and rich in color. This book is gorgeous. I must have for any theater fan. Frances Lincoln $50

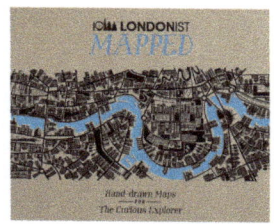

Londonist Mapped

The Londonist is one of my favorite blogs, and I read it every day, so I'm pleased as punch to see them come into book form. I'm a huge map nerd, so their first big book is a tribute to beautiful London maps. They've commissioned special ones but also linseed a few others. The best of London is brought to you by Londonist featuring hand-drawn maps from some of their favorite British illustrators. Whether you're looking for something new to do around Brick Lane or wondering about London's bridges and how they got their names, Londonist's team of contributors know the city and its history inside out. Appealing to map addicts, trivia junkies and Londoners-about town alike, this new compendium showcases hand-drawn maps inspired by some of the best of their writing. It's a beautiful book and a great gift! AA $24.99

Camra's Wild Pub Walks

The best kind of walk in the English countryside is the kind that ends with a visit to a country pub - even if you don't drink. Camra's newest book is dedicated to finding great walks in the English countryside that ends at a pub. The maps are helpful, and the directions are top-notch. Join the author on 22 walks in beautiful remote or mountain landscapes, each with a great pub - often with historical significance - at journey's end. The areas covered are the Peak District, Lake District, Yorkshire Dales and North York Moors, The Highlands and Borders in Scotland, Snowdonia, the Brecon Beacons and Mid Wales. Camra $15.99

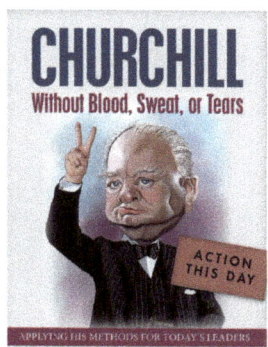

Churchill: Without Blood, Sweat or Tears

Need some motivation in your life? Then This new book by author Lawrence Kryske is an excellent guide to using the accomplishments of Churchill's life and applying the methods of his success to your own. Throughout his life, Churchill was a journalist, politician, author, and painter. How did a renaissance man like this get so much done? With focus, determination and a belief in oneself that they can do great things. Kryske does a great job in summarizing how you can apply these philosophies to your own life. An excellent read for any Churchillian and a great way to get to know Churchill a little bit more. Action This Day! $15.99

THEN - ST PANCRAS - 1895

The Midland Railway Company was responsible for the construction of the station. The firm was founded in 1844 upon the consolidation of the Midland Counties Railway, the North Midland Railway, and the Birmingham and Derby Junction Railway. By the 1860s, the company felt the need to expand itself southward into the nation's capital. William Henry Barlow, as the chief engineer of the Midland Railways, was tapped to design the station. Barlow, along with Roland Mason Ordish and George Gilbert Scott, wanted to create a building that would leave the company's mark on the city. With construction begun in 1866, the station proper only took two years to complete. The Barlow train shed was, at the time, the largest enclosed space in the world: 698 feet long, 240 feet wide, and more than 100 feet high. It suffered the ravages of time and war in the early 20th century. By the 1960s the station was deemed redundant, and it was almost demolished.

NOW

These attempts provoked strong opposition with a campaign led by the Poet Laureate John Betjeman. The station and the hotel were saved from demolition. St Pancras began to suffer from the unloved rot that affected many great Victorian buildings in the 20th century. It became dirty and outdated. But it was given a new lease of life when it was chosen to be the new Terminus for High Speed 1, the high-speed railway that goes directly to France using the Channel Tunnel. This prompted the £800 regeneration of the station. Barlow's shed was restored, the buildings cleaned and modernised, the cellars opened up into a new shopping destination and the glorious Midland Hotel reopened as a hotel and private apartments. Now the station properly introduces European visitors to London and returns St Pancras to being one of the most magnificent railway stations in the world. In honor of the man who helped save the station, there is now a statue of Betjeman on the main concourse level, forever waiting for a passing train.

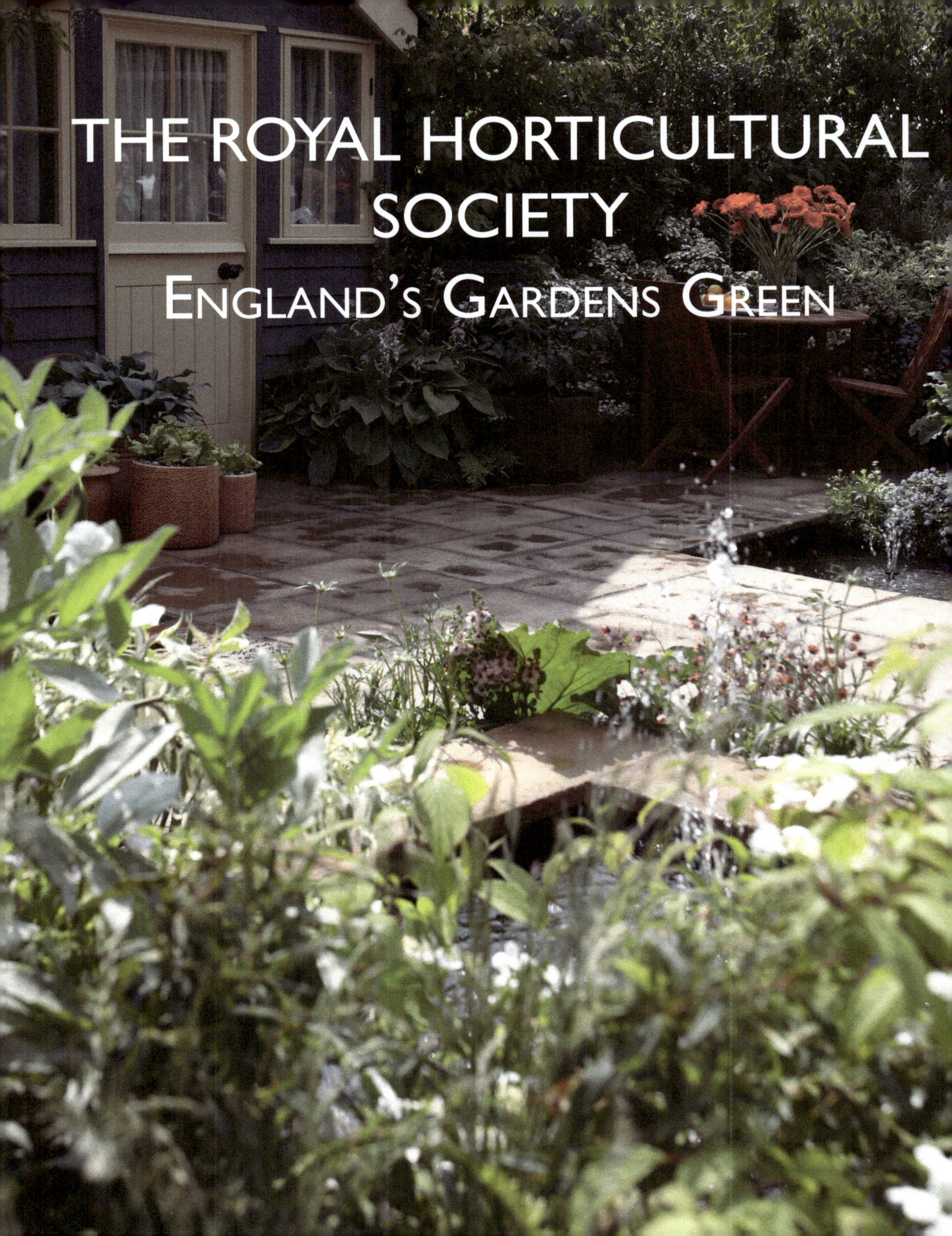
THE ROYAL HORTICULTURAL SOCIETY
ENGLAND'S GARDENS GREEN

The Royal Horticultural Society is more than 200 years old and has been a prestigious organization since its founding in 1804 by a group of famous gardeners and botanists. From its early beginnings, it has grown into an internationally recognised center for horticultural research and knowledge, bridging the gap between the science of botany and professional horticulture and the needs and interests of home gardeners. With royal patronage since 1860, the society has grown to control four and soon to be five gardens across England. Each year it runs the famous Chelsea Flower Show, as well as periodic smaller, seasonal shows at its London headquarters. It owns the world's largest horticultural library and gives its own 'stamp of approval' to plants considered especially suitable for discerning gardeners.

If, as is often argued, Britain is the world's leading country for gardening, then the Royal Horticultural Society is its leading gardening organisation. Having a garden was always an integral part of the British home, whether a castle or a cottage, and in the 18th and 19th centuries gardening was greatly stimulated by the introduction of plants from Britain's colonies and explorations around the world. With a climate that is never too hot or too cold, and rarely too wet or too dry, a wide range of plants can be grown – perhaps wider than anywhere else in the world.

So it was only natural that a group of keen gardeners should gather at Hatchards Bookshop in Piccadilly on the 7th of March, 1804. This was, however, no ordinary group of gardeners. The initial idea had come from John Wedgwood, son of the potter Josiah Wedgwood, and an enthusiastic botanist and gardener, especially of exotic tropical plants and fruits. Meeting with Wedgwood was William Townsend Aiton, Superintendent of the Royal Botanic Garden, in Kew, Richmond; Sir Joseph Banks, the famous botanist and explorer, who was at that time the President of the Royal Society; and William Forsyth, Superintendent of the gardens of St. James's Palace and Kensington Palace, and thus effectively the Royal Gardener. Also at the meeting were nurseryman James Dickson; antiquarian, Fellow of the Royal Society, and passionate gardener Charles Francis Greville; and botanist Richard Anthony Salisbury, who would become the Secretary of the new society. All but Wedgwood would have genera of plants named after them (Aitonia, Banksia, Dicksonia, Forsythia, Grevillia, and Salisburia).

KEY FACTS

- Founded in 1804 by Sir Joseph Banks and other leading garden figures
- Runs the famous Chelsea Flower Show every May
- Combines a scientific outlook with the pleasure and beauty of gardening
- Operates model gardens that have guided and developed the British style

Banks had brought a friend to the meeting - Thomas Andrew Knight – and not only was he accepted as a member in this newly-formed London Horticultural Society but by 1811 he was the President, a post he continued to hold till 1838. These were the formative years of the society. Knight followed the first president, the politician and Fellow of the Royal Society, George Legge, 3rd Earl of Dartmouth. Legge seems to have left little mark on the society, but Knight was a keen horticulturist with scientific inclinations, and he experimented in plant physiology and inheritance. He also researched improved methods of fruit tree growing – and incorporated research into fruit trees into the goals of the society that he drafted at the request of Banks. From the beginning, research was an important part of the society's activities. In 1807 the first issue of their Transactions appeared, complete with hand-colored plates.

In 1818, the society established a garden in Kensington, but this was short-lived, and in 1821 the Duke of Devonshire leased part of his estate at Chiswick to the society as an experimental garden. Beginning in 1827, fêtes and garden parties were held there, and 1833 saw the first of the now-famous competitive garden shows for flowers and vegetables. At this time their headquarters were in Regent Street.

In its early years, despite a solid reputation and social prominence, the society had financial problems which almost led to it being dissolved. However, in 1858 Albert, the Prince Regent, became society President. He proceeded to use the Society to develop an elaborate, Italianate garden

between Prince Consort Road and Queen's Gate, in South Kensington, where the Science Museum, Imperial College and the Royal College of Music now stand. The Queen and Prince made substantial financial donations to the society, and in return, their children were made life-members. The entry of royalty into the society raised its profile dramatically and in December of 1860 the society received a charter to officially call itself 'Royal.'

In 1862 the new gardens were the site of the 'Royal Horticultural Society Great Spring Show,' Chiswick being now considered too inconvenient a location. The show was held there until 1888, when it moved into central London, to the Temple Gardens near the Embankment. It remained there until 1912 when the nurseryman Harry James Veitch organized a one-off 'Royal International Horticultural Exhibition' at the grounds of the Royal Hospital in Chelsea. This venue proved so successful that the following year the Great Spring Show moved there, where it has been every year since, except for some of the war years, evolving into the 'Chelsea Flower Show,' an international event and the highlight of the British gardener's year. This fortuitous outcome earned Veitch a knighthood.

The Chiswick garden continued as an experimental garden until 1903, when the Wisley garden was established. This 60-acre site in Surrey had belonged to the industrial chemist and RHS member, George Fergusson Wilson, where he had been attempting to "make difficult plants grow successfully" since 1878. When he died in 1902, the property was purchased by Thomas Hanbury, a wealthy businessman with China connections and a famous garden - 'La Mortola' - in Liguria. He donated the land to the RHS, and the site has now grown to 240 acres, with extensive gardens and greenhouses. A special feature is a series of model gardens on the scale of a typical home garden, designed to inspire and guide amateur gardeners to grow better gardens.

The continuing success of the RHS for over 200 years was largely the result of the combination of science and aesthetics that was central to the society from its inception. Research in gardening techniques and the control of the naming of plants has always been as central to its activities as the creation of beautiful gardens. The RHS maintains registers of several important groups of plants, as well as awarding special recognition, through the 'Awards of Garden Merit,' to plants of particular value in gardens. Also, the RHS runs training programmes that help spread its methods, as well as awarding medals to those who make special contributions to the gardening world.

At the same time that it acquired Wisley Gardens, the RHS was already constructing a building at Vincent Square, London, for its administrative headquarters. At this time it was another monarch, Edward VII, who also helped give the RHS its first purpose-built exhibition hall for its periodic flower shows. Lindley Hall was built in 1904 in Edwardian Arts & Crafts style by the architect Edwin J Stebbs. The building also contains the Lindley Library, the largest horticultural library in the world, with books dating back to 1514. Lawrence Hall, a second exhibition space, was built in Art Deco style during the 1920s and received an award from the Royal Institute of British Architects.

In recent decades, the RHS has added new gardens to its care. The six-acre Rosemoor Garden in Devon was gifted to the society in 1988. Hyde Hall in Essex was similarly given to the society in 1993, and in 2001 the society merged with the Northern Horticultural Society and acquired Harlow Carr, near Harrogate, in North Yorkshire. Expansion continues and the 156-acre Victorian garden of Worsley New Hall, in Salford, Lancashire, will open as the Bridgewater Garden in 2019.

Sites to Visit

The RHS has four gardens:

Wisley Gardens are the largest, outside London in Woking, Surrey. The gardens and greenhouses are open from 10 a.m. to 6 p.m., every day except Christmas Day.

Rosemoor Gardens are in Great Torrington, Devon. Open from 10 a.m. to 6 p.m or 5 p.m in winter.

Hyde Hall Gardens are at Creephedge Lane, Rettendon, Chelmsford, Essex. Open from 10 a.m.to 6 p.m or 4 p.m in winter.

Harlow Carr Gardens are at Crag Lane, Beckwithshaw, Harrogate, North Yorkshire. Open

Joseph Banks

from 9:30 a.m. to 6 p.m or 4 p.m in winter.

The Royal Horticultural Halls are exhibition spaces used for periodic flower shows and also for other non-horticultural exhibitions and events.

Lindley Hall is at 80 Vincent Square, London SW1. The Lindley Library, in the same building, is open to the public, and registration allows access to the historic collections.

Lawrence Hall is adjacent to the Vincent Square headquarters, on Greycoat Street, Westminster W1.

Membership of the RHS is open to anyone, in any country. Members receive free access for two at all RHS gardens, access to the Chelsea Show on the quieter member's days, and a monthly magazine, The Garden. Some other benefits, such as seeds, are only available to UK and EU members.

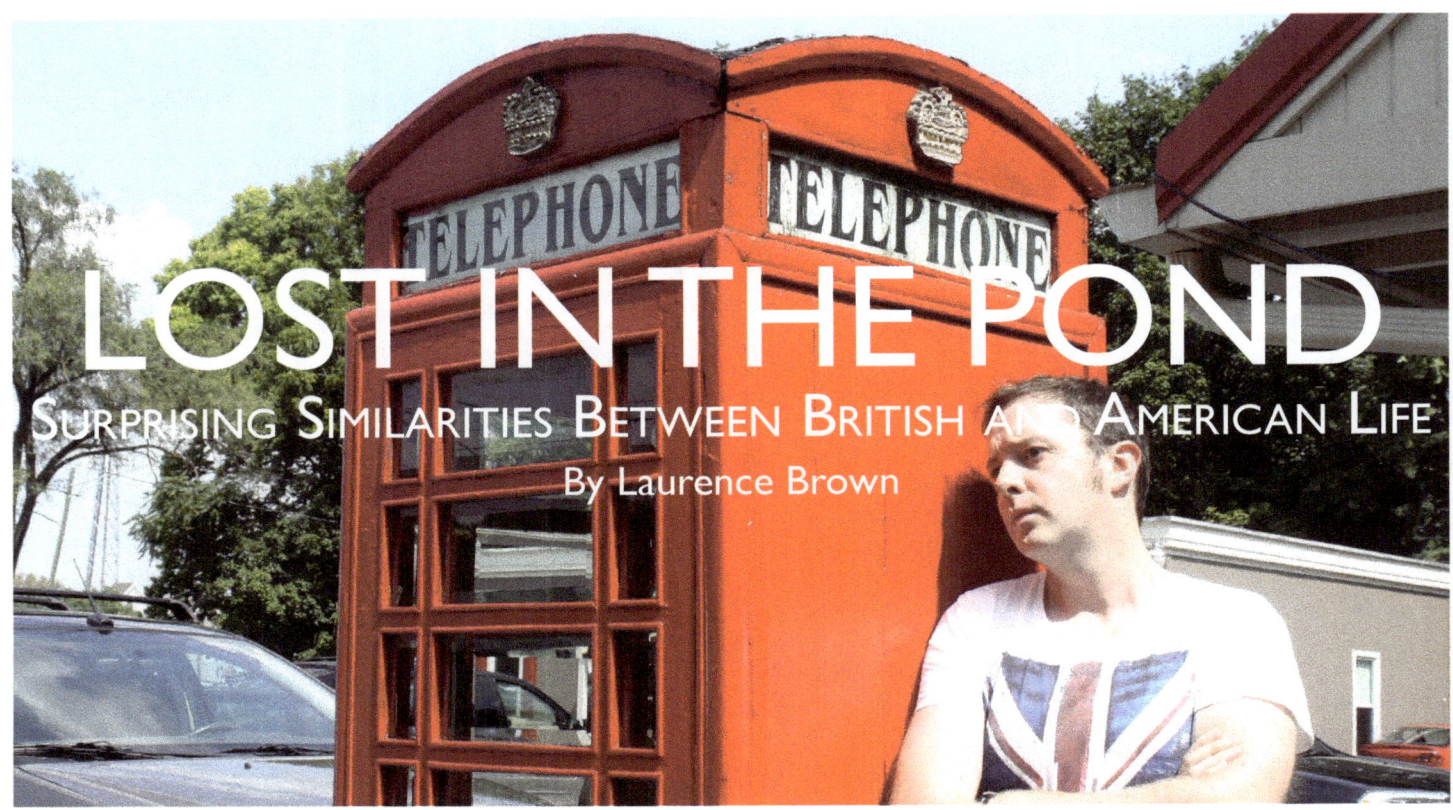

LOST IN THE POND
Surprising Similarities Between British and American Life
By Laurence Brown

As an unofficial British ambassador based in the United States, it has long been a daily exercise of mine to not only notice, but blog about, the numerous ways in which my home country differs from my adoptive one. But seldom have I paused to consider, in fact, that—on some scores—they're not so incredibly different after all.

Sure, we might get hung up—sometimes aggressively so—on the pronunciation of "Vincent van Gogh," but that's neither ear nor there (pun intended). The fact is, there are similarities to be found between Britain and the United States in some surprising areas—ones, dare I say it, that are often overlooked. Here are three such cases.

Spellings

I know what you are thinking: "spellings are precisely the thing that make us different!" It's true that Americans and Brits employee alternate rules toward the spelling of certain words, namely those that—in British English—bear the suffixes -our, -re, and -ise. But while debates over "colour" vs. "color" will likely rage on until English as we know it has evolved into something altogether unrecognizable, it might surprise many of you to know that there are, in fact, one or two instances in which the aforementioned suffixes remain the same on both sides of the Atlantic.

Take, for example, the word "glamour," whose origins lie not within French, but Scotts language. Indeed, it is perhaps due to this origin that Noah Webster—famed lexicographer and writer of An American Dictionary of the English Language—deigned not to alter the spelling. Thus, for the most part, Brits and Americans continue to keep the "u".

Similarly, when considering the -re vs. -er debate, in which Brits will maintain that it's spelled "theatre" and Americans insist on "theater," there are plenty of words within American English for which the suffix was never altered. These include "massacre", "acre", and "mediocre." Moreover, Brits may want to curb their criticism of American -er spellings, particularly because the British, in centuries past, once spelled the twelfth month of the year as "Decembre", but now universally employ the "-er" ending.

And as for the -ise suffix, there remains an incredibly high number of words that did not substitute the 's' for a 'z' in American English, mainly because the words in question—unlike "organize," "realize" and "recognize"—did not originate from Greek. Such words are as follows:

"advise," "arise," "chastise," "circumcise," "comprise," "compromise," "demise," "despise," "devise," "disguise," "excise," "exercise," "franchise," "guise," "improvise," "incise," "reprise," "revise," "rise," "supervise," "surmise," "surprise," "televise," and "wise."

Best-selling Music Artists

Since I earlier made mention of the word "glamour", what better time to segue into a section on popular music artists?

Now it's largely a given that luminaries such as The Beatles are widely recognized on either side of the Pond. Therefore, their likes—along with arguably Elton John, David Bowie, Led Zeppelin, Pink Floyd, Queen, and the Rolling Stones—probably don't belong on a list of surprising similarities between British and American life.

Instead, let's take a look at some of those artists whose transatlantic fame is not quite so easy to picture—until, that is, you've lived in both countries.

For instance, following the success of their 2004 album Hopes and Fears, 2000s indie band Keane continually receives a surprising amount of airtime in the U.S., particularly in bars and grocery stores. The same can also be said of a relatively frequent collaborator of the band in the form of Lily Allen, one of a number of British female singers—including Adele and Amy Winehouse—to have gained traction in the U.S. Moreover, the song "Stars" by Simply Red receives an inexplicably solid amount of airplay stateside, having charted at number 8 in the U.S. Adult Contemporary chart in 1992.

On the other side of the coin, Americans may be interested to know that certain U.S. bands, such as The Killers and Kings of Leon, are just as big (if not bigger) in the UK as they in America. I specifically picked out those two acts, by the way, for the notable way in which they, themselves, project a distinctly British sound.

In general, it makes sense that there exists an overlap in the popular music of each country; after all, since World War II, when the special relationship was forged between Churchill and Roosevelt, countless acts from either country have flourished in the other. It's just that some are far less expected than others.

Goal Posts

Due to America's lack of notable success in the world of football (soccer), it is easy to assume that the only goal structures visible across the country's high schools are those of the American football variety. But, and I'm speaking from a decidedly Midwestern point-of-view here, soccer goal posts often, in fact, outnumber their would-be NFL equivalents.

Indeed, goal posts are a common enough site across public fields in America that it's actually rather surprising that the United States is still as behind at the international level as it is. It could be, of course, that the nation has yet to enjoy the fruits of what is admittedly a rather recent foray into soccer youth development.

Either way, the proliferation of goal posts and soccer enthusiasm among children (Messi and Ronaldo shirts are also a common sight) once prompted me to predict in a BBC America article that the United States will one day win the FIFA World Cup. Three years on, despite the country's failure to qualify for the 2018 World Cup, I still stand by that prediction.

Such a vision of the future would have seemed highly unimaginable in the days before I lived in the U.S. The general stereotype of Americans is that they don't have a clue about the "beautiful game." While this certainly holds true among large swathes of the population, soccer is gaining some ground on the four major sports of baseball, basketball, American football, and hockey. Ironically, it is often the live action from the English Premier League that is driving a lot of this interest, with games often broadcast in pubs—specifically those of the Irish of British persuasion—up and down the country.

Either way, like the UK, those goal posts aren't going away anytime soon.

Laurence is a British writer and humorist who lives in the United States. He also hosts the popular web series, "Lost in the Pond" on YouTube. He has an infuriating habit of taking America to task by pointing out how things are done in the UK. He really needs to stop this behavio(u)r. It's anti-American.

BRITAIN'S ICONIC BRIDGES
TOP 10 ENGINEERING MARVELS IN BRITAIN

By John Rabon

The United Kingdom has some of the world's finest bridges. Of course, most people think of Westminster Bridge, London Bridge, or Tower Bridge when it comes to the country's engineering marvels, but there are plenty of fantastic bridges outside of London. Designed by the very names that made plenty of London's famous landmarks, these bridges are certainly worthy of your attention. From the 18th century to more recent structures, we've picked out ten of our favorites from outside of London and all over Britain.

Iron Bridge

The Iron Bridge in Shropshire earned its name from being the first bridge in the world made from cast iron. It was constructed in 1781 to cross the River Severn and was a symbol not only of what the new material could do but also the industry of Shropshire and the transformation of Britain by the Industrial Revolution. Once dwarfed by factories on both sides of the gorge, the area is now known for its beauty, including this lovely UNESCO World Heritage site.

Pulteney Bridge, Bath

Crossing the River Avon in Bath, Pulteney Bridge is filled with vehicles, people, and shops. It took twenty years to build and has three arches for support. The south side is the more picturesque of the two if looking at it from the river, but both sides of the bridge are excellent examples of the Palladian style when you're crossing it. The bridge has been widened and restored several times over its history, but looks much as it did when it was first built.

Clifton Suspension Bridge, Bristol

Crossing the Avon Gorge in Bristol, the Clifton Suspension Bridge was designed by one of Britain's most famous engineers in Isambard Kingdom Brunel. His design was later modified by William Henry Barlow and John Hacksaw into the bridge that exists today. The bridge has been the scene of many historic moments commiserate with its status, such as the first bungee cord jump, the last Concord flight, and the Olympic Torch Relay.

© Visit Britain Images

Glenfinnan Viaduct, Scotland

Movie fans might recognize this railway bridge as the one the Hogwarts Express would use to take Harry Potter and his friends to school. The bridge was constructed from 1807 to 1901 and rises 100 feet off the ground while spanning 1,000 feet. It's easily the longest railway bridge in Scotland and crosses the River Finnan while carrying the West Highland Line on a single track. It has also been featured on many programmes and films behind the Harry Potter series.

Tees Transporter Bridge

Also known as the Middlesborough Transporter Bridge, the Tees Transporter Bridge is unique as it is a style in which a gondola suspended from the top of the bridge carries people and goods across the River Tees. Sir William Arrol & Co. finished it in 1911. Some notable moments in the bridge's history include being hit by a bomb during World War II and comedian Terry Scott driving his Jaguar off of it after mistaking it for a toll bridge.

Infinity Bridge

The most recent entry on this list, the Infinity Bridge in Stockton-on-Tees crosses the River Tees and opened in 2009. The innovative design has an asymmetric double arch and a suspended deck with mass dampers on the underside to control the oscillation, a necessary feature given its use by pedestrians and bicyclists. One of the best aspects of the bridge is its nightly illumination, which comes in an array of colours and patterns.

Humber Bridge

Crossing over the River Humber, the Humber Bridge opened in 1981 as the longest single-span suspension bridge in the world at 7,280 feet. Now the eighth-longest, the bridge sees vehicle and pedestrian commuters every day and well more than 100,000 every week. Prior to the bridge's construction, travel across the river was mostly done by way of the Humber Ferry. While the bridge is on a toll system, it is the preferable means of traveling between Grimsby and Hull, as the bridge reduced the road distance between the two by 50 miles.

Tyne Bridge

Located in Newcastle and crossing the River Tyne, the Tyne Bridge is one of the most gorgeous outside of London. This through arch bridge opened in 1928 and spans 1,276 feet. It was designed by Mott, Hay, and Anderson based on the Sydney Harbour Bridge and the Hell Gate Bridge in New York. Its towers were built out of Cornish granite and designed to be multi-story warehouses. While many people remember the Olympic rings over Tower Bridge, the largest in the UK were displayed from the Tyne Bridge.

© Visit Britain Images

Forth Bridge

Iron Bridge isn't the only UNESCO World Heritage site that's also a British bridge. Forth Bridge was finished in 1890 as a cantilever railway bridge spanning the Firth of Forth between South Queensferry and North Queensferry. At the time it opened, it was the longest such bridge in the world and continues to be the second-longest single cantilever span in the world at 1,709 feet. The bridge made it onto the UNESCO list by its innovative use of design and materials as well as its sheer size.

© Visit Britain Images

Carrick-A-Rede

Not all bridges are made or iron, steel, and concrete. Carrick-A-Rede is a well-known rope bridge in Northern Ireland that links the mainland to the tiny island of Carrickarede. The bridge is 66 feet long and is suspended 98 feet above the rocks lying at the water's surface. The first bridge was built by fishermen in 1755, and the current bridge was constructed by Heyn Construction in 2008. Those who dare the heights find the bridge to be very exhilarating.

GREAT BRITONS: WILLIAM BEVERIDGE

THE ARCHITECT OF BRITAIN'S WELFARE STATE

By David Goodfellow

William Beveridge was the son of a British civil servant working in India, but he was educated in Britain and graduated from Oxford with top honors. He immediately began working with the moderate Fabian socialists to improve the situation of the poor. He was responsible for devising an early scheme for unemployment insurance in 1911, which he later extended in his Beveridge Report in 1942. The scheme, which provided for healthcare, unemployment, sickness, widow and pension benefits, was implemented by the incoming Labour government in 1945 and provided the foundation for the systems of welfare and benefits still found in Britain today. It was based on what Beveridge saw as the five social evils - Want, Disease, Ignorance, Squalor, and Idleness. Although proposing what is widely viewed as a socialist programme, he was, in fact, a Liberal, supporting the provision of social services through private organizations and charities. He lived a quiet, married but childless life and was made a peer for his work.

Like many Englishmen of his time, William Beveridge was born in India, on the 5th of March, 1879, in British India. His father was in the Indian Civil Service, the elite corps which administered the British Empire in India. As was normal he was sent back to England for his education, and he attended the prestigious Charterhouse School, going from there to Balliol College, Oxford. He studied Mathematics and Classics. Beveridge was a good student and graduated with first-class honors. He went on to qualify for the Bar, but his interest in improving the society around him led him to work as a Sub-Warden at Toynbee Hall, Tower Hamlets, from 1903 to 1905. Toynbee Hall was part of the 'settlement movement,' a system of residences in poor districts where university students and others lived. The goal was to bring about improvement in society by encouraging different classes to live together cooperatively, with the students providing education, day-care, medical services, arts, and culture. In this way, it was hoped that poorer people could be lifted out of poverty by combined, voluntary, social action. The movement was praised for its charitable intent, but criticized by more radical groups for perpetuating class differences.

While at Toynbee Hall Beveridge met Sidney and Beatrice Webb, the founders, along with George Bernard Shaw, of the Fabian Society, a socialist

KEY FACTS

- Born 1879 – died 1963
- Established the principles of the British 'cradle to grave' welfare system
- Believed that full employment was key to making it possible
- A Liberal at heart, although universally admired by British socialists

group that believed in creating a socialist society through the democratic process, rather than through the revolution demanded by other socialists. He became an active promoter of ideas such as old-age pensions and free school meals – both would become features of the future welfare state - as well as the establishment of labor exchanges, which were places where workers could come and find jobs from a pool of work posted by employers.

Beveridge devised a scheme known as unemployment insurance, which took contributions from people in work so that they would receive payments when they were not working. Sidney Webb introduced Beveridge to Winston Churchill, at that time President of the Board of Trade in the Lloyd George Liberal government. Beveridge was invited to develop a system of unemployment centers and an unemployment scheme, leading to the passage of the National Insurance Act of 1911, where both employees and employers contributed to an unemployment fund. The scheme also had a private section, where private organisations organized pension and health benefits through a system of contributions. Webb had written a book - Unemployment: A Problem of Industry – published in 1909 to promote the scheme. However, Beveridge did not support what would today be considered a liberal approach. While wanting to support men who did not work, he wanted a heavy price - complete and permanent loss of all citizen rights – including civil freedom and fatherhood. He was a member of the Eugenics Society, which supported improving the human race by controlling reproduction.

He received a knighthood for his work in WWI, where he was responsible for mobilisation and the

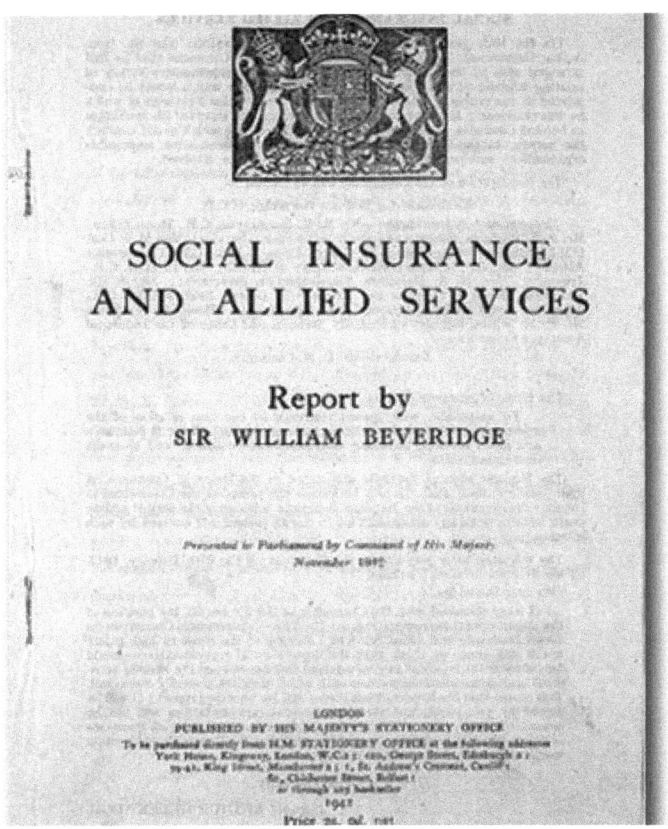

control of manpower in the labor force. At the end of the war, he became director of the London School of Economics and Political Science, which had been founded by the Webbs in 1895 with an endowment from a member of the Fabian Society, so it was largely an instrument of Fabian policies. In that role, he studied potential government social policies for the Society, as well as producing academic work as an economist on prices and wages. In 1936, he wrote *Planning Under Socialism*. He retained his position as director until 1939, having also been appointed Master of University College, Oxford in 1937. During this time he separately worked on helping persecuted academics escape from Nazi Germany, using a body he had set up, the Academic Assistance Council. It is believed that his exit from the LSE was in part triggered by his continuing support for eugenic policies.

When WWII arrived, he had expected to play a prominent role, but instead, he was pushed aside into an obscure position as chairman of an inter-departmental inquiry into the coordination of social services. Churchill did not expect anything from the inquiry until the war was concluded, but instead, in 1942, Beveridge published his Report to the Parliament on Social Insurance and Allied Services. His report quickly sold 70,000 copies, and Churchill suffered his only war-time defeat in the House of Parliament when a motion passed accepting the principles of Beveridge's report. In it he called for a unified system of National Insurance, to cover unemployment, sickness, retirement, and widowhood. It would work in conjunction with a system of National Health (already being planned at the Ministry of Health) to provide a minimum standard of living 'below which no one should be allowed to fall.' More controversially, in support of his ideas of eugenics, he wanted a child allowance, whereby middle-class parents would receive money to encourage them to have more children, while working-class parents would receive a smaller amount, so as to discourage them from reproducing excessively. In the end, a flat-rate of child allowance was introduced.

It should be remembered that throughout the late 19th and early 20th centuries, radical socialism had grown exponentially in Britain. Particularly after the Russian Revolution in 1917, there were real fears of a full-scale revolution in the country. The Fabian Society hoped to prevent that, by instituting more moderate policies to assuage the grievances of the poor, and it was recognised that unless poverty and the conditions of the working-class were addressed, a disaster was in the making for the established ruling class of Liberals and Tories. So Beveridge saw a solution for poverty as vital for the continuation of anything resembling the existing society.

In 1942, he married Jessy Janet Mair, a widow, but they had no children. In 1944, he wrote Full Employment in a Free Society, to describe to the public how his goals could be achieved, and even enhance the economy, by shifting labor costs like healthcare off corporate books and onto the government, and by providing a healthier workforce to increase productivity. He saw 'full-employment' – less than 3% of the workforce unemployed - as a basic goal of social policy, and believed, in his famous phrase, in providing care for the population 'from the cradle to the grave.' He knew that without the tax revenue and low demand for social services that full employment would create, such a system would be difficult to maintain.

He joined the Liberal Party and spent a brief period as an MP, but he lost he seat in the 1945 election when returning soldiers swept the Labour

Party to power in a landslide. Beveridge had sincerely believed that the Liberals would be swept into power, showing his failure to grasp the extent of the disillusionment of the population with 'politics as normal.' Under the new Prime Minister, Clement Attlee, Labour proceeded to carry out the reforms Beveridge had proposed, and more.

In 1946, he was elevated to the peerage, as 1st Baron Beveridge, of Tuggal in Northumberland and went on to become Leader of the Liberals in the House of Lords. His peerage was to die with him, in the absence of an heir. In 1948, Beveridge published Voluntary Action, a book arguing for the implementation of social policy through charities and non-profit organisations, not the state, showing that he was no socialist.

On the 16th of March, 1963, Beveridge died at his home in Northumberland, still working on his last book.

His Legacy

There are two intertwined threads in progressive Britain – liberal and socialist. To oversimplify, liberals recognise the evils of inequality and exploitation and support changes in society that encourage self-improvement through personal action. Socialists see the same evils but believe that only the intervention of a powerful state can distribute wealth effectively. Beveridge was in the Liberal tradition, but he is seen as a hero by British socialists since his report produced the social safety-net of the welfare state. The existence of pensions, unemployment insurance, child benefits, disability allowances and the whole network of support designed to prevent the poorest members of society from falling even lower was the product of his work, but as a believer in the 'small state' Beveridge would have probably preferred to see those goals achieved by voluntary action. His flirtation with eugenics was not as bizarre as we might see it today, and those ideas were held by many liberals and even socialists of those times until they were discredited by the atrocities of the Nazis.

Sites to Visit

Beveridge's grave is in St Aidan churchyard, Thockrington, Northumbrian. It is one of the oldest churches in England.

Further Research

Biographies of Beveridge include:

- William Beveridge: A Biography, by Jose Harris
- Beveridge and the Progressive Era, by Claude Gernade Bowers

THIS ENGLISH LIFE
We Need to Talk About the Special Relationship
By Erin Moore

It has been 72 years since Winston Churchill, on a post-war lecture tour of American universities, first declared that the US and the UK had a "special relationship." Churchill, no longer a Prime Minister, but a private citizen, was eager to further the Anglo-American collaboration. And there is no doubt that these two countries, sharing history, language, and common enemies, have accomplished a lot.

In the years since, some American Presidents have been keener than others. Blair lent Bush a bust of Churchill, a huge compliment. President Obama, standing next to the Queen at a state banquet at Buckingham Palace in 2011, declared he was honored to be in Britain to reaffirm enduring bonds, and thanked the UK for its solidarity.

As for me, even though I wrote a book about British and American culture that was described as a love letter to the two countries, even though the bond between them was first my obsession and then my livelihood, I have never liked the term "special relationship." I felt it had become a lazy cliché, trotted out in every headline, article, and book. I was bored with it, and took it for granted as an idea.

As if this relationship would always be what it was, always be special, and we didn't even have to talk about it anymore.

How wrong I was. I'm positively nostalgic for the term now.

My blues for the special relationship began with Brexit. The fact that my family and I were blindsided by Brexit probably says more about us than you wanted to know. My politics, considering I'm an immigrant and proud dual-citizen who has been lucky to live in the polyglot melting pot of London for 11 years will surprise no one. I'll give you one guess how I feel about Brexit: I hate it.

Not one person I know (with the exception of a couple of British relatives on my husband's side, whose children are furious) voted Leave. Many of our friends are not eligible to vote at all, having been born elsewhere. The night of the vote, we were at a dinner party with a couple of friends who work at big banks. The mood was defiant and confident, if not entirely certain. Everyone stayed up late into the night and some of the discussion was of how their world was set to change if the vote went to the Leavers. Banks were already making plans to move whoever could be forced to move to Paris, Frankfurt or Brussels, sooner rather than later. These orders were coming from upper management. No one on the execution side saw it as anything but a waste of time—a fruitless exercise in hypotheticals.

We went to bed after midnight, still pretty sure the Remainers had it. I'll never forget waking up at 5 a.m., inferring from my husband's hurried preparations for work that the news was very bad. I remember him saying, "You know what this means? Now Trump could win." I decided not to engage in that particular nightmare, and pulled the sheets over my head. It wouldn't be the last time I lost sleep over Brexit.

Later that morning, the fallout was everywhere.

First, there were tears at the school gate: Anne's class has eight nationalities in it. Most of the children were born here in London, but their parents are from all over, and many depend on their work to stay here. We have an architect, a fashion designer and several others in the fashion business, a publisher, a literary agent, a few bankers, a couple of dentists. If their business or their visas dry up, they will have to leave. (Eighteen months later, some already have.)

When I stopped for a cup of tea at the Pitted Olive, my favorite café near King's Cross, the atmosphere was funereal. The proprietors have lived over here for decades and built a popular family business patronised by a diverse community. Everyone from Polish builders to British Librarians to University College London professors and tourists staying in the small hotels around the corner stops for coffee, or crams into the wooden booths for borek gözleme and meze. They were devastated and upset. They felt the vote very personally, like a punch in the stomach. Usually I am in and out with a cup of tea and an apple pastry, but on this day we talked for half an hour. Everyone, it seemed, was looking for catharsis and a way to process the dreadful news.

Back home, there was more Brexit processing with Marie-Laure, our nanny, who has been living and working here for more than 20 years (7 of them with us). She falls into that nebulous category of EU citizens waiting to learn what will be possible post-Brexit. Marie-Laure came here because her opportunities in child care would be far greater and better paid. She moved to West London, where French and English families alike valued her impeccable English and French.

France is a hidebound culture in which many ambitious people, across educational backgrounds and regions, feel thwarted. Many of them move to London. By population, London would qualify as France's sixth-largest city; more French people live here than Bordeaux, Nantes or Strasbourg. Yet, not everyone who comes here to work wants to become a citizen, or can afford to.

I did not start the process of becoming a UK citizen until my daughter was born and acquired her two passports. It took 6 months, was very expensive and involved a lot of daunting forms and a test. I've always been glad I did it, and never more so than now.

About a week after Brexit, a man working the checkout in Primark (assuming from my strong US accent, which he commented on, that I was a tourist) asked when I was going home. When I said I was living here, he said again, this time with an edge, "Right, so when you going home, then?" He made me feel more than unwelcome—his threatening tone made me feel sick. That was a mild experience compared to what friends have been through. An Anglo-Indian friend who was born and raised here has had racial slurs hurled at her that she said she hadn't heard since the 80s. A Japanese friend, traveling with her young girls in the countryside, was threatened in front of her baffled children. They have since moved on to Singapore-- not because they gave up on living here, but because her husband, a banker, was sent to a new post.

I will admit that moving back to the US crossed my mind in the months following Brexit. I did feel less at ease here, and sad to contemplate my kids' future. I suspect the country they inherit will be a lot less interesting, with fewer opportunities and an even higher cost of living. My doctor, whose 18-year-old son is studying at NYU, told me that 90% of his friends had opted to go to universities in the States. American universities love British students, who are, for the most part, more prepared (especially in subjects like writing) and more mature than their US counterparts. British students appreciate the freedom of choice afforded them by the American educational system, where they have until around age 20 to choose their field of study, whereas here they are expected to narrow it down to a few subjects during secondary/high school. Of course, not everyone can pay the steep

fees at US colleges, but the gaps are being filled by scholarships, and off they go: let the brain drain begin.

Despite my Brexit blues, all thoughts of returning to the States evaporated in November of 2016 when Trump became President-elect, It was another bleak, tearful morning bringing more fear about the future.

We moved to London during George W. Bush's tenure. It now seems almost quaint how ashamed we were of him and his actions at the time. As apologetic as we expats were back then, the phrase "not my president" never crossed my mind, as it does daily now. Bush, in retrospect, appears almost statesmanlike by comparison to Trump. The UK responded to the election like a death in the family. St. James Church in Piccadilly put up a sign reading "Evening Prayer: A short service in which to pray and reflect in the wake of the US election."

As of this writing, the special relationship is in tatters. Theresa May reached out, bravely but perhaps fruitlessly, as one of the first foreign politicians to visit Trump in the White House in January 2017. She suggested a State Visit like the one Obama made in 2011 which would involve a banquet full of dignitaries and an audience with the Queen. This proposed visit has since been downgraded and put off indefinitely.

As of this writing, May has rightly condemned Trump's retweeting of anti-Muslim videos by the ultranationalist group Britain First, giving this fringe group an undeserved platform to further their hateful cause. David Lammy, a Labour Party MP, has tweeted. "Trump sharing Britain First. Let that sink in. The President of the United States is promoting a fascist, racist, extremist hate group whose leaders have been arrested and convicted. He is no ally or friend of ours." By the time this issue of the Anglotopia Magazine hits your doorstep, will this seem like the tip of the iceberg? I'm here from the past to tell you that we were pretty upset about this stuff back in early December.

Still, in a moment when the special relationship seems in peril—I see hopeful signs. One is that people I know on both sides of the Atlantic are more socially and politically engaged than ever before. These distressing events have brought an end to the apathy and complacency that was all too easy before. Now we come out and say the things we might not have said: like, I value you and this country is better with you in it. And I hope you stay. And I wish you well.

Whether the Queen and Trump ever meet—and I'm far from convinced that they should—we have a new Royal Wedding to look forward to. When Prince Harry and Meghan Markle marry, they will bring a US-UK alliance back to the front pages for a positive reason for the first time since the US election. And if some journalists decide to couch their coverage in terms of the "special relationship," this time I won't cringe. Because an upsurge of Anglophilia in Trump's America—and hope in Brexit Britain—is just what we need right now.

About the Author

Erin Moore is an American who has been living in London for 10 years. Her book, That's Not English: Britishisms, Americanisms and What Our English Says About Us, is available on amazon.com.

GREAT BRITISH QUESTIONS

Your burning questions about Britain answered truthfully.
By The Anonymous Anglophile

How Can I Get the BBC iPlayer in the USA?

You cannot. The iPlayer is only available within the United Kingdom and as of 2018 access is only allowed to current BBC TV license fee payers. In 2017, the BBC and ITV partnered to launch BritBox and new British TV streaming service for the US market that has thousands of hours of content from the BBC and ITV back catalogs. It's not the iPlayer, but it's the closest we will ever get. It's great. Acorn TV also has a great selection of British TV as well.

How Can I Get British Print Newspapers in the USA?

A decade ago, this was a pretty easy prospect. Most major cities had an international newsagent that offered newspapers from all over the world. But with the advent of digital news, it's practically impossible to buy British print newspapers here in the USA. If you find a newsagent selling them, cherish them. All the major British newspapers now have tablet apps, and you can still read the content of the paper. It's not the same as cracking open a broadsheet, but it's the closest you can get.

I want to visit the Cotswolds but don't want to drive, how can I do this?

Visiting the Cotswolds without being willing to drive is a huge challenge. The area is not served particularly well by train. The major cities have rail access, but the charm of the Cotswolds is the small towns and villages that don't have trains. Buses are infrequent and difficult to decipher. The best way to experience the Cotswolds is to drive yourself or do a guided coach tour, so someone else does the driving. There are also companies that will escort your around the Cotswolds in a private car. It's expensive, but you get a more personal experience.

What Will Meghan Markle's Title Be When She Marries Prince Harry?

I hate to dash the hopes of any would-be princess, but Meghan will not become a princess when she marries Harry. She's a commoner (and an American one at that). You have to be of royal blood to be called a prince/princess and marriage does not confer that. This is the same reason that the Duchess of Cambridge is not 'Princess Kate.' Because she's not a princess. What will likely happen is the Queen will bestow a title on Prince Harry when he marries Meghan (this will be announced on the day). She'll probably make him a Duke and Meghan will become a Duchess. He'll no longer be Prince Harry; he'll be the Duke of Whatever The Queen Says and Meghan will be his Duchess. That will be her official title going forward.

Can I Bring My Pet With Me On A Trip to Britain?

No. Transatlantic flights for pets are absurdly expensive, and pets cannot be in the cabin. Britain is also rabies free and has very strict conditions on transporting pets into the country - that require six months of planning. It's only worth it to bring your pet if you're moving to England, and even then rehoming is usually the better option.

What Happens If I Need To Go To The Emergency Room While In The UK?

First, they call it the A&E. Second, you will be treated. Minor things will not cost you anything but if you get admitted, or something major happens the NHS will still treat you, but they will send you the bill and expect you to pay it. Trip insurance is useful for situations like this but make sure it covers medical!

GREAT BRITISH ICONS: CONCORDE

The Failed Dream of Supersonic Air Travel

There was once a dream that was supersonic air travel. The dream was leaving for lunch in the UK to return to dinner in New York. In the progression of air travel technology in the 20th century, faster was better. Times have changed. Supersonic air travel is now dead and buried. Planes now travel at a relatively slow speed of 600 miles and hour and no faster and there are no passenger planes on the horizon that will go faster. No one wants to break the sound barrier anymore - it's too expensive and passengers aren't willing to pay for it. For a brief time the future looked like Concorde and it flew for almost 40 years. But that future never came.

Concorde was a supersonic commercial airliner that carried just 100 passengers. It was a joint development between Britain and France which began with the goal of revolutionising air travel but floundered on changing habits and the growth of low-cost, mass-market travel. It flew at twice the speed of sound and could cross the Atlantic in 3.5 hours. It's instantly recognisable tilted nose, and swept-back rear wings made it greatly loved by many, and it remains the high point of civil aviation, despite never being replaced by a second generation of supersonic airliners. Despite one fatal crash, it had one of the best safety records of all commercial aircraft. It was used by many dignitaries, from Pope John II to Queen Elizabeth II and by numerous Prime Ministers and Presidents.

Following WWII, there was a boom in commercial passenger air flight. The cinemas were full of films depicting the pleasure of international travel and foreign destinations in Europe, South America and elsewhere. Pilots and hostesses were a highly respected and envied class of workers, and for the first time, ordinary people could take vacations outside the confines of their own country. Airline manufacturers responded with larger, more luxurious planes. In particular, the shift to jet engines instead of propeller-driven planes ushered in the 'Jet Age,' with the Boeing 707 being the first and most successful of a new generation of aircraft.

The shift to jets was in large part triggered by technical problems that developed with more powerful propeller engines, particularly the noise, shock waves and turbulence created when the tip of the whirling propeller passes the speed of sound. The only practical way to make faster, more powerful engines was to move to jet propulsion,

KEY FACTS

- A Joint British and French development
- Flew London to New York in just over 3 hours
- Flew Paris to New York in 3.5 hours, at a speed of 1,300 mph
- Flew commercially between 1976 and 2003
- Failed because of changes in the air passenger market

opened up the possibility of creating aircraft that could travel faster than the speed of sound. Although planes in a dive had already exceeded that speed, usually with a dangerous loss of control, it was on the 14th of October 14, 1947, that the American military pilot Chuck Yeager became the first man to break the sound barrier in level flight, in a Bell X-1. This plane was the result of a joint US-British project, using information from early British research into supersonic flight. However, the US reneged on the terms of the agreement and refused, as required, to share the results of their own research.

As a consequence, Britain went it alone in the early 1950s, when the Royal Aircraft Establishment, the research wing of the Royal Air Force, set up a committee to study supersonic transport. At first, no feasible design could be developed, until Johanna Weber and Dietrich Küchemann, of the RAE, came up with a new wing concept called the 'slender delta.' This wing created powerful vortexes above it, greatly increasing lift, and although it required a sharp take-off angle, this innovation opened the door to supersonic travel.

In 1956, the Supersonic Transport Advisory Committee was formed and began work on a design based on this new wing and in 1959, a study contract was awarded to the Hawker Siddeley and Bristol aircraft companies. The goal was to develop a production model by 1960 to beat the US, who it was rumored, were also working on a supersonic aircraft.

Simultaneously, in France, researchers were unknowingly going in the same direction and

Concorde Prototype at Fleet Air Arm Museum

following a design contest the Sud Aviation Super-Caravelle won. Fearing that US designers were already working on a supersonic plan for the transatlantic routes, the French set their sights on a shorter-haul plane that would not have to compete with the Americans.

In April 1960, Pierre Satre, the technical director of Sud Aviation traveled to meet Bristol designers to discuss a partnership. France needed British engines, and both parties had no experience in metals for the high temperatures that would be generated by the flights, so a partnership seemed the best way forward. However, Britain still wanted to build a larger 150-passenger plane for transatlantic flights, so for a while, the two parties worked on parallel designs to their own specifications. It became increasingly clear that a single design would benefit both sides, so by late 1961, a single design for a transatlantic plane had emerged. The goal was to reach Mach 2 (twice the speed of sound) since the metal technology of the time could not cope with the temperatures created by flying at Mach 3.

On the political front, things did not go so well. Although the French were much more interested in partnering with the UK than with the US, the British government were reluctant to invest in a project that seemed unlikely to have any financial benefits to the country. However, in the end, a longer-term view won the day, arguing that without this plane Britain would be locked out in the perceived rush for supersonic flight and that the partnership with France would smooth the way for Britain's entry into the Common Market (as the EU was then known). Rather than a commercial agreement, an international treaty was signed on the 29th of November, 1962.

In 1965, construction began on two prototypes, one built by Aerospatiale at Toulouse, and the other by BAC at Filton, Bristol. In 1967, sales efforts began and the consortium secured 100 non-binding orders from 15 different countries. The first test flights took place in early 1969, and the planes were first seen by the public at the Paris Air Show in June of that year. In 1971 and 1972, the planes began to tour the world to secure orders. The French plane was the first to visit the US, where in 1973 it landed at Dallas/Fort Worth to mark the official opening of the new airport.

However, at this point, things began to unravel

for Concorde. At the Paris Air Show in 1973 the rival Russian supersonic plane, the Tupolev Tu-144, crashed, killing 12 people and destroying 15 houses. In the public mind, the romance with air travel was beginning to tire, and concerns about noise, pollution, and high-altitude radiation were becoming more common and focused on this new and untried plane. Since the US had canceled its own supersonic programme in 1971, it has been suggested that some of this concern was encouraged by the US government in a display of sour grapes and protectionism. Due to concerns about noise, Concorde was only ever allowed to fly to John F. Kennedy Airport by US regulators, which meant that the plane would never get the orders from major airlines it needed to be a game-changer in aviation. Other contributing factors were the 1973 oil crisis, which made airlines cautious of high-consumption planes; and the development of wide-body planes, like the Boeing 747, which shifted the market from air-travel as a luxury activity to a low-cost, no-frills means of transport.

In the end, only Air France and British Airways took up their orders, and this, combined with spiraling costs which brought the price to £23 million in 1977, meant that Concorde never went into full-scale construction. Despite legal opposition that reached the Supreme Court of the US, Concorde began scheduled flights between Paris and London to JFK Airport on the 22nd of November, 1977. The first scheduled flights had begun a little more than a year earlier from London to Bahrain and from Paris to Rio de Janeiro (via Dakar). Concorde took 3.5 hours to fly Paris to New York, against 8 hours for conventional aircraft. The plane cruised at 56,000 feet, well above the altitudes of other planes. The average cruise speed was 1,334 mph, about 800 mph above that of commercial planes of the period.

Initial ticket prices across the Atlantic were around $800, $100 more than conventional first class. By 1981, the British Government, which shared ownership with British Airways, had lost money every year, so was persuaded by British Airways to sell its share to the company. Market research showed that people thought Concorde tickets should be expensive, so BA regularly raised prices to match that perception, and in this way kept the aircraft profitable. Concorde became a plane that only the rich could afford to fly on. Supersonic air travel never came to the masses. Concorde was chartered quite a bit and flew all over the world, but regular passenger service was limited to JFK/London and JFK/Paris.

On the 25th of July, 2000, disaster struck. A Concorde leaving Charles de Gaulle Airport crashed, killing all 100 passengers and nine crew members, plus four people on the ground. Following safety improvements, the plane returned to commercial flights on the 11th of September, 2001, landing in New York shortly before the Word Trade Center attacks. Although commercial flights continued for a few more years, the death-warrant for the plane had been signed. The French crash, declining air-travel following 9/11, an aging cockpit design and rising maintenance costs all conspired to lead Air France and British Airways to simultaneously announce on the 10th of April 2003, that flights of Concorde were to end. It was a shocking, short-term decision. Concorde was generally thought to be profitable, but it was now deemed more trouble that it was worth. Sir Richard Branson, the founder of Virgin Atlantic, made an unsuccessful bid to buy the BA fleet but his old rival declined. The last Air France transatlantic flight took place on the 30th of May, 2003. BA made a series of 'last flights' to America and around the UK in October of 2003, culminating with the rare illumination of Windsor Castle as a tribute.

The Concordes were donated to various museums. Some now live in august institutions like the Smithsonian. Some sit outside, open to the elements, their airframes rotting away. Concorde will never fly again. Their hydraulics, the lifeblood of an aircraft, have been drained. Once they made their final flights, they could no longer fly anywhere else. Occasionally groups make headlines by saying they want to bring a Concorde back to flight but they usually fade away - the cost to do so would be astronomical, and Airbus is completely unwilling to service Concorde which means it can never get the necessary paperwork to fly. Nostalgia is not enough to get one of these in the air again.

One of those final destinations was Bristol Filton Airport, where every Concorde was built and had its first flight. It was only fitting that one of the final ones would go there. It's now marooned there. The airport has been closed and redeveloped. It took over a decade for planners to finally build a museum around the Concorde (it sat outside for

Left and Above: New Concorde Hanger at Aerospace Bristol

the intervening years). That new museum is now called Aerospace Bristol and it just recently opened. The museum is a guide to all the important flight developments that occurred at Bristol Filton, but by far the most important attraction is the new Concorde Hanger.

Set back from the rest of the museum in a separate building, a British Airways Concorde now sits properly in a dedicated hanger, with a multimedia experience all around it to educate visitors on the history of Concorde. Best of all you can walk around and under the Concorde and take in its immense size in person. What's striking is how HUGE Concorde is when you see it in person. But then how small it is on the inside when you see how cramped the seats were. There's a great video projected onto the side of the plane that gives a 10-minute history.

Upstairs, there's a small museum display for Concorde that features various artifacts from its history. And then you're treated to be able to onto the plane itself. Previously one would have to pay thousand of dollars to go on board a Concorde, now anyone can. It looks exactly as it did when they stopped flying. Unfortunately, you're not allowed to sit in the seats to get a real feel for what it would have been like to fly in the cramped interior.

If you're a fan of Concorde and aviation, a visit to this new museum is highly recommended. Looking around, though, you're hit with a realization. Once they brought Concorde into her new hanger, they sealed her in by building a wall. You get a huge feeling of sadness when you realise that there are no hanger doors. Concorde is trapped inside and can never get out. She belongs in the air but will never taste it again.

Concorde died for lots of reasons but mostly because the airline industry doesn't have a vision beyond operating as cheaply as possible for passengers who want to pay as little as possible. The audio guide on the overhead speakers talked about how Concorde had revolutionised air travel, but really, it didn't. The revolution died with Concorde's last flight in 2003. Supersonic air travel is dead. There are glimmers of hope it might return again one day on a smaller scale, but it's still unlikely. Concorde will now spend its future forever as a selection of really cool museum pieces.

Sites to Visit

A non-functioning Concorde shell is on display at the Brooklands Museum in Weybridge, Surrey. A second is on display at Le Bourget Air and Space Museum in Paris. This plane has been partly restored, and there are plans to make it possible to taxi the plane on the runway. Club Concorde, a group of enthusiasts, has expressed the desire to buy this plane and have it flying again by 2019 (something that's highly unlikely). The last British Concorde is now housed at Aerospace Bristol, at Bristol's former Filton Airport and was open as of January 2017.

Locations of the remaining Concordes

Prototypes

- G-BSST - Fleet Air Arm Museum, England
- G-AXDN - Imperial War Museum Duxford
- F-WTSS - French Air Museum at Le Bourget Airport
- G-BBDG - Brooklands Museum Weybridge, Surrey
- F-WTSB - Aeroscopia Museum near Airbus Toulouse factory

British Airways

- G-BOAC - Manchester Airport
- G-BOAA - National Museum of Flight Edinburgh
- G-BOAB - Lives at Heathrow (not open to public)
- G-BOAD - Intrepid Sea, Air & Space Museum New York
- G-BOAE - Bridgetown, Barbados (Museum)
- G-BOAG - Museum of Flight Seattle
- G-BOAF - Aerospace Bristol

Air France

- F-BVFA - Smithsonian Institution National Air and Space Museum's Steven F. Udvar-Hazy Center
- F-BVFB - Sinsheim Auto & Technik Museum in Germany

The New Aerospace Bristol Museum

- F-BVFC - Aeroscopia Museum near Airbus Toulouse factory
- F-BTSD - Air and Space Museum at Le Bourget, France
- F-BVFF - On display at Charles de Gaulle Airport in Paris

Further Research

There are several biographies of Concorde, including:

- *Concorde: The Rise and Fall of the Supersonic Airliner*, by Jonathan Glancey
- *The Concorde Story*, by Christopher Orlebar
- *Concorde: A Designer's Life: The Journey to Mach 2*, by Ted Talbot
- *Vintage Champagne on the Edge of Space: The Supersonic World of a Concorde Stewardess*, by Sally Armstrong
- *Concorde and the Americans: International Politics of the Supersonic Transport*, by Kenneth Owen

GEORGE IV
The Lavish Regent Turned King

The fourth and last Georgian king, King George IV's reputation is one of the worst of any British monarch. A wild and reckless youth, George grew into a feckless and extravagant adult. As Prince Regent, he had little to do with state affairs unless he was asking for handouts to cover his debts and as king, his approach to sovereignty did not change. Two marriages, one secret and one failed, combined with George's taste for excess and penchant for horse-racing made him unpopular with the public. The 'first gentleman of England,' George may have had fine manners and impeccable style but his reign was ineffective in every way, and he died without a friend in the world.

As the first child of King George III, George was born directly into the title of Duke of Cornwall and Duke of Rothesay. He was also given the titles Prince of Wales and Earl of Chester a few days after his birth. Said to have been a very capable student, George's education and upbringing were of a standard you would expect for a future king, and he quickly became fluent in French, German and Italian. By age 18, George was given a house of his own, and he took to his new freedom with glee.

Wildly extravagant, the young Prince socialised constantly, drank heavily and kept many mistresses. When he turned 21 and took up residence in Carlton House his partying and spending increased tenfold. Despite obtaining a grant of £60,000 (equivalent to £6,45 million today) from Parliament as well as a hefty annual allowance from the King, George managed to spend himself into debt. King George III despaired of his son's behaviour and his political leanings which opposed the king's own conservatism.

On the 15th December 1785, at the age of 22, George married Maria Fitzherbert, a twice-divorced Roman Catholic, and a commoner. Of course, the King did not give his consent to this union and the 1701 Act of Settlement that barred the spouse of a Catholic from succeeding was still in place making this marriage void. As a Catholic, Maria believed the laws of the Church to be superior to the law of State and considered herself the wife of the King for the rest of her life. In 1787, overcome by debt and all but estranged from his father, George went to his political allies in Parliament for help. They came through, and on the condition that his marriage to Fitzherbert be publicly denied, gave him enough money to clear the worst of his debts and improve

KEY FACTS

- George IV was born at St James' Palace on the 12th of August 1762.
- George succeeded as the King of Great Britain and Ireland and King of Hanover on the 29th January 1820 at the age of 57.
- He was married in December 1785 to a twice-divorced Roman Catholic lady named Maria Fitzherbert although he repudiated the marriage. George was also married in 1795 to his cousin Caroline Amelia Elizabeth.
- George died at Windsor of various complications to do with obesity on June 26, 1830, aged 67, having reigned ten years.

his residence Carlton House.

George was married again ten years later on the 8th April 1795 to his cousin Princess Caroline of Brunswick. The marriage took place very much against George's will; he was forced to agree to the union so that his father and Parliament would pay his astronomical debts, and the marriage was disastrous. The pair separated after the birth of their only child, Princess Charlotte, and so convinced was Caroline that George hated her she claimed on her deathbed in 1821 that he had poisoned her.

By 1811, George III's mental illness had become so severe he could no longer play his role in government and on the 5th February 1811 the Prince of Wales became Prince Regent of Great Britain and Ireland. Little changed in Britain as a result of this as the regent played an even lesser role than his father in governmental affairs. In 11th May 1812, the Prime Minister Spencer Perceval was assassinated, and the Napoleonic Wars raged on, but George spent these years refining himself into the 'first gentleman of England,' taking an active interest in fashion and culture.

King George III died on 29th January 1820, and the Prince Regent became King George IV. In similarity with his lifestyle up to this point, King George's coronation was an obscenely costly

The Bristol Pavilion

and extravagant affair. But despite the hit to the taxpayers' pocket it was a popular event and the British public were relieved to see a king in the flesh after so many years under the reign of a recluse. George banned his legal wife Caroline from his coronation and refused to recognise her as Queen, even going as far as to have her name removed from the Book of Common Prayer.

King George IV embarked on a royal tour in 1821 visiting Ireland, the first monarch to do so since Richard II and Scotland, the first since the mid-17th century. A born collector, George also began to establish an impressive royal art collection and transformed Windsor Castle and Buckingham Palace. The 'Catholic question,' the issue of when and how Catholic people would be emancipated from the various discriminations they faced was a major concern of parliament during George's later reign, but he intervened mainly to complicate matters. In 1829, George was forced by his ministers to agree to the Catholic Emancipation, against his will and his interpretation of his protestant coronation oath.

George's taste for excess in all things led to a massive decline in his health in his later years. Obese, addicted to laudanum and suffering from gout, dropsy and possibly porphyria, he became completely incapacitated. On the morning of the 26th of June 1830, King George IV took his last breath. George was buried on the 15th July 1830 at Windsor Castle.

George may have fathered many children given his proclivity for mistresses, but his only legitimate child was Princess Charlotte of Wales. Sadly Charlotte died of complication following the birth of a stillborn baby in 1817. Prince Frederick, Duke of York and Albany, George's younger brother had died childless, and so the third son of George III, Prince William, Duke of Clarence took to the throne as William IV.

Legacy

George IV's legacy is not a positive one. His reputation was poor amongst the British public due to rumors about his marriage to a Catholic, constant philandering and excessive spending that saw him rack up the equivalent of millions of pounds of national debt. His moniker 'the first gentleman of

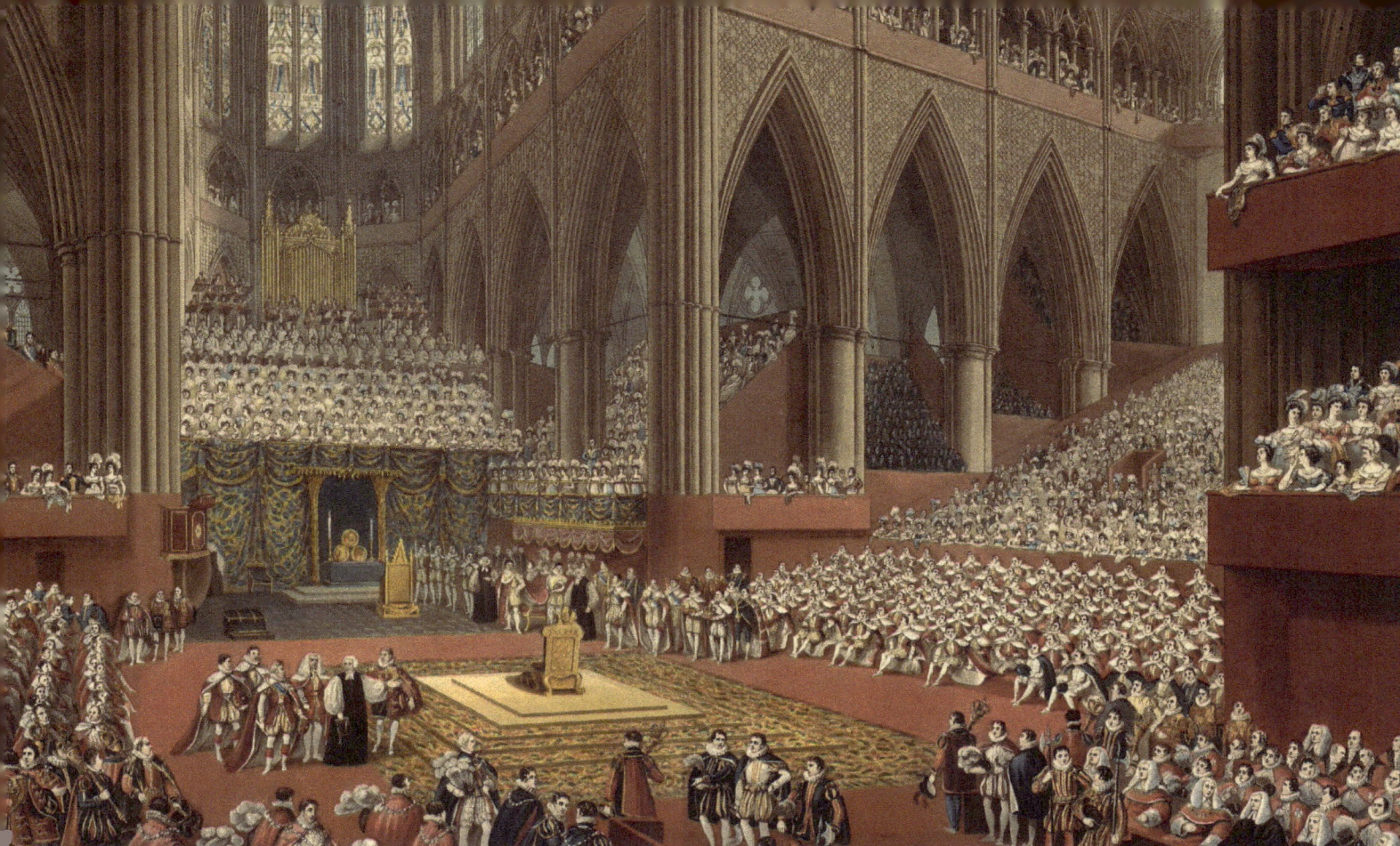

Coronation of George IV

England' is an ironic one given George's indulgent lifestyle and moral weaknesses. A patron of the arts, George nevertheless had a huge influence on the architecture, fashion, and style of the day. Perhaps George IV is best summed up by the comment ran in *The Times* newspaper after his death that read, he would always prefer 'a girl and a bottle to politics and a sermon.'

Film & TV

- This Charming Man (2006)
- Poldark (1996)
- A Royal Scandal (1996) TV documentary
- Vanity Fair (1987 and 1998) TV series
- Princess Caraboo (1994)
- The Madness of King George (1994)
- The Scarlet Pimpernel (1982) TV drama
- Prince Regent (1979) TV documentary
- Lady Caroline Lamb (1972)
- The First Gentleman (1948)
- The Scarlet Pimpernel (1934)

Further Research

- Hibbert, Christopher (2015) *George IV*
- Baker, Kenneth (2005). *George IV: A Life in Caricature*
- Parissien, Steven (2001). *George IV: The Grand Entertainment*
- David, Saul (2000). *Prince of Pleasure: The Prince of Wales and the Making of the Regency.*
- Smith, E. A. (1999). *George IV*
- De-la-Noy, Michael (1998). *George IV*

Locations to Visit

- George IV was born at St James's Palace in London, died at Windsor Castle in Berkshire and was buried at St George's Chapel in Windsor. All of these locations are open to the public.
- There are many statues of George IV, but two of the most famous are located in Trafalgar Square, London and the Royal Pavilion in Brighton.

AUNTIE BEEB

The Fascinating History of the BBC

By John Rabon

While no longer alone amongst Britain's media powerhouses, at one time, the British Broadcasting Corporation (BBC) was the only game in town. Since its incorporation in 1922, the corporation has been responsible for informing and entertaining the British public, tasks for which it continues to excel at 95 years later. Over this time, the BBC has provided not only the United Kingdom but the world, with reliable news and some of mankind's most legendary programmes from "Doctor Who" to "Monty Python's Flying Circus". Its personnel have influenced radio and television, and its buildings are some of the most famous in Britain. As we delve into the near-century long broadcasting history of the BBC, we invite you, dear reader, to join us on a journey from the first radio signal to the present and discover what a fascinating chronicle this media giant possesses.

The United Kingdom's first radio broadcast took place in June 1920 at the Marconi factory, and from there, radio became so prolific a communication tool that the General Post Office had to step in as the licensing official to control the growth of the medium. By 1922, the GPO had more than 100 requests for licenses from manufacturers and other organisations, and so to ensure a measured development of radio broadcasts, the GPO recommended issuing only one license to a consortium of manufacturers (including Marconi) under the title of the British Broadcasting Company, Ltd. The company formed officially on 18 October 1922, and made its first broadcast on channel 2LO from the seventh floor of Marconi House on 14 November that year.

To head this new broadcasting conglomerate, the government appointed John Reith as the first General Manager for the BBC in mid-December 1922. Mr. Reith had served in the army during World War I and had had no experience in broadcasting before applying for the manager post on seeing a newspaper advertisement for the position. He was admittedly out of his depth for the position, having to deal with copyrights, patents, music publishers, artists' associations, performance rights, and more, though he felt he had the credentials to "manage any company" given his military background. Despite this lack of prior experience, he proved to be an immensely capable manager who helped shape the BBC

John Reith

during its formative years and remained in charge until 1938. Making up the rules as he went along, Reith proved an innovative leader who had to use his army engineer's background to craft standards and practices that the corporation would follow for decades.

In September 1923, one of the BBC's most influential documents began publication with the first issue of the *Radio Times*. The periodical provided a schedule of the corporation's limited programmes, but also served as an educational resource for budding amateur enthusiasts as well as carrying the manufacturers' advertisements for the newest radio equipment. The RT was also the only place to find the radio schedule, as newspapers viewed it as a competing medium and thus refused to publish it. The magazine began as a joint effort between the BBC and publisher George Newnes, and the latter type-set, printed and distributed the RT himself until the corporation bought the publication fully under its control in 1925.

The BBC's first major test came during the General Strike in 1926. At the time, the BBC was in renegotiations with the GPO over its license, an issue that was left up to the Crawford Committee. Several of the manufacturers wanted out due to the unprofitable nature of the consortium, while Reith wanted the BBC to become a public service. Reith wanted the BBC to maintain its monopoly and serve the public interest, feeling its expansion should be funded by the government for the general welfare. Meanwhile, the General Council of the Trades Union Congress was trying to get the British government to stop wage reduction and improve the conditions for the nation's coal miners. Negotiations between the TUC and the government broke down, and the strike began on 3 May 1926. The strike had an effect of temporarily halting newspaper production, rendering the BBC the only source of regular news.

Behind closed doors, Reith was firmly on the side of the government with regards to the strike, even letting the Prime Minister broadcast from his own home. This helped to keep the government out of the BBC's business insofar as it did not attempt to use the radio service as its mouthpiece. The BBC then presented some of the most even coverage of the strike, representing the viewpoints of both the workers and the government during the work stoppage. This cemented the BBC's audience as well as establishing its reputation for fair and balanced reporting. The company came out of 1926 in a strong position, and the Government accepted the Crawford Committee's recommendation that the BBC have a new status as a non-commercial, Crown-chartered organisation in 1927, then becoming the British Broadcasting Corporation. The original 1927 charter established objectives, powers, and obligations of the BBC, entrusting John Reith as its Director-General to execute the document's provisions.

1928 would see another leap for the BBC as construction began on Broadcasting House. The corporation had operated its radio broadcasts out of Marconi House and buildings in the Strand and Savoy Hill, but Broadcasting House would be its first purpose-built headquarters for radio broadcasting. G. Val Mayer designed it in an Art Deco style for the exterior, while Raymond McGrath designed the interior in a similar vein. Its Portland stone structure contained all the studios, and the building's steel shell provided acoustic "buffering." For a time, its construction was held up as nearby residents were concerned about it blocking the natural light for their homes on Langham Street. It took four years to complete, and programmes slowly began moving over in 1932, with the first broadcast being that of Henry Hall and the BBC Dance Orchestra on 15 March. That same year, King George V would become the first monarch to use radio as a broadcast medium to reach his subjects.

Meanwhile, as Broadcasting House was going up, something else revolutionary was being born. Scottish engineer John Logie Baird had been experimenting with television since 1924, beaming the first images across a room and later demonstrated his experiments at Selfridge's and the Royal Institution. He also used BBC frequencies to broadcast some of his images from studios at Covent Garden in 1929. In 1930, he would broadcast the BBC's first televised drama, "The Man with the Flower in His Mouth", ushering in the television era for the broadcaster. Baird's technology could only broadcast thirty lines of resolution, as opposed to 2,160 lines of resolution by the latest 4K televisions. Limited regular broadcasts then began in 1934, and the BBC established its first television studio at Alexandra Palace in 1936 along with starting the BBC Television Service.

By 1937, technology advanced enough that televisions had 405 lines of resolution. 1937 would also see the BBC's first outside television broadcast as the corporation filmed the coronation of King George VI. Unfortunately, the outbreak of World War II in 1939 would see a suspension of the television service for the duration of the conflict. In response to the danger presented by the London Blitz, the BBC would move much its radio broadcasting out of London to Bristol and then Bedford. St. Paul's Church in Bedford actually became the home studio for the daily service until 1945. The BBC Television Service would resume on 7 June 1946 with Jasmine Bligh as the first presenter back on the air. October 1946 would see the beginning of television programming dedicated solely to children, with shows such as "Muffin the Mule" being broadcast from the corporation's new television studios at Lime Grove.

One of the biggest changes to the BBC to occur post-war was the introduction of the television license. As mentioned earlier, at the advent of the company back in 1922, the General Post Office

Clockwise from Top Left: Blackadder, Doctor Who (Tennant Years), Yes Minister, House of Cards

was responsible for issuing licenses to amateur and professional radio operators. Besides broadcasting, those who wanted to receive radio broadcasts paid a fee of 10 shillings. With the resumption of the BBC Television Service in 1946, the Post Office merged the receiving radio broadcast license with television reception, and the cost for both was a mere £2 (roughly £76 today). With the advent of color television in the 1960s (more on that later), a surcharge was added to cover the new technology. The cost has subsequently risen nearly every year, though the license fee was frozen in 2016 at £145.50 while the BBC's Charter was renegotiated and now sits at £147 as of April 2017. While some try to get by without the license, the penalty for owning a television and not having a license is roughly £1,000 plus any incidental legal costs and compensation.

Television would only grow as a medium with Newsreel beginning in January 1948 and the first televised Olympic Games in the summer. While only 100,000 British homes had televisions by this time, the BBC still broadcast 68.5 hours of live coverage during the games. The next year would see the return of live weather broadcasts that had been pursued tepidly before the war. Things were relatively quiet until ITV came along in 1955 to challenge the BBC's monopoly on the television airwaves. The new company was a direct result of the Television Act 1954, which created the Independent Television Authority (later the Independent Broadcast Authority) to regulate the growing medium and license franchises. More insight into the government was provided during the 1950s as the first live broadcast proceedings of the House of Commons were made in 1950 and the coronation of Queen Elizabeth II was transmitted in 1953.

One major event that took place in 1956 was the establishment of the Radiophonic Workshop. The workshop was established because the BBC wanted to develop its own music and sound effects for the radio and television programmes it produced. The workshop would craft some of the most innovative

The former BBC Television Centre (now closed)

sounds over the next few decades, including Doctor Who's famous TARDIS dematerialisation sound effect and the programme's theme tune. The Radiophonic Workshop would not close up shop until 1993 when the corporation determined the department was no longer viable. In 1958, one of the BBC's most important children's programmes would be born when "Blue Peter" premiered on 16 October. Head of Children's Television at the time, Owen Reed, wanted a programme that catered to children ages 5 to 8 and represented a "voyage of adventure." Still running today, it would have a major influence with lines such as "And now for something completely different" and the famed Blue Peter Badge becoming established parts of British culture.

Blue Peter would also become one of the first television programmes to move into the famed BBC Television Centre when it opened in 1960. Much like Broadcasting House before it, Television Centre was purpose-built for TV broadcasting. The building was designed by Graham Dawborn, who was initially stumped by having to design a building for the triangular property. The story goes that he went to a local pub where he drew the boundaries of the land on an envelope with a big question mark over it. This ended up becoming the basis for his design that would permit eight tv studios, offices, production galleries, recording studios, and separate entrances for guests and delivery trucks.

Construction on Television Centre actually began in 1950, but government restrictions on the building made the process a lengthy one. The sanctions on building and the licensing of materials stopped the construction until 1953, and in the meantime, the BBC opted to renovate its studios at Lime Grove, Hammersmith, and Shepard's Bush Empire. Stage One including the TVC scenery block was the first part of the center built, while Stage 2 and the canteen block followed in 1954. The next year would see work begin on the circular office block that composed Stage 3. By the time the building opened in 1960, studio TC3 was the first to be completed. The studio would become home to many of the BBC's most famous programmes from "Monty Python's Flying Circus" to "Strictly Come Dancing".

When the Independent Television Authority determined that ITV didn't have enough quality programming, it gave the license for a new television station to the BBC, ultimately creating BBC Two in 1964. The new station caused the name of BBC Television Service to change to BBC One. BBC One would become the home to most of the mainstream and popular programmes over the years, while BBC Two was populated with the more intellectual programmes and films, including documentaries such as "The Ascent of Man", and eventually automotive magazine "Top Gear". BBC Two would also become a testing ground for other shows that would eventually move to BBC One such as "Have I Got News for You" and "The Great British Bakeoff". The channel later broadcast the corporation's first dedicated block of morning children's programming, which would eventually evolve into CBBC and CBeebies.

Science-Fiction television programming would change forever in 1963. The BBC's then Head of Drama, Sydney Newman, wanted a new programme that would help teach kids about history by using time travel. The programme that he eventually developed with the corporation's first female producer, Verity Lambert, would become the worldwide phenomenon that is "Doctor Who". Featuring the alien known as The Doctor, his granddaughter Susan, and her teachers Ian and Barbara, the first episode hit a stumbling block as it was overshadowed by news concerning the death of US President John F. Kennedy when it premiered the same week. The first episode was rebroadcast a week later, but the programme really took off with the introduction of the Doctor's most famous enemies, the Daleks. After leading actor William Hartnell was forced to leave the show in 1966 due to ill health, the writers came up with the concept of regeneration so that Doctor Who could continue with a new actor as the Doctor. This plot device kept the original version of the show going until 1987, coming back for a 1996 television pilot film and the current programme that began in 2005.

1966 would also see another major innovation for the BBC with the advent of color television. The corporation announced that it would soon bring color to television screens in 1966, though it would be another year before its first colorised broadcast to the public. The BBC had actually experimented with color transmissions for the first time in 1957 with broadcasts made to both houses of Parliament, but would not bring the technology to the masses for another nine years. BBC Two was

Anglotopia's Top 10 BBC Comedies

1. Yes, Minister
2. Monty Python
3. 'Allo 'Allo
4. As Time Goes By
5. Blackadder
6. Dad's Army
7. Fawlty Towers
8. Keeping Up Appearances
9. Only Fools And Horses
10. Red Dwarf

the first to experiment with color broadcasts when it televised Wimbledon with the new technology on 1 July 1967. BBC Two Controller David Attenborough said at the time that at least five hours of programming per week would be dedicated to color, but by December, 80% of the channels shows were in color. At the time, a color receiver cost about £250 along with the supplemental license fee. Color would be extended to BBC One in 1969 and was completely in effect by 1976.

Local radio stations such as Radio London also began to appear at the time, spurred on by the existence of pirate radio ships. These maverick stations, such as Radio Caroline, were headquartered on ships anchored in the North Sea and broadcast popular music that wasn't as widely available on BBC Radio. As they weren't government sponsored, they also featured copious amounts of advertising that eventually forced the BBC to permit nationally based advertising services. The corporation was also encouraged to diversify its broadcasts across multiple stations, having Radio 1 play popular music to compete with the pirates, Radio 2 featured "easy listening," Radio 3 had classical music and cultural programming, and Radio 4 focused primarily on news and information.

The 1970s continued to push innovation as the BBC partnered with Open University to bring higher education to the masses through early morning and late-night educational programmes. Even today, Open University and the BBC's partnership continues to bring new ways of

> **Anglotopia's Top 10 BBC Dramas**
>
> 1. Doctor Who
> 2. Pride & Prejudice
> 3. Upstairs Downstairs
> 4. Life on Mars
> 5. House of Cards
> 6. Call the Midwife
> 7. The Forsyte Saga
> 8. Bleak House
> 9. All Creatures Great and Small
> 10. Our Friends in the North

learning to the public through online videos that cover everything from the color spectrum to how cars are built. 1972 saw the introduction of news programming aimed at children and young people called "Newsround". With John Craven at the helm, "Newsround" brought kids current events from all over the world and even broke news stories such as Pope John Paul I's assassination and the Challenger explosion. 1974 then saw the introduction of Ceefax. Ceefax was a Teletext service that originally begun as a captioning system for the corporation's programmes but grew to provide full pages of information on news, sports, and more. It ceased to be used in 2012 when the information service switched over the being completely digital.

Many of the BBC's most endearing television programmes also got their start in the 1970s. Leaving Monty Python to follow his own path, John Cleese started the show "Fawlty Towers" with his then-wife Connie Booth. Other comedies such as "Are You Being Served?", "Last of the Summer Wine" and "Porridge" also kept audiences laughing. However, comedy wasn't the only new programming that got viewers attention. Now known the world over for his exceptional nature documentaries, David Attenborough began broadcasting his "Life of Earth" series in 1979, which led to decades of bringing the true majesty of nature to the public.

The 1980s marked new challenges for the United Kingdom and the BBC. With the premiership of Margaret Thatcher beginning in 1979, her Conservative government brought a wave of deregulation that further loosened the BBC's grip on the radio and television industries in Britain. Under the Broadcasting Act 1980, the Independent Broadcasting Authority became further empowered to create another TV license. Competitor ITV was joined by the commercially-sponsored Channel 4 in 1982 and its Welsh counterpart, S4C. However, audiences were still tuning into the BBC in droves thanks to new programmes such as "Eastenders" and "Breakfast Time", as well as major events including the Falklands War, Live Aid, and the Wedding of Prince Charles to Diana Spencer, the non-royal who became beloved as the "People's Princess."

New technology drove innovation in the 1990s. The 24-hour news stations that had become popular in the United States convinced the BBC to launch its own constant news channel in 1997. While the BBC was only second to get into the game in Britain, BBC News 24 immediately made its impact in a world where constant-access to the news was becoming necessary to keep the public informed. BBC Radio also expanded itself to BBC Radio 5, which also covered news, opinion, and sports in 1994. 1997 saw the advent of the BBC's website, bbc.co.uk, and the corporation provided its first digital channel the next year with BBC Choice. Choice not only offered news and information on demand but also played host to many "behind the scenes" shows that let audiences in on how they're favorite programmes were made. This station became BBC Three in 2003, airing more innovative programmes such as "The Mighty Boosh" and "Being Human" until it was finally closed in 2016, becoming a web-only service.

As the British government instituted a devolution of its powers at the beginning of the millennium to national assemblies in Wales, Scotland, and Northern Ireland, so the BBC split off some of its responsibilities to regional branches in Cardiff, Glasgow, and Belfast. This meant that the regional headquarters had more ability to produce their own programmes not only for local audiences but for national consumption as well. This was perhaps best exemplified by the revival of "Doctor Who" in 2005, which was produced and largely filmed at BBC Broadcasting House Cardiff. Meanwhile, much of the original drama and comedy production moved to Broadcasting

House Belfast and much of the national television production, including many beloved panel shows, started to be done out of BBC Pacific Quay, which opened in 2007. BBC North also gained expansive responsibilities in the mid-2000s at New Broadcasting House in Manchester. Other regions under the corporation purview include BBC West, BBC North West, and BBC Yorkshire, amongst others.

The digital frontier was even more firmly embraced come the 2000s as iPlayer was launched so that anyone could view BBC programmes on the computers and electronic devices, that way they wouldn't miss a moment of the revived "Strictly Come Dancing". The "Red Button" was introduced the next year that permitted viewers to get more information on the programme they were watching, answer quiz questions, and interact with their shows in an all-new way. All these innovations were put to use in 2012 for the Summer Olympic Games in London and part of the revamping of Broadcasting House, which underwent a major renovation from 2003 to 2013. The new wings and renovations brought everything under one roof after Television Centre had closed in 2012. One of the best programmes that really shows off the revamped Broadcasting Centre is "W1A", which features Hugh Bonneville as the new Head of Values, tasked with promoting the core purpose of the BBC while constantly flummoxed by his subordinates.

In 2016, another chapter in the ongoing saga between the BBC and the Conservative Party began as the corporation's charter was due to be renewed. The BBC's Royal Charter only lasts for ten years, thus requiring it to be renewed periodically, which naturally has a tendency towards some executive meddling by Her Majesty's government. When the charter came up for renewal most recently, some ministers desired to move the corporation away from reliance on the government, while others wanted more monitoring of the BBC's programming and approval of the charter by both the Lords and the Commons. The approved charter, while championing diversity in programming and presenters that should please regional audiences, has also been criticised for allowing communications regulator Ofcom to have more say over how the news is presented. The new charter also closed the loophole that let people watch BBC programmes through iPlayer without a television license and

W1A - Comedy Set in the BBC Headquarters

a "unitary board" replacing the BBC Trust as the governing body of the corporation. In a further attempt to privatise the BBC's production, the charter permits private companies to have the opportunity to produce BBC programmes, taking some of the shows out of the house. In one good move, the new charter will last for eleven years instead of ten to make it less likely that it will become a political football for parties to use in election years.

Even as the new charter changes the workings of broadcasting, the BBC continues on its purpose, established by John Reith at the corporation's outset, to: "Inform, educate, and entertain." Since its creation in 1932, the BBC has sought to excel in all three areas amidst vesting improving technology and increasing competition. Today, it continues to give audiences the very best in programming with "BBC News", "Doctor Who", "EastEnders", "QI", and more. Joining forces with ITV to create Britbox, the BBC ensures that its reach continues not only across the United Kingdom but the whole world. Always embracing new technology and methods to meet its core mission, one can only

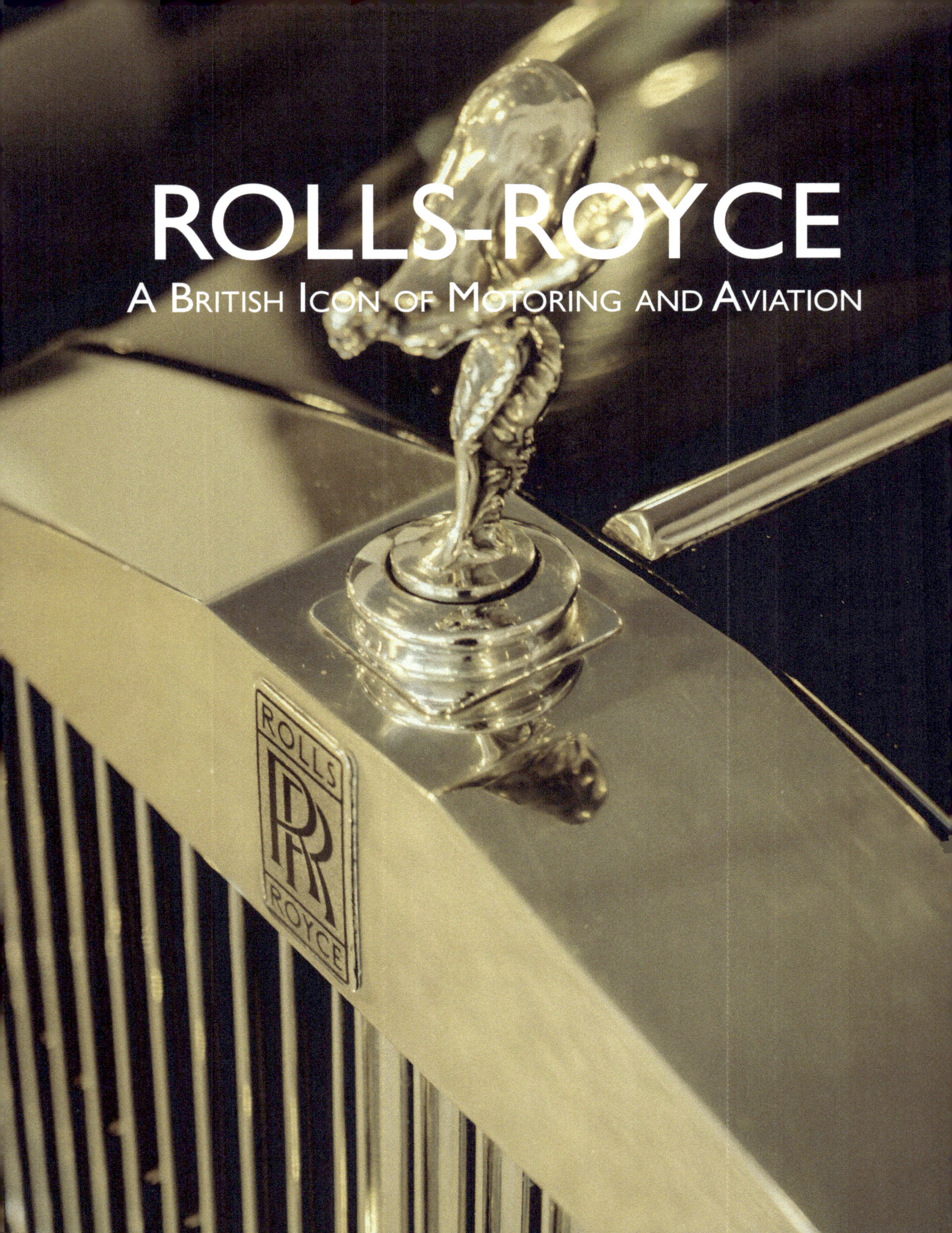

ROLLS-ROYCE
A British Icon of Motoring and Aviation

Two men who could not have been more different created the brand of Rolls-Royce. One, Charles Rolls, was a wealthy playboy with a love of engines, who died aged 32 when his airplane crashed. The other, Henry Royce, was a working-class engineering genius, who developed not only car engines, but airplane engines too, creating the engine for the Spitfire fighters and the Lancaster bombers that would save the UK in WWII. Their brand became synonymous with luxurious and reliable motor cars, and in airplane engines for innovation, endurance, and power. After the death of Rolls, Royce ran the company with such attention to detail that he made himself seriously ill. Even then he continued to arrange every detail, until his death in 1933. After the war, the business foundered on the costs and complexities of airplane-engine development and went into receivership in 1971. After a period of government ownership, it returned to public hands as two separate companies – one for cars and one for engines. Both remain in business today.

The late 19th century saw the first motor cars on the roads of England, but they were made in Germany and France. The earliest British-made cars employed European components, and it was probably Richard Stevens, a Welshman, who produced the first all-British car in 1897. Following the lifting of the 2-mph speed limit in 1896, driving became more popular, and in 1900 Herbert Austin began what was to soon become, backed by the Vickers brothers, Wolseley Motors Limited in Birmingham.

So when another Welshman, Charles Stewart Rolls, met Frederick Henry Royce at the Midland Hotel, Manchester, on the 4th of May, 1904, they were certainly still among the pioneers of motor car manufacturing on the British Isles. Before the end of the year, they had their first car, the Rolls-Royce 10 hp, ready to show at the Salon de l'Automobile, or Paris Motor Show, held in December of that year.

Neither man was a novice with cars. Henry Royce was already 41 and had suffered the loss of his father when he was only nine years old. His father's flour-milling business had failed, forcing the family to move to London from their home in Huntingdonshire. In those years, children began school at an older age, and after his father's death Royce was forced to leave school, after only one year of education, to sell newspapers and deliver

KEY FACTS

- Founded in 1904 by Henry Royce and Charles Rolls
- Pioneered luxury car manufacturing in the UK
- Pioneered airplane engine development globally
- Suffered in the general post-WWII decline of British manufacturing

telegrams. With the financial help of an aunt, he was apprenticed to the Great Northern Railway Company at its engineering works in Peterborough when he was fifteen. After only three years, he was forced to move on again, and drifted into work with electrical lighting, for the Electric Light and Power Company. Then, in 1884, with a friend as a partner, he went into business making household electric fittings. They started making dynamos and electric cranes for businesses and enjoyed some success. By 1899, F.H. Royce & Company had gone public, with a share offering. They had outgrown their factory in Hulme, Manchester, so opened a second one nearby in the Trafford Park neighborhood. Increased competition from Germany and the USA presented a threat to the continuing strength of the business, so Royce, who had become fascinated by motor cars, bought some early models. HIs De Dion and a two-cylinder Decauville seemed to him to be poor quality, and after trying to improve them, he decided instead to make his own car. In 1904 he made three cars, one of which he gave to a director of Royce & Co. named Henry Edmunds.

Edmunds was a friend of Charles Rolls, and there could hardly have been a man more different from Royce than Rolls was. The son of John Allan Rolls, 1st Baron Llangattock, he had been born in a house in prestigious Berkeley Square, although the family home was at The Hendre, a country house north of Monmouth, in Wales. Charles had been to Eton, and from there he went to Trinity College, Cambridge, but he and Royce did have one common interest – engines. Rolls had been tinkering around with them at Eton, earning himself the nickname 'Dirty Rolls,' and at Cambridge, he studied

Charles Rolls (Left) and Henry Royce (Right)

mechanical and applied science. When he was just 18, he went to Paris, joined the Automobile Club of France, and bought a Peugeot Phaeton. The year was 1896, and he became the very first car owner in Cambridge. He became a founding member of the Automobile Club of Great Britain and campaigned to remove the speed limit imposed on early drivers.

Realising he was more of a promoter and salesman than an engineer, he persuaded his father to give him £6,600 to form C.S. Rolls & Co., one of Britain's first car dealerships, importing French and Belgian cars. By comparison, Royce had saved just £20 to invest in the founding of F.H. Royce & Co. Rolls dealership began in early 1903, and it was there, the following year, that Henry Edmunds took that first car made by Frederick Royce. Rolls interest was seized, and that fateful meeting for the 4th of May was arranged.

The success of their car in Paris led to a partnership, Rolls-Royce Limited, formed in 1906. Rolls brought money and a head for business, while Royce had the technical and engineering skills. Their cars soon began winning awards for quality and reliability, and they were soon selling in the USA. Their cars offered smooth, quiet rides which appealed to the luxury market, and moved away from the Toad of Toad Hall image of motoring. The introduction of the 40/50, a powerful 6-cylinder car, cemented the company's reputation for quality and luxury.

The younger Rolls, with no real need for the money, soon lost interest and was a sleeping partner by 1909. He turned to airplanes, bought a Wright Brothers plane, and became a pilot. The following year, at an air-show at Hengistbury Airfield, Bournemouth, he died in a crash, becoming the first air fatality in the UK. He was just 32 years old.

Royce was now in charge, but he had his own problems. A workaholic to the point where his health suffered, he became seriously ill in 1902, and again in 1911. In 1912, he underwent major surgery and was given a few months to live. As one might have predicted, he ignored that and went back to work, although he was not allowed to go to the factory. So he managed things remotely, living either in West Sussex or the south of France, while the factory, laid out in 1908 to his meticulous requirements, was in Derby, in England's north-west.

Despite his prognosis, Royce did not die, and the government invited him to diversify into aircraft engines. His first was the Eagle, two of which powered the first trans-Atlantic flight by Alcock and Brown in 1919. The 1920s were the great age of airplane racing, and Royce began building aluminum-body engines specifically for maximum power with minimum weight. Starting with the Kestrel in 1927, he developed the larger Buzzard, and from that the Rolls-Royce R, a 37-liter supercharged V-12, delivering 2,800 horsepower from a 1,640-pound engine. With it fitted into a Supermarine S.6B seaplane and funded by the UK government in the interests of national prestige, he won the Schneider Trophy in 1929. A few months after that race, the plane broke the world air-speed record, reaching 407.5 mph.

On the motor car front, the company had introduced a smaller, cheaper car in 1922 – the Twenty. This was followed by the Phantom, and it was then that the older 40/50 was transformed into the Silver Ghost. A factory was established in Springfield, Massachusetts, manufacturing Silver Ghosts for the American luxury market. In 1931 it acquired the ailing Bentley business, turning it into a smaller, more 'sporty' car to compliment the sedate Rolls-Royce image.

Royce saw the military benefits of the 'R' engine, and with no government interest, but war-clouds gathering over Europe, he worked on the project himself. By 1932 he had the 'PV-12' under development – 'PV' stood for 'Private Venture.' Although he died before its completion, the engine was to become the Rolls-Royce Merlin, which powered both the Spitfire fighter and the Lancaster bomber, changing the course of history. Royce received an OBE in 1918 and was made a Baronet in 1930, putting him finally in the same social class as his old partner, Charles Rolls. He became ill again and died at his home on the 30th of April 1933.

After WWII, all car production moved to the Crewe factory in Cheshire, where the airplane engines had been made during the war. But the post-war years of austerity were not an ideal time to be selling luxury cars, so they began to concentrate on engine manufacturer, producing their first diesel engines for cars in 1951. They also began producing turbo-prop airplane engines, as the industry transitioned into jet propulsion, and began producing jet engines, notably the RB163 Spey, used to power numerous early jet aircraft. The development of jet engines was notoriously expensive, and the financial rewards uncertain and far off. Consequently, the company entered a period of financial hardship, culminating in a voluntary entry into receivership at the beginning of 1971. This was despite a series of government loans and subsidies aimed at shoring-up the company and protecting its 80,000 employees, as well as its technical prowess. At the time, it was developing the RB211 turbofan engine for the Lockheed Tristar, so trans-Atlantic relations were put under threat, but after a fire sale of assets and a complete company reorganisation, Lockheed finally got their engines just over a year later, but too late to avoid being beaten by the McDonnell Douglas DC-10 to be the first long-range jet plane.

The car division limped along under receivership through the 1970s, and public confidence in the business was so eroded that when a share offering was floated in 1973, 80% of the shares were not taken up, and subsequently bought by the government to preserve the jobs of employees. After further restructuring, and a merger with Vickers, the engineering company, the government was able to successfully reprivatise the company in 1987, by selling its shares to the public. Today, 'Rolls-Royce' is the airplane engine company, with 50,000 employees and an income of £5 billion a year. Rolls-Royce Motor Cars operates entirely separately, as a subsidiary of the German luxury car maker, BMW.

Sites to Visit

- Rolls-Royce Motor Cars has a large showroom at 15 Berkeley Square, Mayfair, London W1.
- Visits to the Heritage Centre of the Rolls-Royce headquarters in Derby (aeronautics manufacturer) can be arranged by prior appointment. Contact Jayne Rogers, +44 (0) 1332 823888; heritage.trust@Rolls-Royce.com

Charles Rolls

- His grave and family memorial are in the Church Cemetery of Llangattock-Vibon-Avel, 5 miles west of Monmouth.
- The Hendre, his family's country home, in the village of Llangattock-Vibon-Avel, is now the clubhouse of the 'Rolls of Monmouth Golf Club.'
- There is a circular memorial stone set in the ground at the Upper School location of St Peter's Catholic Comprehensive School, built on the site of Hengistbury Airfield, where he died.
- There is an 8-foot statue of Rolls in Agincourt Square, Monmouth, Wales. It was erected in 1911. Having been planned as a celebration of his successes, it became a memorial to his death. There is another statue of him on Marine Parade, in Dover.

Henry Royce

- There is a plaque on the interior wall of Alwalton Church, Derbyshire, the village where Royce was born. It may contain his ashes, but they are also kept in an urn, at the company's headquarters.
- There is a blue plaque on the gate pillar of Quarndon House, in the Derbyshire village of Quarndon, where he lived between 1908 and 1911.
- There is a memorial stained-glass window in Westminster Abbey, erected in 1962.
- There is a statue of Royce outside the company headquarters of Rolls-Royce, on Moor Lane, in the town of Derby.

THE SLANG PAGE
British Railway Terms

Tube - Nickname for the London Underground

Railway - Railroad is an American term; do not use this term when talking about Britain's rails.

Heritage Railway - Usually a steam railway, but sometimes diesel operating on disused lines

Beeching Cuts - Dr Beeching famously cut many of Britain's branch lines in the 1960s leading to closure of stations all across the country. Some argue the system has never recovered.

Varsity Line - The line that used to connect Oxford to Cambridge. Fell out of use and is now being rebuilt.

HS1 - The high speed railway incorporating the Eurostar service to mainland Europe through the Channel Tunnel.

HS2 - High Speed 2 - A brand new high speed railway that will be constructed in the 2020s and link London to Birmingham.

Bogie - The undercarriage assembly of rolling stock incorporating the train wheels, suspension, brakes and, in powered units, the traction motors

Main Line - A principal rail artery.

Branch Line - A minor line that branches off the main line, usually has less frequent service.

Parliamentary Train - A train service that operates solely because it has to be in order to keep a train franchise. It's often cheaper to just run these 'ghost' trains than go through the process to kill a route/line/station.

Points - Where trains connect and divege on a line. Points failure is a common problem that causes delays.

Signal Failure - When the train signals break, which means trains can't operate safely because the train driver does not know if the tracks ahead are clear.

Sleeper Service - Train service where you can book a bed and sleep overnight and wake up in your destination. Currently the only two left are the Cornish Rivera Sleeper and the Caledonian Sleeper (to Scotland).

Terminus - Where a railway line ends or terminates.

Trainspotter - Person with an intense interest in trains, many will keep track of every locomotive they come across in a notebook.

East Coast Mainline - Mainline railway that runs roughly along the east coast of Britain north to Scotland.

West Coast Mainline - Mainline railway that runs roughly along the west coast of Britain north to Scotland.

Great Western Railway - Famous railway built by Brunel that services the west of England and the west country.

Footbridge - Bridge that allows you to cross tracks safely to get to another platform at a station.

Single Day Return - A single ticket that allows a return journey.

Level Crossing - Street-level crossing of railway tracks.

Network Rail - Quasi-state owned company that owns all the railway tracks and most stations. Responsible for maintaining the tracks and other infrastructure. Train operating companies lease access to the network and pay for its use.

British Rail/British Railways - The former state owned company that ran Britain's railways from the 1940s to the 1990s.

Nationalisation - Catch-all term used to define the policy of taking the railways and the operating companies completely back into public ownership.

Through Station - Station where the trains pass through rather than terminate.

ANGLOTOPIA
THE MAGAZINE FOR ANGLOPHILES
ISSUE #10   SUMMER 2018

Letter from the Editors

Summer in England is a remarkable time. After the dreariness and damp of winter, England is resplendent in green, earning the mantle 'Green & Pleasant Land.' While we enjoy being in England at any time of the year, no matter the weather, there is something truly special about a Great British Summer.

I've just returned from a lovely May trip to England. Summer had started early. I was over to cover the Royal Wedding (article about that in the next issue) of Prince Harry to Meghan Markle. The sun shined every day I was there. It was not too hot and not too cold. I could not have asked for better weather - nor a better experience. Royal Weddings are amazing events, and I now count myself lucky that I've been to two.

Now a bit of housekeeping. We're moving to new software for managing subscriptions. When we started the magazine more than two years ago, we used the best software we could find. But it proved inadequate, mostly in the renewal department. Emails wouldn't get sent reminding people to renew and then when they were sent, people couldn't reset their passwords. I'm just as sick of it as everyone else is, so after much search, we found a new subscription management software.

And the good news is that it actually works. All new subscriptions will now go through it, and over the next few months, we'll transition current subscribers over to the new system so that when it's time for you to renew, you can start fresh with the new system. The biggest change is that we can now auto-bill, which is something people have asked for in the beginning. You don't have to actively renew - you'll just keep getting the magazine as long as your payment information is securely on file.

Also, in between this issue and the last, we finally unveiled long-gestating plans to launch a London-themed print magazine. Issue #1 will be shipping this summer. The format is slightly different than this magazine, with a shorter page count and different binding. If you love London and want an entire magazine dedicated to it, please consider subscribing.

Cheers,
Jonathan & Jackie
Publishers
Anglotopia

Table of Contents

Abandoned Tyneham..2
Poem 10
Brit Book Corner..12
Then & Now...14
Exploring Leeds..16
Lost in the Pond...26
Great Britons: Cecil Rhodes..................................28
This English Life...32
St Paul's Triforium Tour...34
The Suez Crisis...40
The Monarchs: Edward III....................................48
Churchill's Chartwell..52
Beside the Seaside...60
Slang Page: British Police Slang...........................64

About the Magazine

The Anglotopia Magazine is published quarterly by Anglotopia LLC, a USA registered Corporation. All contents copyrighted and may not be reproduced without permission.

Letters to the Editors may be addressed to:

Anglotopia LLC
1101 Cumberland Crossing #120
Valparaiso, IN 46383
USA

Photos: Cover: St Paul's Cathedral Nave, This Page: Windsor During Harry's Wedding, Back Cover: Garden at Snowshill Manor, Inside Back Cover: View of London from Highgate

Printed in PRC

ABANDONED TYNEHAM
THE DORSET VILLAGE LOST TO TIME

By Jonathan Thomas

It was a typical chilly autumn in 1943 along the Dorset Coast. The village of Tyneham was nestled in a valley between the coast and the hills of the Isle of Purbeck. It was always shielded from the worst the sea would throw at it. But its fate could not be saved from World War II, despite its remote location.

Its very remote location, in fact, would destroy the village and hundreds of years of tradition.

That autumn, the residents of Tyneham received a letter from Winston Churchill's War Cabinet that told them they had one month to leave their homes. Their village was needed for the war effort. Don't worry, the letter said, you can return after the war is over.

They never did.

The village was a microcosm of rural village life in Britain. Home to a little more than 200 people, most of whom who worked on the Tyneham estate and nearby Tyneham House, Tyneham had several small, but cozy dwellings, a schoolhouse, a church, a post office, a newly installed phone box (in 1929).

The town's history goes back to the Roman era, with evidence found all over the valley. The town was first mentioned in the Domesday Book, William the Conqueror's inventory of his new kingdom. It was called Tigeham which means "goat enclosure." There's a 12th-century record calling the place Tiham. The church has been dated to have been in existence in some form since the 1300s.

However, Tyneham, despite its beautiful location, was not some bucolic paradise. The residents basically lived a feudal existence, with most people working on the surrounding estate. None of them owned their homes. Industrialisation of farming led to them to already coping with depopulation in the 1930s. The school closed in 1929 due to a lack of students. Increasingly, it was looking like there was no reason for the village to exist.

Britain's War Office agreed and didn't think it would harm too many people to push them out. Britain was planning, in secret, for the eventual D-Day invasion. And Tyneham's location near the coast and the village's architectural similarity to Northern France made it a perfect place for soldiers to practice. The village and 7,500 acres of surrounding heathland and chalk downland around the Purbeck Hills, were requisitioned just before Christmas 1943 by the War Office for use as firing ranges for training troops.

It was a time of war. If something like this happened now, the social media firestorm over displacing people from their homes would make sure it could never happen. But it was 1943, people had a sense of duty to do their bit. And they had to keep it secret. The Official Secrets Act was a very real and dangerous set of laws to go up against.

When the final residents left, a note was left on the church door.

"Please treat the church and houses with care; we have given up our homes where many of us lived for generations to help win the war to keep men free. We shall return one day and thank you for treating the village kindly."

When the war was over, the village was never given back to the residents. It wasn't theirs anyway. It was now a strategic asset. World War II wasn't the end of Britain's foreign military adventures. Tyneham still had a purpose to serve and that purpose was target practice. But as time has gone on, the need for the target practice has declined with Britain's military presence around the world. So, the Ministry of Defense now opens the place to the public on select days of the year.

The residents begged to return home. Former resident John Gould wrote to Prime Minister Harold Wilson in 1974 and urged him to hand it back to the people. "Tyneham to me is the most beautiful place in the world and I want to give the rest of my life and energy to its restoration … Most of all, I want to go home," he wrote.

His pleas were ignored. But the MOD started to slowly release control and now allows visitors. The Lulworth Range is still used for army practice and local windows in surrounding villages are known to rattle when the Army is at it. It's rather disgusting to think of such a peaceful place being defiled in such a way on a regular basis. Sure, it's quiet and beautiful when it's open to the public, but when the range is active, it's a hellscape of noise.

In the 15 years that we've been traveling to Dorset, I have always wanted to visit Tyneham. It's a hard place to visit because the abandoned village sits in the middle of the Lulworth Range, a British military area that is still closed to the public except

Pictures: Clockwise from Left to right 1. Rare Phone K1 Phone Box, 2. Home Ruins, was two levels, 3. The Restored Schoolhouse, 4. Chilling Warning Sign (these are dotted all over the site).

on certain days of the year. And even then, you're very restricted in where you can visit because there is a danger of unexploded bombs all around you.

The signs warn you to stay on the roads and signposted footpaths. Every time we've had a chance to visit, something has gotten in the way. The first time, it was a sudden fog that rolled into the Isle of Purbeck and forced them to close the access road. The second time we tried, during a family trip in 2013, Dorset was hit by storms so massive we had to completely stay away from the coast. When we tried last year, the Lulworth range was closed on short notice. This year, finally, we were able to visit. So, one quiet New Year's day, after checking that the range was indeed open, we hopped into our hire car and drove from Shaftesbury to Tyneham, a village lost to war and time. It was a humbling and fascinating experience.

When you visit, you're struck by the silence. Only interrupted by the occasional crash of waves over the hill if the wind is right and the rushing of a stream into the local pond. The village has been left in an arrested decay. The wartime damage has made most of the building uninhabitable and none of the houses even have roofs.

It's a ghostly, yet beautiful scene. The jagged roofs of the small cottages just into the air, awaiting roofs that will never be rebuilt. Water drips onto well-worn flagstone floors. There are bullet holes if you know how to look for them. Fireplaces sit cold and quiet, never to have a fire again. There is beauty in dereliction. But also sadness.

It's a popular place for explorers and walkers to visit. There are several walking paths that run through and around the site (with those aforementioned warnings to stay on the path). So, we were not alone during our visit. But their numbers were few and it was easy to get a sense of place. It's a quick stop anyway. You can survey the entire site in less than an hour. The warning signs all around you don't really inspire one to linger.

I love visiting abandoned ruins in Britain. Every county in Britain has a ruin of some kind, whether it's a castle, abbey or Roman settlement. But it's a little strange to explore the ruin of something so recently abandoned. This is not a place burned to

Pictures: Top - One of the abandoned farm houses. Bottom - The beautifully restored parish church.

the ground by Henry VIII. This is a place that was ruined within living memory.

The former residents of Tyneham campaigned for years to get their village back, but the Ministry of Defense has always refused. The land is too important and too dangerous to clean up (it's filled with unexploded bombs and toxic waste). However, there are signs of life in Tyneham. The schoolhouse has been restored to its final form - a 1920s British classroom. There's a small exhibition and several artifacts on display. It's like stepping back in time and going to school in 1929. It's remarkable.

The church has also been restored and is cared for. Services are occasionally held for former residents. Some that died in recent years have requested to be buried in the churchyard, so there are signs of fresh burials. The desire to move back to Tyneham will die as the final residents pass on. The village will join the ruins of Britain.

But it's not a 'proper' tourist attraction. There is no cafe or gift shop and this provides the place a certain level of authenticity to the experience of visiting. It's free to visit, but there's a small donation box asking anyone who uses the car park to pay £2 towards the upkeep of the paths and village. £2 well spent and you should leave more.

The most shining artifact left in Tyneham is the rare 1929 K1 Mark 236 Telephone Booth. But it turns out this isn't the original. The original was damaged during filming for the 1986 film "Comrades". The film company was obliged to source a replacement and they did. It's still a rare site and a great example of early British phone box design - a precursor to the famous K6 Red Phone Box we're all so familiar with.

While the place is no longer suitable for human habitation, due to the abandoned state of the surrounding land, it's become a haven for wildlife. While walk amongst the ruins and have a look into the church, you can hear the song of nature all around - the place is positively teeming with life, which is a strange experience. A great example that humans are not necessary for a beautiful natural environment.

While the village was the heart of life in the valley, the Manor House was the source of all their employment. It was originally built in 1523 and the three-story Elizabethan mansion was set in beautiful grounds with immaculate lawns, lime trees, palms and other tropical plants that were able to survive

Photos: Above - The row of cottages from the rear. Right - View of the beautiful Lulworth Range from the villages.

in the humid micro-climate of the valley. It's a magnificent tumble down old English house. It was abandoned along with the village and survived as a ruin until it was finally pulled down by the MOD in 1967. When you think of how jealously Britain now protects its stately home heritage, it's inconceivable that this would be done now. It would have been restored if the ruin has survived.

Inside each ruined house, there's a plaque that tells you about the family that lived there. For example, No 4. The Row was a Shepherds Cottage. It was the home to the Upscale family from 1925-1929. They worked on the estate and tended the sheep. The family focused on Dorset Horned Sheep, a popular sheep that is unique in that it 'lambs' (breeds) twice in one year.

It's moving to imagine the rhythms of village life and the lives of the people that lived in these home. As you walk through them, you can almost hear their whispers. The cottages are surprisingly roomy but they would have been rather crowded since most families were rather large and probably had lodgers staying with them to make ends meet.

World War II changed Britain a lot and in many cases, still dictates many aspects of British Culture today. This is one of those relics - a lost village. A composite of the rural fantasy we all like to attach to Britain. They won the war - but what did they lose? A place like Tyneham would never have survived in aspic. If it was still a living village, it would likely be a holiday settlement with people buying the cottages as second homes for the access to the nearby Dorset Beaches as has been the fate of many small villages along England's coastlines.

Still, it's nice to visit this special place and have a wander and imagine what it would have been like to live there before war ripped the community apart. The villages were never allowed to return to their homes, but their sacrifice allows us to visit and remember them, acknowledge their loss and hope that we never have to do something like it again. It's important that we respect the villagers' final wish on that posted notice - to treat the place with care and respect.

THE PASSIONATE SHEPHERD TO HIS LOVE
CHRISTOPHER MARLOWE

The Cotswolds Near Snowshill Manor

Come live with me and be my love,
And we will all the pleasures prove,
That Valleys, groves, hills, and fields,
Woods, or steepy mountain yields.

And we will sit upon the Rocks,
Seeing the Shepherds feed their flocks,
By shallow Rivers to whose falls
Melodious birds sing Madrigals.

And I will make thee beds of Roses
And a thousand fragrant posies,
A cap of flowers, and a kirtle
Embroidered all with leaves of Myrtle;

A gown made of the finest wool
Which from our pretty Lambs we pull;
Fair lined slippers for the cold,
With buckles of the purest gold;

A belt of straw and Ivy buds,
With Coral clasps and Amber studs:
And if these pleasures may thee move,
Come live with me, and be my love.

The Shepherds' Swains shall dance and sing
For thy delight each May-morning:
If these delights thy mind may move,
Then live with me, and be my love.

BRIT BOOK CORNER

THE EAST END IN COLOUR 1960-1980

If you're a fan of the hit show "Call the Midwife", then this is the book for you. This wonderful collection of photos from the 1960s to 1980s London is an incredible time capsule of what life was like in the East End of London during this era. These pictures are gritty, real, and beautiful in their own way. It's a London depressed and down on its heels. It's not a sepia-toned vision of London that never existed but rather a look at the real London. Many of these places still exist, but the East End of London has gone through an incredible regeneration in recent years - partly due to the 2012 Olympics and partly due to the fact that London is a place many people want to live - which has turned many depressed areas into desirable places to live. This London is long gone, but the pictures captured in this collection discovered in the Tower Hamlets Local History Library & Archives and lovingly curated by Hoxton Mini Press will provide a record of the East End's past. Hoxton Mini Press $22.95

SECRET COTSWOLDS BY SUE HAZELDINE

The Cotswolds are Anglophile paradise. The beautiful landscape of the Cotswold Wolds along with the honey-coloured houses creates a stunning environment that always warms the heart when you see them. There is tons of history in the Cotswolds, and a new book by Sue Hazeldine is an excellent look at the rich and varied history of these old wool towns. The book is divided up into chapters that focus on a particular place or subject related to the Cotswolds. From Broadway Tower to Malmesbury Abbey, you'll learn tons of fascinating history. Any lover of the Cotswolds will appreciate this lovely little book. Amberley $21.95

UNSEEN LONDON

London is one of the world's most photographed cities, so it's fair to say you probably might think there's nothing left to see. But you'd be wrong. In *Unseen London*, you can see the city anew through the eyes of 25 contemporary photographers where you can venture along hidden canals, around notorious housing estates, through surreal street scenes and deep underground. This is London as it is today, and as you've never seen it before. The photos in this book are an eclectic mix of strange, beautiful, and downright odd. It paints a portrait of a living city where you can see how people actually live rather than the sanitized version that popular entertainment creates of London. Hoxton Mini Press $34.95

SHAFTESBURY THROUGH TIME BY ROGER GUTTRIDGE

Shaftesbury is our favorite town in England, so I was delighted to see this beautiful new book about the town's history. We consider it our 'hometown' when we're in England so we like to learn everything about its history. The author has found an excellent collection of old photos for this book - many more not previously published. They're also helpfully presented next to pictures of what the same place looks like currently - which is lovely. I love then & now comparisons. The captions are fascinating and provide an interesting insight into why things in Shaftesbury look they way that they do. It's a treasure of Shastonian history. Amberley $18.99

FOR THE LOVE OF LONDON: A COMPANION BY JULIAN BEECROFT

A book that's an entire love letter to London. Filled with fascinating trivia about London, this book is a great companion to this wonderful city. Have you ever wondered: Why the Queen asks permission to enter the City? Where in London you are required to drive on the right? What is the history behind Pearly Kings and Queens? From the garden suburbs to the action-packed center, the city of London reveals layer upon layer of history, culture, delights—and secrets. Whether you're intrigued by London's rich history or fascinated by its glittering cultural scene, *For the Love of London* will take you on a tour encompassing architecture, royalty, landmark events, historical figures, crime, culture, and a host of surprising facts about the world's finest city. Summersdale $14.95

TEA GARDENS BY TWIGS WAY

A sunlit lawn, blossom-laden trees, rustic chairs around tables laden with teapots and cakes, the tinkle of teacups and the murmur of conversation – what could be more British than a tea garden? As a nation obsessed with tea drinking and gardening, it is not surprising that the British combined the two. The popularity of tea gardens took hold in London in the 18th century, and grew during the Victorian and Edwardian eras, when suburban family parties joined cycling clubs and charabanc outings to sample tea gardens far and wide. Despite the British weather, tea gardens have thrived for more than 200 years. This beautiful new book from Shire books is an excellent guide to the history behind famous tea gardens with plenty of inspiration to create your own. Shire Books $12.95

LONDON NIGHTS

London at night has a certain romance to it and this new book, released to coincide with an exhibition of the same name at the Museum of London, it's a triumph. It's entirely dedicated to images that capture London in the night - from the first pictures from the Victorian Era to the Modern Day. It paints an interesting portrait of a dynamic city. There's a wide range of photographers on show and tons of variety amongst the subjects. Some pictures are hauntingly beautiful. Some are rather disturbing (and there's some light nudity in the book). This book is a treasure and beautifully put together by Hoxton Mini Press. $27.85 Hoxton Mini Press

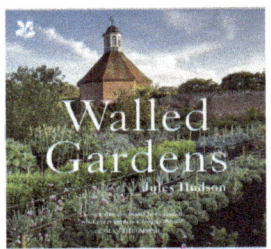

Walled Gardens by Jules Hudson

I love a good National Trust book. This new one is by Jules Hudson, the British presenter known for pottering about National Trust properties. This book takes you on a fascinating pictorial voyage of discovery around some of Britain's most beautiful and productive walled kitchen gardens. For centuries, walled gardens have provided a wealth of food, fruit, and flowers for England's great houses. Beginning as simple medieval enclosures, they evolved into powerful status symbols and centres of world-class horticultural expertise. This book charts the history of these unique English spaces and shows how they've adapted to the modern era. Filled with exciting history and tons of beautiful pictures. Trafalgar $24.95

THEN - Burford 1939

Burford, a bustling market town in the Oxfordshire Cotswolds was built on the wealth of 'white gold' - wool. Burford high street, pictured above with its gently sloping hill, is considered the most beautiful street of honey-coloured cottages after Chipping Camden. This photo, originally published in 1939 in the book *Cotswold Country* by Ward, Lock & Co in London, shows a town before it would be inevitably changed by World War II.

NOW - Burford 2012

We visited Burford in 2013 when we were in the UK for the Queen's Diamond Jubilee Celebrations. Burford hasn't changed much since the picture on the left was taken. Many of the same cottages remain, though some have notable additions. But the gently sloping hill bordered on each side by beautiful trees still remain. Burford is bustling - it's a busy town with lots of good shops and restaurants. Now considered the "Gateway to the Cotswolds' - we highly recommend at least stopping for tea & cake.

EXPLORING LEEDS

Your Complete Travel Guide to This Yorkshire Hotspot

By Laura Porter

INTRODUCTION

This West Yorkshire city is well worth a visit. Located in the eastern foothills of the Pennines and less than 20 miles from the Yorkshire Dales National Park, Leeds is that sought-after combination of a modern city close to stunning English countryside.

Leeds is the UK's third-largest city and is about 190 miles north of London, so it can be reached by train in a little more than two hours. They take shopping seriously here as it is the principal regional shopping center for the whole of the Yorkshire. And once you've bought the perfect outfit, there's plenty of nightlife too.

HISTORY

Many have heard of Leeds for its woolen cloth industry. When Kirkstall Abbey was built in the 12th century, the monks kept sheep, and by 1290 they owned 11,000. The land offered plenty of space to feed and breed the animals, and the soft, pure water of the area was ideal for washing wool. The river could also be used to move goods to and from ports such as Hull, on the east coast of England.

Home manufacture of cloth and woolen cloth trading was known in the area from the 14th century. 'Yorkshire Broadcloths' – cheap, good quality cloths produced in the surrounding areas – helped the growth of Leeds in the late 16th and early 17th century.

The Industrial Revolution of the late 18th and early 19th centuries brought about the biggest growth for Leeds with the building of cloth mills with new machinery making mass production possible. This major industrial city became known as 'the city that made everything.'

In 1880, the population had reached 100,000, and there were more than 100 coal mines in and around Leeds. This proximity of cheap coal made Leeds into a powerful industrial and manufacturing center. Coal was extracted on a large scale and the still-functioning Middleton Railway, which opened in 1812, was the first successful commercial steam locomotive railway in the world.

While the Middleton Railway was for moving coal, the first passenger railway in Leeds opened in 1834. Both the waterways and the railways meant that Leeds had good transport links to bring in coal and other raw materials cheaply and easily and to export manufactured goods to all parts of the world.

Although it was the largest city in Yorkshire by 1890, Leeds did not officially become a city until 1893.

While Leeds is no longer a centre for manufacturing, its contemporary economy has been shaped by Leeds City Council's vision of building a '24-hour European city' and 'capital of the north'.

ARCHITECTURE

There are more listed buildings in Leeds than in any other city outside London, so this is definitely a 'look up' city as the Victorian architecture is fantastic. As well as the shops and theatres, the civic buildings are outstanding.

A favorite is the Central Library and connected Leeds Art Gallery gothic masterpiece with its spectacular staircases and archways, stone beasts and mosaic tiling designed by George Corson and opened in 1884 as the Leeds Municipal buildings.

Yorkshireman Cuthbert Brodrick is an architect forever associated with Leeds. His greatest career break was in 1853 when he won a competition for the design of Leeds Town Hall. The competition was judged by Charles Barry – the English architect, best known for his role in the rebuilding of the Houses of Parliament in London during the mid-19th century. The Town Hall was opened in September 1858 by Queen Victoria, the first time a reigning monarch had visited Leeds. To get to see inside a book for one of the really good selection of shows on from classical music and

> ## INSIDER TIPS
> - Museums are closed on Mondays.
> - Free water taxi to Royal Armouries from behind the train station.
> - Knowledgeable staff in the Visitor Centre under Leeds Art Gallery.
> - Easy access to Leeds from London by direct trains from King's Cross - takes a little more than 2 hours.

Photos - Clockwise from Left to Right - 1. Just Grand Vintage Tearoom, 2. Kirkgate Market, 3. Clever Kit in the Arcades, 4. Royal Armouries

opera to comedians and evenings with well-known personalities.

Brodrick had visited France and Italy in 1844, and this influenced his architectural styles. He built the Corn Exchange next which opened in 1864. Still considered to be one of Britain's finest Victorian buildings, its ingenious roof gave an even northern light for the careful inspection of grain by merchants. The Grade I listed building was imaginatively remodeled and reopened in 1990 as a place for independent boutiques and quirky cafés.

His Leeds trio was completed with the Leeds Institute in 1868, now the home of Leeds City Museum. And his name is remembered in a more modern way with a large Wetherspoons pub called the 'Cuthbert Brodrick' in Millennium Square.

Other notable landmarks include the Civic Hall in Millennium Square, with golden owls adorning the tops of the twin spires. There are also four golden owl sculptures in front of the building which were added in 2000. Do look out for owls all across the city as there are 25 owl locations and a trail to follow to see them all.

And the shopping structures are not all new as the Victorian arcades are beautiful. While the high-end stores may mean you only visit for window shopping, it's certainly worth taking a stroll through the Victoria Quarter to admire the elaborate architecture and decoration including the dramatic stained glass roof and paneled mosaic floors.

SHOPPING

Leeds is the shopping capital of the north. The city is very compact and walkable with a large pedestrian zone. Briggate is the main shopping street and is one of the oldest streets in Leeds dating back to the 13th century. There was a market held here and shops built in the 19th century along with arcades and theatres. Fans of the High Street should head to Trinity Leeds, while if you are after something more high end, go to the Victoria Leeds.

Trinity Leeds

With 120 High Street shops including M&S, Superdry, River Island, and Hollister, plus eateries and a cinema, this is a popular destination. It feels like an out-of-town shopping center but is still in the city center. Even those who don't enjoy shopping are grateful to have it here as it brings people to the city every day.

There's a stylish glass roof over the whole centre, but it's not a closed environment so it can still be cool on a cold weather day.

Even if you're not looking to shop, the top floor Trinity Kitchen is a fantastic place to grab a bite to eat. Possibly the UK's coolest food court, there are neon signs and lights and a unique mix of temporary food vans and permanent restaurants offering a variety of exotic cuisines. It's quite loud here but the food is good, and the shoppers love it.

Victoria Leeds

The city's most recent retail addition is the impressive Victoria Gate which houses one of the largest John Lewis stores in the UK as well as other desirable brands. It's a stunning building although it doesn't gel with the surrounding architecture.

The Victoria Quarter is notable for its high-end luxury retailers and impressive architecture. Retailers here include Mulberry, Jo Malone, LK Bennett and Louis Vuitton and sitting in the heart of the center is department store Harvey Nichols, which chose Leeds for the site of its first store outside London back in 1996.

The Victoria Quarter was built in 1900 by theatrical architect Frank Matcham who was also responsible for the London Coliseum. Its gilded mosaics, marble floors, ornate wrought-iron metalwork and polished mahogany, make the area a real delight. In the 1990s, Queen Victoria Street was covered with Britain's largest stained glass roof to make a new arcade forming the Victoria Quarter along with the restored County Arcade and Cross Arcade.

More Arcades

Thornton's Arcade was the first to open in 1878. Named after Charles Thornton, who had the ingenious idea of covering up the shopping alleys that connected Briggate to its side streets. He also owned the Old White Swan in Swan Street where in 1865 he opened the music hall that is now the City Varieties Music Hall. Today, the arcade has cool shops such as the Welcome Skate Shop and OK Comics.

Queen's Arcade opened in 1889 and has stores such as Levi's, Office shoes, American Apparel, and Jones the Bootmaker, as well as independents like Accent Clothing, Aladdin's Cave Jewellery and Mary Shortle – a doll shop that probably delights and scares in equal measure.

Near to the Leeds Grand Theatre and Opera House, Grand Arcade opened in 1897. It has become my favourite of the great eateries (see below) and Our Handmade Collective – a lovely shop offering gift ideas from more than 60 designer-makers. They even have craft evenings with the makers so you can learn something new.

Corn Exchange

This iconic rotunda has more than 30 creative, independent retailers and salons along with food outlets. If you are looking for something quirky and individual, then this is where you need to come shopping.

My favorite store was The Great Yorkshire Shop where you'll find rhubarb blend tea and rhubarb chocolate, plus prints, bags, cards, and gifts. (Yorkshire is known for early forced rhubarb.)

And if you're looking for locally made treats, I can also recommend The Yorkshire Soap Company on Albion Street where the soaps look like cakes. You can't miss the shop as they have bubbles coming out of a window above the shop.

Kirkgate Market

And finally, do allow time to meander through the maze of one of Europe's largest indoor markets. Open since 1857; it was designed by the celebrated architect Joseph Paxton who was responsible for the iconic Crystal Palace in Hyde Park, London. The market today sells well-priced fresh meat, fish, fruit, veg, and flowers, plus street food to eat now. There are vintage fairs here on the first Saturday of the month.

Did you know the very first M&S goods were sold in Leeds from a 6' by 4' trestle table? From a humble market stall to one of Britain's most successful retailers, M&S started at Kirkgate Market.

Back in 1884, Polish immigrant Michael Marks opened his penny bazaar stall in Leeds Market before forming a partnership with Tom Spencer a decade later. There's a replica of the Penny Bazaar inside the market selling M&S goods.

MUSEUMS

Royal Armouries

The one place everyone told me I had to visit was the Royal Armouries. You can catch a free water taxi from Granary Wharf, behind the train station, or walk for 15 minutes from the city center.

This free museum opened in 1996 on the south bank of the River Aire as Britain's national museum of arms and armor. It's set out across two connected buildings with four floors of exhibits. There are more than 8,500 objects including an armoured elephant, Samurai disemboweling weapons, and Henry VIII's horned helmet.

Inside you can try the crossbow range for a small fee, and it stages regular displays of jousting, falconry, and sword-making outside.

Sadly, I found the museum quite dated and there are no interactives with the displays so I'm not sure how entertaining families would find it. As an adult, I found it quite dry and in need of modernisation. While historic exhibits won't change, how you present them can affect the visitor experience.

The Tetley

In the same part of town is The Tetley – a center for contemporary art located in the Art Deco headquarters of the former Tetley Brewery. It's more of a 'project space' than an art gallery but most visit for a meal and to enjoy a pint of Tetley's in this historic setting.

Photos Right - Top - Corn Exchange, Bottom - Leeds Town Hall

Leeds Art Gallery

Keeping with the free contemporary art theme, Leeds Art Gallery is said to have the best 20th-century collection outside London. The gallery reopened in 2017 after renovations with a vibrant wall-painting by Lothar Götz by the staircase.

It's not all modern though as I found a lovely gallery with an 1847 painting by John Everett Millais and a centerpiece of marble busts. These paintings and busts were acquired in the first 12 years of the gallery's life (1888-1900).

You won't need long to visit the gallery so do stop at the Tiled Hall Cafe, shared with the adjoining Central Library. It has a beautiful ceiling that is worth admiring with a cuppa.

Henry Moore Institute

On the other side of Leeds Art Gallery is the Henry Moore Institute, connected inside via a bridge. This sculpture research center and gallery only needs a quick visit as it seems to be aimed at academics more than visitors. But you can see Henry Moore's Reclining Woman outside the Leeds Art Gallery.

Leeds City Museum

While the previous galleries had been quite uninspiring, Leeds City Museum was much better than expected. The Cuthbert Brodrick-designed building is striking from the outside, and inside there are four floors of galleries with simple interactives.

The curators here have struck the right level of information on the walls and an excellent range of exhibits from an Egyptian mummy and Roman stones in the 'Ancient Worlds' gallery to impressive stuffed animals in the 'Life on Earth' section. 'The Leeds Story' takes up most of one floor and really brings to life the history of the city.

By the entrance to the café, you'll find the Leeds Tiger. It was shot in the Himalayas in 1860 and was displayed as a rug before being presented to the museum in the 19th century. The pelt was then combined with one or more other tigerskins and rather inexpertly stuffed with straw. While it's a saggy specimen, it is well loved locally so the museum won't change him.

Museums Outside of the City Centre

Kirkstall Abbey is one of the best preserved Cistercian monasteries in Britain, and you can explore the ruins set within parkland. At the same location is Abbey House Museum with three recreated Victorian streets, and toys and games from years gone by.

Leeds Industrial Museum is at Armley Mills, once the world's largest woolen mill. There is industrial machinery, railway locomotives, Victorian workers' cottages, and one of the UK's smallest cinemas.

At Lotherton Hall, you can explore a fine Edwardian country home with extensive grounds, red deer park, and gardens, plus Wildlife World with penguins, flamingoes and more.

Temple Newsam is four miles from the city centre. It's a country mansion set within 1,500 acres of parkland, complete with a rare breed farm too.

Feel the force and power of a fully restored 1820s water-powered mill and explore the beautiful and tranquil island rich in wildlife at Thwaite Mills.

Based in an old workhouse at St James's Hospital, the Thackray Medical Museum has displays featuring gruesome twists, and it plays up to its reputation with exhibitions on the history of leeching, and a recreated Victorian street that comes complete with authentic smells.

SPORT

No article on Leeds could miss Headingley Stadium, just 10 minutes from the city center. Home to Yorkshire County Cricket Club, Headingley is a famous Test match venue which also stages one-day internationals. Rugby League fans will know Headingley is also home to Leeds Rhinos. And footfall supporters can see Leeds United FC at the 40,000 capacity Elland Road Football Stadium.

EAT AND DRINK

Eating out is a popular pastime in Leeds, and there's a huge choice of dining opportunities. As Yorkshire tea is the local drink, the first meal I wanted to try here was afternoon tea. I know I'm used to London prices, but I was amazed at the posh tea and cake bargains in Leeds.

Just Grand! Vintage Tearoom in Grand Arcade is a lovely venue. Drinks are served in mismatched crockery, and the menus are on old LPs. There's a huge choice of teas and a really well-priced afternoon tea (just £13.50!) with sandwiches, a scone with cream and jam, and a slice of fruit cake with local Wensleydale cheese on top of the cake stand. If the tables are taken inside, there are colorful Granny-crocheted blankets on the seats outside to keep you warm.

Other afternoon tea locations include the 13th floor Sky Lounge at the DoubleTree by Hilton at Granary Wharf, although the modern twist menu doesn't include scones. The Tetley has an afternoon tea menu with a beer fruit scone included (£14), and the Fourth Floor Café at Harvey Nichols has a small outdoor terrace that overlooks Briggate and afternoon tea for just £20. The staff here is lovely, and this is a great place for a breakfast, lunch or a glass of wine too.

Head back to Grand Arcade for lunch or dinner as there are some other excellent options here including Roots and Fruits vegetarian café that's been in Leeds for more than 20 years, the wonderful Casa Colombiana restaurant and Latin cocktail bar, and Zaap Thai street food on the corner of Vicar Lane – popular with families for the fun atmosphere.

If you'd like a full Sunday roast with Yorkshire puddings, there are traditional pubs in the city center. John Betjeman described Whitelocks as "the very heart of Leeds." Dating back to 1715 and owned by the Whitelock family since around 1880, the pub has a ceramic-tiled bar, old woodwork, and stained glass windows. Leeds Brewery's The White Swan, adjoining City Varieties theatre, is a gastropub and does a popular Sunday roast too.

The city seems to have really embraced the idea of rooftop dining. Belgrave Music Hall and Canteen offers music, art, film, and food on three floors, including the roof terrace. And East 59th is a Manhattan-style rooftop bar with contemporary American dining in the day then cocktails and DJs to dance the night away.

For Michelin-starred, ultra-modern dining book a table at The Man Behind the Curtain to try chef Michael O'Hare's tasting menu. It's all rather avant-garde, but you're paying for the experience as well as the food. Home also specialise in tasting menus so you can 'taste the season' and pair wines.

The glamorous Restaurant Bar and Grill is in the old General Post Office in City Square and is loved for steaks and evening cocktails. And French eatery Brasserie Blanc is housed in a converted Victorian warehouse by the canal. The vaulted brick ceilings, cast iron pillars, and candlelight make for a relaxed evening out with friends and family.

For quick eats, the Trinity Kitchen's street food market is recommended. Five different trailers are winched up to an upper floor every six weeks, and the rotating vendors trade alongside permanent outlets. Or stop in the Corn Exchange at Humpit for deliciously creamy hummus with fluffy pita bread to wipe it up. The Old Red Bus Station on Vicar Lane is a bar, music club, and canteen that has a £2.50 coffee and cake deal, making it a great place to stop.

Fuji Hiro was the first Japanese restaurant in Leeds. It's a family-owned restaurant serving Japanese staples such as fried noodles and steaming bowls of ramen. It's at the back of the Merrion Centre, so near to the First Direct Arena.

NIGHTLIFE

Theatres

Leeds Grand Theatre and Opera House was built in 1878 and has been Opera North's home since 1978. Known as "the Drury Lane of the North," the idea to build the theatre began when Queen Victoria and Prince Albert came to Leeds to officially open the Town Hall in 1858. It is alleged that Prince Albert commented that "Leeds seemed in need of a good theatre, and that nothing was more calculated to promote the culture and raise the tone of the people."

The Grand is where you can see the plays and musicals from London's West End, but do beware when booking as the theatre is said to be haunted by the friendly 'Lavender Lady' who visits Box D in the Dress Circle.

The Swann Inn (now The White Swan) had a singing room added in 1766, and this is now the City Varieties Music Hall. Charlie Chaplin, Buster Keaton, and Harry Houdini are among the entertainment greats to have trodden the boards at this Victorian theatre, and it's still pretty much as it was in 1865 although it has been restored. As well as a fun pantomime in the winter, you can enjoy music hall evenings here throughout the year.

West Yorkshire Playhouse has plays, dance, comedy, and West End transfers. While the theatre is about to undergo major redevelopment, they have transformed one of the workshop spaces to create a 350-seat theatre to continue running a full and varied programme. Leeds College of Music, close to the Playhouse, has a packed concert schedule too.

Carriageworks Theatre in Millennium Square has a good range of shows, events, and activities including plenty for families.

Music

Leeds has one of the most vibrant live music scenes in the UK. Not only is Leeds home to the 13,500-capacity First Direct Arena with live music, comedy and more, but you can also enjoy regular gigs at The O2 Academy, The Wardrobe, Brudenell Social Club, Headrow House, and Belgrave Music Hall. The Domino Club has live jazz but is a particularly cool venue as you enter through Lord's Barbering in Grand Arcade and head downstairs to a darkened room with candles, dimmed lights and a fantastic atmosphere.

ASK A LOCAL

To get an insider's tips on the best nightlife in Leeds, I had a chat with Alex Simmons, a man brimming over with confidence and a big love of his city. Alex was a world-renowned DJ and now runs Rugby AM.

Mojo on Merrion Street is a small cocktail and rum bar with a great vibe. It gets louder throughout the evening and dancing is encouraged. Regulars have seats with their names on them, so look out for the plaque for popular radio DJ Chris Moyles.

For slow-cooked meats and the hottest sauces, Red's True Barbecue on Call Lane is a favorite. Run by two guys from Leeds, Alex told me they went to the US and came in fourth in the world in a hot sauce competition.

There's no bouncer outside The Maven Bar, so you just have to look for the door with an M on it on Call Lane. Head upstairs to a real hidden gem cocktail bar with darkened windows and subdued lighting. Based on a 1920s US Prohibition speakeasy but with its own style too, creative cocktails are served in teacups.

Bar Fibre is a four-floor super bar on Lower Briggate. Owned by local legend Terry George, the bar has just celebrated its 17th birthday. It's a gay bar that's straight-friendly and plays good local sounds. On Bank Holidays they have a courtyard party with the next door bar, and it can get packed with thousands of people.

Legendary dance club reunions in Leeds to look out for including Back to Basics which is the longest-running house night in the UK. It launched the careers of artists such as Daft Punk and Groove Armada. SpeedQueen offers one of the best straight-friendly dance nights in the UK. And Habit, where Alex was the resident DJ up to 2011, has regular reunions.

FURTHER AFIELD

If you are fortunate enough to be here longer than just a weekend, Leeds provides the perfect base to explore the incredible landscapes of the Yorkshire Dales, North Yorkshire Moors, and dramatic Yorkshire coastline.

Just 10 miles south of Leeds is the Yorkshire Sculpture Park at West Bretton. It's home to works by Barbara Hepworth, Henry Moore, Joan Miró and Anthony Gormley in 500 acres of 18th-century parkland.

Open from April to October, Harewood House is a Georgian property 7 miles from Leeds that sits within a Capability Brown-designed landscape. The House has incredible art collections and rare Chippendale furniture.

Roundhay Park is one of the biggest city parks in Europe and is just 3 miles from the city center. It's more than 700 acres of greenery wrapped around a couple of lakes and a handful of cafés, plus an indoor wildlife park called Tropical World making Roundhay Park the most visited family attraction in Leeds.

TV soap fans will love The Emmerdale Studio Experience where you can see set reconstructions, preserved props, and costumes and discover the secrets behind stunts and special effects.

ACCOMMODATION

There are some excellent hotels in Leeds City Centre. I stayed at the Leeds Marriott which is in a quiet courtyard; just a few minutes walk from the train station. The rooms are impressively spacious, the on-site (including in-room) dining was above expectations and the staff is wonderfully welcoming and friendly. There's a Leisure Club with a pool and free use of an app for newspapers and magazines.

Other good choices are the stylish Malmaison or Dakota. The Radisson Blu is almost next to Leeds Art Gallery, and the independently-run Quebecs is in one of the most distinctive terracotta brickwork buildings in Leeds.

If you'd like a spa break, Chevin Country Park Hotel & Spa is about 10 miles from Leeds in Otley and has spa day options if you prefer to stay in the city.

WHAT'S ON

You've heard of the Tour de France but do you know about the Tour de Yorkshire? This annual bike race takes in 169 villages, towns and cities along the way with a thrilling finish in Leeds. *3-6 May 2018*

Every summer, Millennium Square hosts live music, screenings, and festivals for Millennium Square Summer Series. One of the not to be missed events is the incredible Symphonic Sounds of Back to Basics on 27 July 2018, featuring a unique collaboration between the Orchestra of Opera North and legendary Back to Basics DJ Dave Beer. *May-August 2018*

What better introduction to cricket than an international match at the Yorkshire County Cricket Club's home? Headingley has been hosting international cricket since 1899 and in 2018 will host three internationals; England vs. Pakistan Test Match on 1 June, England vs. New Zealand Royal London Women's One-Day International on 7 July and England vs. India One-Day International on 17 July. *June & July 2018*

Leeds Pride celebrates the LGBT* community with a parade through the center of the city and partying until the early hours. A true celebration of Leeds' diversity and equality, it's the biggest event of its kind in Yorkshire. *5 August 2018*

The UK's largest family-friendly Volkswagen show is the VW Festival at Harewood House. A full weekend of live entertainment, live music, VWs galore and a great venue with a laid-back atmosphere. *10-12 August 2018*

Leeds Festival is one of the UK's largest music festivals, held over the August bank holiday weekend each year, with a number of stages across Bramham Park hosting some of the biggest names in rock and indie music. *24-26 August 2018*

Leeds West Indian Carnival is Western Europe's longest-running authentic Caribbean carnival parade. 2018 is the 51st carnival, and you can expect amazing costumes, infectious tropical rhythms, mouth-watering food, and entertainment for everyone. *27 August 2018*

As the nights draw in, October sees the return of Light Night. This family-friendly two-night festival of arts and light transform the city centre after dark into a sea of light and sound. *4-5 October 2018*

LAURA'S LEEDS TOP 10

1. Shopping!
2. Visit Leeds City Museum
3. Admire the Victorian Architecture
4. See a show at The Grand
5. Have a drink on Call Lane
6. Do the owl trail
7. See live music
8. Enjoy afternoon tea at Just Grand! Vintage Tearoom
9. Chat to a local – everyone's really friendly!
10. Book tickets for the Millennium Square Summer Series (especially 'The Symphonic Sounds of Back to Basics')

LOST IN THE POND
The Differing Medical Terminology of the British and American Hospital
By Laurence Brown

If you ask a British person newly transplanted to America what he or she misses most about Britain, two of the leading answers notably bear only three letters: BBC and NHS. In the case of the former, streaming services such as Britbox help to alleviate that particular craving; whereas the latter gives way to a healthcare system famously distinct from its tax-funded equivalent in the United Kingdom.

But even once you cut through the political red tape, another element of the medical field reveals itself in the form of terminology. At this point, the linguistic divide between Britain and the United States is well documented; so much so that the differing medical terms ought to have their own dictionary.

As someone who—after 10 years residing in America's Midwest—recently underwent his first major brush with the world of American hospitals, I would indeed welcome such a dictionary.

After all, the last thing on your mind as your arm reluctantly receives its fourth jab is the fact that Americans refer to this as a "shot." And by the time the ensuing pain from said shot subsides, you might—if you're paying attention—notice that "Elastoplast" and "plaster" have since made way for "Band-Aid", an adhesive bandage that, like "Elastoplast, is a genericised brand name.

And speaking of names, even the buildings that make up a typical hospital often assume unfamiliar monikers. A regular checkup with your GP (a term not used in the United States) will necessitate a visit not to the "surgery" but to the "doctor's office." In fact, the use of "surgery" in this sense tends to confuse Americans, who only associate that word with operative care.

Should you be unfortunate enough to find yourself in an accident of the life-threatening variety, you'll almost certainly end up in the American equivalent of A&E. For American readers, this stands for "Accident & Emergency" and—unless you have a dark sense of humor—is distinct from "Arts & Entertainment". As it happens, though, it was the world of entertainment that brought the American equivalent to the attention of the British. "ER", the show that catapulted George Clooney to superstardom, ran concurrently with the BBC show "Casualty", another British name for the emergency department.

And while an ambulance might be your means of travel on either side of the Pond, the number with which to summon it is famously different. However, while the British emergency code of "999" might be a fraction quicker to dial than America's "9-1-1", it is worth noting that this was not the case during the days of rotary phones.

Either way, someone's going to hospital. Except that this precise phrase is another one that tends to jar with Americans; dropping the determiner "the" is seen, stateside, as confusing or unnecessary, and so "going to the hospital" is much preferred. It has been said that the British version only exists to distinguish between a hospital in the notional sense and hospital in the specific sense. In other words, Brits might say "I'm going to the hospital on the far side of town" to indicate a particular location, but will say "I'm going to hospital" if the location is unimportant to the conversation.

Regardless of your preferred sentence structure, though, further terminological confusion might even arise once you are diagnosed. For instance, should you be unfortunate enough to contract glandular fever, bear in mind that Americans refer to this as "mono" (or mononucleosis). When my sister-in-law first reported that she was suffering from this mysterious illness, aside from imagining how horrible it must have been, I couldn't help considering the following two things: 1) Mono must be very rare—I've never heard of it; 2) Stereo must be twice as bad. Turns out she just kissed too many boys.

On a more serious note, if you happen to suffer from epilepsy, be sure not to describe your most serious symptom as an epileptic fit. American medical professionals know this as a "seizure." Moreover, while Britain might have multiple other uses for the word "fit"—to mean 'in shape', 'attractive', or 'ergonomically compatible'—Americans don't use it in the sense of an episode brought on by synchronous neuronal activity. The nearest usage to this stateside is "conniption fit", another way to describe a tantrum.

Of course, should you find yourself feeling nauseous (a word more prevalent in America than Britain), you might—excuse the lovely visual—find yourself vomiting. You're probably familiar with American terms such as "hurl" or "barf," but what you may not know is that Americans don't tend to refer to the resulting mess as "sick." They do use the verb to be sick, just not the following noun phrase: "I flushed the sick down the toilet." Okay, moving on from what I will affectionately call the "word vomit" section, let's focus on some terms associated with your recovery. One place that specialises in that very thing is, of course, the chemists—the building where, for example, you pick up your paracetamol. Except Americans refer to this building by one of two names, a pharmacy or a drugstore, and you're unlikely to find any container bearing the name "paracetamol" in America; instead, its US equivalent is known as "acetaminophen".

Of course, while you're navigating all of the above terminology differences, there's a subcategory of linguistic variances you might want to pay attention to and that's spelling. Scores of medical terms, while lexically consistent on either side of the Pond, employ subtly different letters. For instance, Britain's tendency to use the Latin grapheme æ in words like "enclyclopaedia" is not shared by Americans, so words such as "paediatric", "leukaemia", and "gynaecology" become "pediatric", "leukemia", and "gynecology". Similarly, the Latin grapheme œ is dropped from the likes of "oesophagus" and "diarrhea", while "paralyse" becomes "paralyze", "tumour" becomes "tumor", and "ageing" becomes "aging."

Thankfully, variations in spelling and terminology are quite easy to figure out after a while. The same, however, cannot always be said of America's healthcare system, but that's another story for another time.

Laurence is a British writer and humorist who lives in the United States. He also hosts the popular web series, "Lost in the Pond" on YouTube. He has an infuriating habit of taking America to task by pointing out how things are done in the UK. He really needs to stop this behavio(u)r. It's anti-American.

GREAT BRITONS: CECIL RHODES
Businessman, Politician, Imperialist

Cecil Rhodes was a businessman and politician who made his fortune in the late 19th century Scramble for Africa by the European powers. After cornering diamond production in South Africa and forming De Beers Consolidated mines to maintain high diamond prices, he moved into politics and served as Prime Minister in the colony from 1890-1896. He then undertook a commercial and political land-grab of the countries of the eastern part of Africa, almost succeeding in bringing a continuous strip from the Cape to Cairo under British control. His attitude to Africans led to him being described as the father of apartheid. After his death, his considerable personal fortune created the Rhodes Scholarship, which brought overseas students to Oxford University and began the careers of many prominent people. Cecil John Rhodes first set foot in South Africa when he was 17, having been sent there for his health by his Church of England clergyman father. Cecil was asthmatic and so sickly he had been taken out of Grammar School, in Bishop's Stortford, Hertfordshire, where he was born on 5 July, 1853.

Rhodes landed in the Colony of Natal, which had been annexed by the British is 1843, joining the formerly independent Boer province to the larger Cape Colony. Rhodes brother Herbert had set up a cotton farm in Natal, and Cecil joined him. The venture failed as the climate and soil were not suitable for cotton. A diamond rush had just begun at Kimberley in the Cape Colony, and the brothers went there to try their luck. At first, they rented water pumps to miners, but he used the profits of this enterprise to start buying small diamond mine claims, helped by the financial backing of the London banking family Rothschild.

Cecil did return for a term at Oxford in 1873 but quickly returned to Kimberley, where he continued to expand his operations. In 1876, he returned to Oxford for a second term, and it was there that he attended a lecture by the polymath John Ruskin, who presented an idealised view of the British Empire as a force for good, lifting up the 'lower races' and spreading peace and prosperity across the Earth. This inspired Rhodes to adopt the cause of British Imperialism and take the view that Britain, through its excellence, had a right to rule. At the same time he joined the Freemasons, and in his first will, written in 1877, he left money for a secret society with but one object; the furtherance

KEY FACTS

- Born 1853 – died 1902
- Businessman and founder of De Beers diamond mines
- Carried out extensive imperial purchases and seizures of African lands
- Established the Rhodes Scholarship to Oxford University after his death

of the British Empire and the bringing of the whole uncivilized world under British rule, (and) for the recovery of the United States.

Back in the Cape, his chief partner was John Rudd, another young Englishman seeking his fortune. They found a rival in Barney Barnato, a Cockney Jew, who had seized control of the diamond market and was manipulating prices. Rhodes and Barnato were both racing to consolidate all the tiny mines into a large company, and after complex financial maneuverings they combined forming De Beers Consolidated Mines, which at one point controlled 90% of the world's diamonds. By being able to control production and keep supply close to demand, Rhodes was able to maintain an artificially high price for diamonds, and create a large fortune for Rothschild Bank, Barnato, De Beers, and of course, himself.

In 1880, Rhodes entered the Cape Parliament, and within 10 years he was Prime Minister of the Cape Colony. His first task was to remove black Africans from land required for industrial development and, in his words, show them that in future, nine-tenths of them will have to spend their lives in manual labor, and the sooner that is brought home to them the better. By setting limits on the amount of land black people could own, and setting the level for the right to vote above that limit, he succeeded in preventing them from developing as a political force, arguing that the native is to be treated as a child and denied the franchise. He also attempted to overthrow the neighbouring Boer Republic of Transvaal, launching, with the approval of the British government, the Jameson Raid over the New Year weekend of 1895–1896. The purpose

was to send a small force to encourage an uprising by British settlers in the Transvaal, but it failed completely, forcing Rhodes to resign as Prime Minister. A brother, Frank Rhodes, was jailed and nearly executed in Transvaal for treason, and the raid was a factor in the outbreak of the Second Boer War.

Driven by his belief in the right of the superior British race to rule, and by a desire to increase his fortune, Rhodes began to purchase mining concessions from local chiefs and simultaneously expand the control of the British government over the areas he purchased. By covering the costs of administration and having his companies administer the areas thus occupied, he prevented the perhaps more benevolent direct rule from Britain that distressed missionaries and others wanted while keeping these territories legally British. This gave him the security and legality needed to sell shares in his mining operations to investors. In this way, he was instrumental in keeping Britain dominant in the so-called Scramble for Africa with other European countries, especially in the eastern half of the continent. Many of his tactics were secretive and technically illegal, but a blind-eye was often turned by the British government. Rhodesia (now Zimbabwe and Zambia) was the jewel in Rhodes' Cape to Cairo Red Line, a reference to the desire to have red, the traditional color on maps of British territories, run the length of Africa. By 1914, only the German colony of Tanzania broke the continuity, and that country also fell into the hands of Britain via the WWI peace treaties. The railway line Rhodes dreamed of, from the Cape to Cairo, was never completed.

Rhodes never married, arguing that he didn't have time, but it has been suggested, without any definitive evidence, that he was gay. Rhodes kept no diaries and wrote very few personal letters, so his private life remains largely concealed. His name has been associated with several potential lovers, the last of which was Leander Starr Jameson, who had led the Jameson Raid. Jameson was with Rhodes during his final illness, was the residual beneficiary of his will, giving him Rhodes mansion, and although Jameson died in England, in 1920 his body was re-interred in Rhodesia beside Rhodes.

In the end, Rhodes' lifelong ill health kept him regularly ill after he turned 40 and he died of heart failure on the 26 March 1902, just 48 years of age. His body was carried on a funeral train from the seaside cottage on the Cape where he died to a hilltop in Rhodesia called 'World's View,' where his grave remains today. Tribal chiefs attended his internment there.

His Legacy

Rhodes' greatest legacy was the Rhodes Scholarship, established by Nathan Rothschild, the administrator of his estate, in compliance with the terms of Rhodes' will. This was the world's first international study programme and allows students from any current or ex-British colony to study at Oxford. Important recipients include J. William Fulbright, Dean Rusk, and President Bill Clinton.

With the collapse of the Empire and the de-colonisation that followed WWII, Rhodes' reputation began to decline, and today it has reached a veritable nadir, with recent attempts to remove his statue from Oxford University. His racist views are widely considered to make him the father of the apartheid system that blighted South Africa, but he should perhaps be seen as being a product, as much

as a maker, of his times.

Sites to Visit

- His grave is part of Matobo National Park, Zimbabwe.
- There is a statue of Rhodes on the façade of Oriel College, Oxford University.
- His birthplace is now the Rhodes Arts Complex & Bishop's Stortford Museum, containing records and artifacts of his life. It is at 1-3 South Road, Bishop's Stortford, Hertfordshire, and is open Monday to Saturday from 10am-4pm.
- The Rhodes Memorial stands on the slopes of Devil's Peak, Cape Town.

Further Research

Biographies include:

- Cecil Rhodes Man and Empire-Maker (1918), by Princess Catherine Radziwill, is still available. The princess was infatuated with Rhodes, and when he refused to marry her, she engineered a court-case for fraud based on false allegations she made. Although she lost the case, she went on to write this contemporary biography.
- The Founder: Cecil Rhodes and the Pursuit of Power (1988), by Robert I. Rotberg.
- Cecil Rhodes and His Time (2012), by Apollon Davidson
- Cecil Rhodes, His Private Life (2013), by Philip Jourdan

THIS ENGLISH LIFE

This Old House: England Edition
By Erin Moore

Our place was built in 1823. It's a tall, narrow row house, about the size of the average suburban American home, inconveniently spread over five floors. It has all the problems you might imagine: holes between the floorboards big enough to lose Legos in. Windows you can feel a breeze through. Suspicious damp spots that suddenly appear high up on the walls. Ancient electrics that need to be replaced. Inadequate heating system. Something is always going wrong, and nothing that goes wrong is inexpensive or simple to fix. It is, in fact, a bona fide money pit that takes up a lot of my free time. And yet, I love it. Did I mention it's beautiful? It's my dream. You could blame a childhood spent watching "This Old House" reruns. But I blame hurricanes.

I grew up on Big Pine Key, Florida, an island about 30 miles from Key West that few people had heard of before it was nearly wiped off the map by Hurricane Irma last September. Irma was the worst hurricane to hit the Keys in many years. In my lifetime there have been several that caused severe damage including Hurricane Irene in 1999, which cost $600 million to clean up. NOAA estimates Irma at $50 billion, which translates to countless lost homes and businesses belonging to people I love. They are devastated, but they are rebuilding, determined that their community will come back stronger.

It is largely because of storms like Irma that few buildings in the Keys are very old. Aside from the picturesque Conch Houses in Key West (the oldest of which dates back to 1829), there isn't a lot of romance to them, either. It isn't hard to see why someone like me, from a place like that, would be looking for stability: a house made of brick. Our house is solid. Despite its age, it's hard to imagine it blowing away. After all, in Hertford, Hereford, and Hampshire (say it with me!) hurricanes hardly happen.

Americans have a reputation for liking new things. I don't think that's a fair generalisation. What seems a more likely explanation is that the old things Americans like are not considered so very old elsewhere. I grew up being taken to flea markets and tag sales by my grandparents. In a small town, these were social events to look forward to. (Not to mention the delicious flea market fried sugar doughnuts, an approximation of which can also be found on the Kent coast. They make me weepy with nostalgia.) Nana and Grandpa liked old things. They liked a bargain and the thrill of the chase. Grandpa would focus on fishing and boating equipment, while Nana inspected modern rarities like Hummel figurines, needlepoint kits, thimbles (which she collected for me), secondhand hardcovers, and assorted knickknacks. She would take her purchases home wrapped in the previous day's edition of the Key West Citizen and catalog them in a series of red notebooks. I imagine the notebooks were kept for my parents' benefit, for the far-off someday when it all would be handed down to them. I learned to appreciate things with a bit of history, emphasis on story. Things like that are at home in an old house, and so am I.

What a house this age lacks is storage. We have one measly closet and it is dark and tiny, hidden away under the stairs with the old paint cans, bags of cat litter, tools and gardening supplies. It is for this reason I have become one of the new renunciates—Marie Kondo acolytes, hounding my local charity shop weekly with increasingly random assortments of cast-offs. One recent haul included a bundt cake pan, two suit jackets and a pair of vertiginous heels from New York publishing days, five pairs of outgrown kids' shoes (about which I used to get emotional, before I understood how many dozens of pairs they would outgrow in their childhoods, and decided to save my tears) and some books.

Divestment is my new religion. But on the flipside, I'm drawn to antique shops of the type that aren't supposed to exist anymore: mellow, musty and usually empty of other customers. Full of "brown furniture" of the type that not many of us covet anymore, at sub-Ikea prices. Georgian picture frames and sets of glinting glassware. I have a weak spot for any item whose use has to be explained to me, and I'm still smarting over missing two old club ballot boxes that could have been used to "black ball" someone in the last century or before. I love things that have been knocked around, used and abused and loved before I was born. Unlike Nana, I don't go in for delicate or breakable things—with a cat and two kids, ours is not a knick-knack-able life.

The comedian Harry Enfield has a recurring sketch about a Notting Hill antique shop called I Saw You Coming. The curmudgeonly old proprietor, Marcus, sells junk to gullible luvvies. His eyes light up as a pretty blond comes through the door, jingle jingle. "Trustafaria! Darling! Mwah, Mwah. Have I got just the thing for you. This rusty old lantern is just the kind of toss you'll be into." "How much is it?" "Well it cost me a fiver at a car boot sale, but you have a good eye. All the scratches are actually organic. And I saw you coming—so I'll give it to you for a grand…"

The shops I go to are nothing like this, you understand. My favorite, Fisher on Gray's Inn Road, is owned by a young woman named Hilary. She will offer you a glass of sherry on arrival and sell you a regimental drum. Or a ceramic dog. Last November, I bought a Georgian lazy Susan that I use as a cake stand. For my husband's birthday, a watercolor of a crab with a deep and glossy wood frame. In London these days, shops like hers are rare, and if we want them to last, we support them. I'll take an old thing over a new thing any day. My husband is just the same. On a recent trip to Paris, we could think of no better use for a Saturday afternoon than patrolling the Marche aux Puces for tarnished silver and papery antique table linens. We love to meet the people selling them, and the fact that we never know what crazy thing we will find around the next corner. Last visit, a vast needlepoint tapestry of a bare-breasted mermaid. Alas, we lack the wall space…

My parents have lately fallen into the business of old things. When my grandmother died, faced with the task of dispersing decades of her accumulated collections, they started having garage sales. Before long, they rented a booth in an antique mall in Ocala, the central Florida town where they now live. They are still working through Nana's back catalog, but their greater love is picking their own stock around Southern estate sales, tag sales, and junk shops. They like old things; they like a bargain and the thrill of the chase. They have been very successful at it. They have an eye, a way with their customers, a gift for imaginative merchandising and dozens of retailing ideas up their sleeves. In the age of eBay, people still love to browse their shop in person.

When they visit us in London, they comb the stalls of the Portobello Road, Spitalfields, and Camden Passage. They find the most extraordinary things: a 19th-century child-size steel foot brace, a Napoleonic cannonball, dozens of cut glass prisms from a defunct chandelier. They pack them up and take them back to Florida, where their customers are enthusiastic about them. For a while, the steampunks of Florida couldn't get enough old pocket watches on chains. Someone bought the foot brace to donate to a medical museum. And any horse or racing-related memorabilia find an easy home in horse-mad Ocala. Anything from England is automatically old enough and odd enough to be an antique—at least an honorary one.

They don't live in the Keys anymore, so they missed this latest and worst hurricane. But we remain in touch with many old friends on Big Pine, and we know there is cause for hope. Every weekend, teams of neighbors form to help clear debris, remove fallen trees and repair homes. Tropical foliage comes back quickly. Within a few years, everything will be greener and more beautiful than ever before. Relationships stronger, too. But some people have lost everything. Reminding us that choosing what to let go of is an absurd privilege. In the charity shops, my parents and I frequent, most of the things are the cast-offs of the dead. To be alive, and to have too much, is a guilty gratitude. Then I go back to my crumbling house and know, no matter what, it will outlast me.

Erin Moore is an American who has been living in London for 10 years. Her book, That's Not English: Britishisms, Americanisms and What Our English Says About Us, is available on amazon.com.

THE TRIFORIUM
BEHIND CLOSED DOORS AT ST PAUL'S CATHEDRAL
By Jonathan Thomas

St Paul's Cathedral is the most magnificent building in London. We've visited it often and even climbed the dome, all the way to the top. We try to visit whenever we can. It's one of the most historically important buildings in London and the view of the cathedral from various angles in London are actually protected - no building can block St Paul's. So, when I learned last year that there's a secret tour you can take that goes behind the scenes, I had to book in as soon as possible.

Every major cathedral has something called a Triforium. It's a weird space, often closed off from the public. But the massive scale of a cathedral by design creates a Triforium. What is it? By the stricter definition, it's a gallery or arcade above the arches of the nave, choir, and transepts of a church. Because of the height and accessibility, they are almost always closed off to the public.

As a consequence, these spaces are much more shall we say, institutional, than the rest of the public-facing cathedral. More often than not, they're used as a storage area for the cathedral. It's where they put stuff they need out of sight or don't have room for elsewhere. St Paul's Triforium is generally closed to the public, but it's occasionally offered in special tours a few days out of the month.

The St Paul's Triforium is special though, because it provides an insight in the very construction of the cathedral by Sir Christopher Wren after the Great Fire of London. To say I was excited about exploring what is essentially the attic of St Paul's Cathedral is an understatement.

We arrived early for our tour (after a marathon drive from Dorset to make it there in time). So, we went down the crypt for a quick lunch before our tour started. The group was small, no more than 10 people. After we were all gathered around, we were led to the main public staircase and up a few flights of stairs. Then we stopped and waited as the tour guide unlocked the door that's normally closed to the public. What a treat.

Once we were through the door, we were lead along a corridor and finally arrived at a spot that offered up an incredible view across the entire nave of St Paul's. They call this the 'BBC View' as this is where cameras are usually placed for big state occasions. The perk of this tour is that we were allowed to take pictures, something that's usually forbidden in St Paul's. So, all of us took tons of pictures. How could we not when the rare treat afford by this view?

We were then led through a corridor that had low ceilings but was filled with artifacts. They ranged from works of art no longer needed to various stone artifacts from the cathedral's history. There has been a church of some form at the site of St Paul's Cathedral since 604 AD. The star of this room, though, were the pieces of the original 'Old St Paul's' that burned down its great fire. They're just sitting there on a shelf, away from the public eye, which is a real shame because they're remarkable.

Then we're led to another corridor where the choir and clergy store their robes. You get the sense that this is a very private space. There you'll find detritus from the cathedral's history from old altars to sketches of possible architectural plans.

And then the real highlight of the tour. Sir Christopher Wren faced lots of challenges trying to get across his vision for a new cathedral and his designs went through many iterations as various stakeholders tried to have their say. Finally, when Wren wanted to convince the patron who mattered the most - King Charles II, he did something rather drastic. He built a massive wooden scale model of his vision. So big that the King could go inside it to get a sense of scale.

This wooden model, a treasure of national importance, still exists and is the main attraction you see on this tour. It's in a special room that was originally supposed to be the second library but instead has been turned into a permanent exhibition for the wooden model. Made to scale of 1:25, this model represents the design. It was intended to be a permanent record, in case Wren died to show clearly his vision. It was designed to be walked through at eye-level to suggest the experience of the real interior. The model was made from full-size drawings scaled up by Wren and his assistant Edward Woodroffe, working at a large table in the Cathedral convocation house.

The model was completed in 1674 and cost about £600, a princely sum of money equivalent to the cost of a good London house at the time. Initially, it was painted stone colors inside and out, with grey for the lead of the domes, gilded details, and fictive relief, but the paint has chipped and faded away with time leaving a beautiful dark wood structure in immaculate condition. The King was impressed, and Wren was allowed to continue to

Photos - Top - 1. Full view of Wren's Wooden Model, 2. (left) Close-up of wooden model, 3. (right) Interior of wooden model, notice the details and the faded paint.

Photos 1. Top - St Paul's Library, 2. Bottom - the Dean's 'Money-maker' Staircase.

pursue his vision though the final cathedral which differs quite a bit from the model.

We spent a good amount of time in the room, and it was incredible to see in person. Sadly we were not allowed to go inside of it, which was fine. It was treat enough to be able to see it. You really don't get an idea of just how massive this model is. Imagine a child's 'Wendy House' and triple the size to give you an idea of scale. Around the modern are framed drawing of Wren's various incarnations of the designs. And these are reproductions; these are Wren's actual copies. Remarkable!

After the treat of the model room, it was time to venture towards the library. When the giant creaky door was opened to the library, you're immediately hit with the most magnificent smell. A mixture of old leather, paper, and ink. If you could bottle the smell, it would make an excellent perfume for book nerds. The room is filled wall to wall with old books, with only a few dating back to before the cathedral was constructed. But many were donated as part of a massive collection.

The library's collection was almost mostly destroyed in the Great Fire of London. Wren's library chamber was restocked by the Commissioners for rebuilding St Paul's: They bought collections, including valuable Bibles and liturgical texts, and were fortunate to receive a generous bequest in 1712 of nearly 2,000 volumes from the library of Henry Compton, late Bishop of London. In 1783, the library of John Mangey, Vicar of Dunmow and Prebendary of St Paul's, was added. In the 19th century, extensive collections of ecclesiastical tracts and pamphlets were brought in.

It's a remarkable place, filled with treasures beyond compare. The librarian was there, and he was kind enough to talk to us about the books in the collection and how they care for them, ensuring that they survive the ravages of decay. The library was rather dark, but as it was late in the afternoon, occasionally a beautiful golden sunlight would enter the room and then leave, providing the most beautiful light to admire the collection. When we were ushered out of the library, I didn't want to leave. From July 2018, the library will be closed off from the public tours as it will undergo an 18-month conservation program. It was a privilege to take part in one of the last public tours.

After the library, we were led to a staircase, but not just any staircase. This is the Dean's

Above: Ruins of old St Paul's.

Staircase, and the cathedral staff jokingly call it the moneymaker. Because you've seen it countless films - most recently in the Harry Potter films. The cantilevered staircase is perfectly balanced. It's not supported in any way. Each stair is anchored to the wall, and that's it. Architecture and math in its purest form. The staircase is more than 300 years old and shows no signs of buckling under its own weight.

After that, we returned to the 'BBC View' where we were allowed to take as many pictures as we like. Back through the first corridor, down the stair and back to the floor of the cathedral. We lingered for a bit, enjoying the stunning architecture, but it was closing to tourists as the evensong was beginning (something we highly recommend doing). It was a real treat to visit the St Paul's Triforium, and we highly recommend it to anyone who has an interest in the architecture and construction of the cathedral. Even with the closure of the library for the next 18 months, it's still very much worth taking the tour.

If you go: To book, watch this web address: https://www.stpauls.co.uk/sightseeing-times-prices/guided-tours - you'll get an idea of dates and times. You have to email or call to book your tickets. You can't book online. There are 141 steps up to the Triforium, and there are no lifts, unfortunately, so it's not accessible for those in wheelchairs. It's £8 (about $10) on top of your admission ticket to the cathedral.

Showdown at Suez: Eden, Nasser and the End of Empire

By Christopher Saunders

On 26 July 1952, Egypt and Great Britain, awoke to a shock. The Young Officers, a coterie of nationalist Egyptian soldiers, ousted the pro-British King Farouk in a near-bloodless coup. Though Mohammed Neguib became Egypt's head of state, observers knew that the 38-year-old Colonel Gamel Abdel Nasser wielded real power. Now British officials confronted a new government with little intention of respecting Western authority, and whose charismatic leader dreamed of a pan-Arab state.

For Anthony Eden, then Foreign Secretary, Nasser's rise to power "happened so quickly that no one was aware as late as the morning before." While Winston Churchill advocated "positive action," hinting at a coup or invasion, Eden urged restraint. "While I do not expect the new Egyptian government to show any marked friendliness towards us," he wrote, "they do seem to be approaching Anglo-Egyptian problems in a more practical way and this is at last beginning to show results." One expected nothing less from England's leading diplomat.

In his third term as Foreign Secretary, Eden enjoyed a reputation as a polished statesman and man of principle. He served with distinction in the First World War, then entered politics; he resigned from Neville Chamberlain's cabinet in February 1938, unwilling to appease Hitler and Mussolini. His second tenure, under Churchill's wartime premiership, showed brilliance navigating the complex relationships among the Allied Powers. More recently, he negotiated West Germany's entry into NATO and Vietnam's independence from France.

Fifty-eight when he became Prime Minister in April 1955, Eden retained considerable charm and culture. He collected modern art, spoke fluent Arabic and Farsi, read French literature and Shakespeare, even dabbled in photography and travel writing. His second wife, Clarissa (Churchill's niece), was two decades his junior, a witty, engaging woman beloved of London society. He retained his good looks, with peppery hair and a matinee idol mustache, reminding novelist Robert Graves of actor Ronald Colman.

Yet Eden was vain, resistant to criticism, and savagely temperamental. His secretary, Evelyn Scheckberg, remembered that with Eden, "you can have a scene...of great violence with angry words spoken on both sides, and ten minutes later the whole thing is forgotten." Less charitably, a Conservative colleague, Rab Butler, called him "half mad baronet and half beautiful woman." Eden's health exacerbated these traits: a botched gallbladder operation in 1953 severed his bile duct, causing excruciating pain which Eden combatted with painkillers.

Eden's better half dominated early dealings with Nasser. He negotiated the withdrawal of British troops from Egypt in 1954, aside from a small force defending the Canal. Nasser assured Eden that "if this question were settled, a great friendship would exist between us." Along with American President Dwight Eisenhower, eager to woo Nasser away from the Soviet Union, Eden urged funding for the Aswan Dam, a massive project to develop the Nile. It seemed like Britain and Egypt would finally end their colonial relationship and part as friends.

Then Eden actually met Nasser, and their relationship imploded.

The fateful meeting occurred in Cairo on 20 February 1955, two months before Eden assumed the Premiership. Nasser and his entourage arrived in uniform; they were embarrassed when Eden, his wife and staff entered in civilian dress. Afterwards, Eden tried to impress his hosts by reciting Arabic proverbs, striking Nasser as arch and condescending. Their conversation turned to policy, with the two sparring over Nasser's anti-Western rhetoric and Britain's relations with the Arab world.

Their discussion was polite, if stilted and occasionally combative. Egyptian journalist Mohamed Heikal felt the Prime Minister "was the sort of person [Nasser] could do business with." But Nasser complained that "it was made to look as if we were beggars and they were princes!" For his part, Eden dismissed Nasser as suffering from "jealousy" at Britain's power and "a frustrated desire to lead the Arab world." In turning Eden and Nasser against each other, the conference provided a curtain raiser on a tragedy.

England and Egypt's destinies intertwined after Admiral Nelson destroyed Napoleon's fleet in Aboukir Bay in 1798. As the British Empire grew, policymakers saw Egypt, due to its crucial position astride both Africa and Asia, as a key linking England and India. The Suez Canal's creation in 1869 made the connection even more crucial: the Canal, jointly owned by Britain and France,

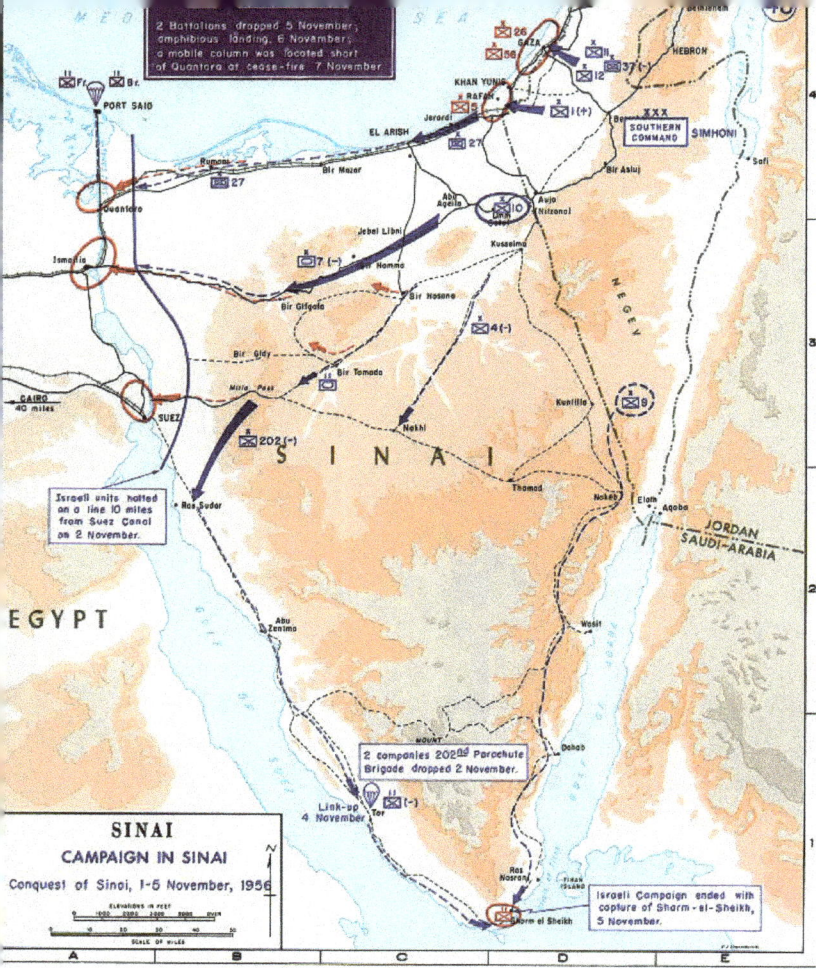

Engagement Area

by escalating clashes between British troops and Egyptian police in Ismailia, Egyptian mobs rampaged through Cairo, destroying European businesses and murdering nine Britons.

All prelude to the coup of June 1952. While Western policymakers initially saw Nasser as "an Arab Ataturk," a secular, modernising nationalist eschewing extremist Islam, he also showed a discomforting independence, espousing a Middle East free of Western rule. Britain, still clinging to its imperial past, saw him as a nationalist troublemaker; America, obsessed with the Cold War, wondered if he was a Communist.

Egypt's relations with the West swiftly deteriorated. Frustrated by America's reluctance to sell him arms, Nasser purchased Czech rifles and Soviet tanks instead. He further irritated Eisenhower by recognizing Red China. Then Nasser enraged the British by criticising the Baghdad Pact, Eden's attempt to form an alliance of Muslim states against Soviet influence.

Now Eden saw Nasser's hand in every setback Britain experienced. When King Hussein of Jordan dismissed John Glubb, British commander of the Arab Legion in March 1956, Eden blamed Nasser. When rioters stoned Foreign Secretary Selwyn Lloyd in Bahrain, Eden again accused "the Egyptian" of causing trouble. He labeled Nasser both a fascist and a communist, "as much in Khrushchev's hands as Mussolini was in Hitler's."

Nasser laughed at his opponent's insults. While Nasser hardly mourned the unrest in Iraq, Jordan and other British allies, he played little role in affecting it; he felt Eden blind to anti-Western resentment that transcended Egypt's borders. In conversation with Mohamed Heikal, Nasser joked that Eden thought he "only had to press one button on [my] desk and a demonstration erupted in Amman; another button and there was a riot in Aden."

Anthony Nutting, Eden's protege in the Foreign Office, didn't find the Prime Minister's paranoia amusing. One evening in March, while hosting American diplomat Harold Stassen, he received a phone call from Eden. In response to increased tensions with Nasser, Nutting had prepared a memorandum on neutralising Nasser through diplomatic and economic pressure. This wasn't enough for the Prime Minister, who demanded more drastic action.

provided a vital link for east-west trade, especially in oil. However, British imperialism proved incompatible with Egyptian aspirations.

Britain occupied Egypt outright in 1882 in response to a nationalist uprising. Their relationship remained rocky and often violent, culminating in riots and assassinations following World War I. Britain granted Egypt nominal independence in 1922, while retaining a huge military garrison. During World War II, British troops forced King Farouk to depose a Prime Minister suspected of pro-German sympathies. This incident enraged the young Nasser, who said that "there is something which is called dignity that one must be ready to defend."

Nasser joined the Young Officers, which formed the nucleus of anti-British agitation. During the war, their agents (including future president Anwar Sadat) contacted Axis officials for assistance expelling the British. War's end only increased tensions, from the disastrous war with Israel to anti-Western riots and economic turmoil, culminating in January 1952's Bloody Saturday. Incensed

"What's all this nonsense about neutralising [Nasser]?" Eden demanded. "I want him murdered, can't you understand?"

Maintaining his composure, Nutting suggested that removing Nasser without an "alternative" would only create chaos. "I don't give a damn if there's anarchy and chaos in Egypt!" came the reply. A shaken Nutting returned to dinner, fearing that a lunatic inhabited 10 Downing Street.

Eden's subordinates entertained harebrained ideas to affect his wish. One plan involved encouraging the Muslim Brotherhood to kill Nasser; on their own, they had already tried the previous year. (This fell through, as MI6 felt it couldn't trust the fanatical Brotherhood to uphold Western interests.) Other plots seem hatched from an Ian Fleming novel: nerve gas pumped into Nasser's office, paying Nasser's doctor to poison him, even an exploding razorblade.

For now, the British and Americans settled on economic pressure. The Americans dragged their feet funding the Aswan Dam, which became a symbol both of Egyptian aspirations and Western aid to third world nations. On 19 July, Secretary of State John Foster Dulles, who saw events purely through a Cold War prism, announced the cancellation of the Western loan. Dulles gloated afterwards that Nasser "is in a hell of a spot and no matter what he does can be used to American advantage."

Publicly, Egypt shrugged off Dulles' decision. "Naturally it upsets our plans," Nasser's aide Aly Sabry told reporters, "but the High Dam will be built." Privately, Nasser considered it a "slap in the face." He ordered Mohammed Younis, an Army engineer, to organise a coup de main that signified Egyptian independence. He told few others, even his inner circle, about his decision.

On 26 July 1956, Nasser made a long, angry speech in Alexandria denouncing Anglo-American perfidy. Repeating the themes of "strength and dignity," he excoriated Western arrogance ("imperialism without arms") and defended his own actions as necessary for Egyptian independence. Then, referring to the President of the Suez Canal, he commented: "I began to look at Mr. Black...and I imagined that I was sitting in front of Ferdinand de Lesseps."

As Nasser evoked Suez's architect, Younis and 30 picked followers moved to seize the Canal. ("I told

Nasser

them that one man in each group...had instructions to shoot on the spot anyone who violated secrecy," Younis recalled. Mohamed Heikal claimed that Younis punctuated this threat by slamming a revolver on his desk.) Moving swiftly, his men overwhelmed the Canal's British and French operators without firing a shot.

Back in Alexandria, Nasser announced: "Brothers of yours, sons of Egypt, are rising up to direct the canal company and undertake its operation." He proclaimed the Canal "a part of Egypt and the property of Egypt." Nasser received delirious applause from his listeners. It was the apotheosis of his career: In a stroke, he captured the Canal and threw down a gauntlet Eden and Eisenhower couldn't possibly ignore.

The West reacted with fury. Eisenhower denounced the "deliberate, unilateral seizure" and demanded United Nations intervention. The British press responded with near-hysteria, with the Times calling it "an act of international brigandage" and claimed that Egyptian pilots lacked the skill to run the Canal (which Younis's men disproved

Churchill with Anthony Eden

within 24 hours). Others evoked fascism, with the Daily Mirror encouraging Nasser to "remember Mussolini…[who] ended up hanging upside down by his feet."

The Mirror's intemperance echoed the Prime Minister. Eden (whose immediate response was commenting that "the Egyptian has his thumb on our windpipe") told Eisenhower that "Nasser is not a Hitler…but the parallel with Mussolini is close." He took the analogy public in a televised address in August. "We all know this is how fascist governments behave," Eden said. "And we all remember, only too well, what the cost is in giving into fascism." In other words, stop Nasser or risk World War III.

This miscalculation, more than Eden's health, temper or even his personal dislike for Nasser, explains the Prime Minister's actions. Nasser, though a saber-rattling strongman, lacked Hitler's strength or even his intent; he envisioned an Arab state unified through politics, not an empire forged by conquest. But Eden, who made his reputation opposing appeasement two decades earlier, felt he couldn't take that risk. As historian Keith Kyle writes, "The battle against Neville Chamberlain, lost in 1937-1938, must be won at Suez."

The Americans weren't so sure. Secretary Dulles assured Eden that America would force Nasser to "disgorge" the Canal. Yet Eisenhower, facing reelection, had no intention of embroiling America in a Middle Eastern conflict. He warned Eden of "the unwisdom even of contemplating the use of military force at this moment," encouraging instead diplomacy. Frustrated, Eden turned to two other allies, less powerful but equally anti-Nasser: France and Israel.

France hated Nasser even earlier than England. Fighting a brutal war in Algeria, French officials blamed Nasser for the FLN's terror campaign. Indeed, Nasser housed FLN refugees, gave inflammatory speeches supporting them, and even authorised arms shipments. Jacques Soustelle, Governor of Algeria, called Nasser "the octopus whose tentacles have for so many months been strangling North Africa;" Robert Lacoste, a Socialist MP, proclaimed that "one French division in Egypt is worth four divisions in Algeria."

Guy Mollet, France's Prime Minister, took office promising to wind down the Algerian War. Now he proposed to expand it. A humiliating visit to Algiers changed his mind, as enraged European Pieds-Noir pelted him with eggs and tomatoes. Now Mollet (a former Resistance fighter who survived Nazi imprisonment) latched onto the anti-Nasser hysteria, echoing Eden by comparing Nasser to Hitler and his writings to *Mein Kampf*.

Israel needed little encouragement. Nasser backed harsh rhetoric about Israel with action, supporting fedayeen militia units who murdered Israeli soldiers and settlers in the Gaza Strip. Israel, in turn, instituted a brutal policy of retaliation, sending commando teams to annihilate Arab villages in revenge. David Ben-Gurion, recently returned to power, eagerly seized the opportunity to smash a mortal enemy.

Their conspiracy climaxed in the Paris suburb of Sevres on 22 October. Selwyn Lloyd met with Christian Pineau, Mollet's Foreign Minister, General Challe and Israeli officials including David Ben-Gurion and his one-eyed Chief of Staff, Moshe Dayan. Over the next three days, these allies hatched an incredible plot to justify Western intervention. Israel would attack Egypt, Britain and France would call for a ceasefire and intervene, seizing the Canal in the process.

The charade disgusted even those who planned it. Moshe Dayan thought Lloyd's "whole demeanor expressed distaste - for the place, the company and the topic." Lloyd had protested to Eden beforehand, and afterwards vented his spleen to Anthony Nutting, who decided that he "cannot stay in the Government if this sordid conspiracy is carried out." Christian Pineau admitted that "I wonder how Eden could have thought for one moment that the Arab world would swallow such a story."

Only the Israelis left Sevres happy. As an incentive for their cooperation, Pineau promised Ben-Gurion and Dayan not only territory in the Sinai, but French cooperation in constructing a nuclear reactor. After the British departed, Mollet and Pineau treated the Israelis to a toast, ushering in Israel as a nuclear power. The balance of power in the Middle East took another fateful turn.

British and French forces massing on Cyprus had little idea of this duplicity, still less how to proceed with their operation. Eden alarmed Field Marshall Bernard Montgomery by saying that he wished to "knock Nasser off his perch." A pithy phrase, Montgomery thought, but what did it mean? He pressed the Prime Minister for details: Did he want Nasser overthrown or merely humbled? Did he want to reoccupy the Canal Zone or Egypt entirely? The Prime Minister didn't elaborate, convincing Montgomery that any invasion was foredoomed.

Ultimately, General Sir Hugh Stockwell, commanding the invasion, proposed a dual operation called Musketeer. After an intense aerial and naval bombardment, paratroopers would seize key points along the Canal, while amphibious forces attacked Ports Said and Fuad. The French commander, Andre Beaufre, ridiculed Musketeer as "a second-rate copy of the Normandy landings." Eden wasn't the only one trapped in a World War II mindset.

Israel invaded the Sinai on 29 October, their French jets and tanks smashing Egyptian resistance. Eden and Mollet issued their ultimatum, to American befuddlement, Soviet indignation and Arab fury. The United Nations condemned the conspiracy, with America and the USSR in rare agreement. It particularly enraged Eisenhower, then working to support Hungary's anti-communist revolt. "I just can't believe it," Ike told Dulles. "I can't believe [Eden] would be so stupid."

Nor were Britons universally supportive, with only 40 percent approving intervention (briefly spiking to 53 percent once fighting began). Eden's strongest support came from working class Britons, who felt that "the Gyppos had hit us, [and] we should hit them." Others were sharply divided: when several Oxford dons published an open letter attacking the Prime Minister, other professors responded with a supportive missive. Even Queen Elizabeth, who privately questioned Eden's policy, wrote that "My lady-in-waiting thinks one thing, one private secretary thinks another, another thinks something else."

On 3 November, Eden gave a televised broadcast appealing for national unity. (Clearly nervous beforehand, he looked so pale that Clarissa had to darken his mustache with mascara.) His tone was at once resolute and pleading, forthright and dishonest. "All my life I've been a man of peace: working for peace, striving force peace and negotiating for peace," Eden assured viewers. "I could not be other, even if I wished. But I am utterly convinced that the action we have taken is right."

The next day, 30,000 antiwar demonstrators swarmed Trafalgar Square, London's largest public protest since 1938. The demonstrators carried placards reading "Law Not War" and chanting "Eden must go!" They listened to fiery orators (including Aneurin Bevan, the Welsh MP who proclaimed Eden "too stupid to be Prime Minister"), threw firecrackers and ball bearings at counter-protestors, then tried to march on 10 Downing Street. There, mounted police set upon them, arresting or injuring dozens.

Eden's cabinet heard this commotion as they made their final deliberations on using military force. His ministers were divided, with several urging Eden to cancel or postpone the invasion. Then came word that Israel rejected the ceasefire. Clarissa Eden, who witnessed the scene, recalled that "everyone laughed and banged the table with relief except Birch and Manckton, who looked glum." Their vote became unanimous.

On 6 November, British and French troops attacked Port Said. After a preliminary bombardment, airborne troops landed outside the city. The French paras, battle-hardened in Algeria, fought with matchless skill and brutality: Pierre Leulliette recounted numerous atrocities among his

The aftermath in the canal

unit, from executing prisoners to looting and even rape. "A prisoner is sacred but so's a sentinel," he explained.

British units suffered from poor coordination and outdated equipment: many paratroopers discarded their easily-jammed Sten guns for Egyptian rifles. The red-bereted soldiers of 3rd Para Battalion suffered heavy antiaircraft fire, then fought bloodily for every inch of ground: They stormed a causeway defended by artillery, a cemetery bristling with rifles, and a heavily-guarded airfield.

Meanwhile, the second wave (40 and 42 Commandos of the Royal Marines) landed on Port Said's beaches, already burning from heavy bombardment. They too faced stiff resistance, with Egyptian machine gunners blasting away at close range, along with snipers and militiamen sniping from buildings along the waterfront. The Marines made little progress until landing several Buffalo tanks, which shrugged off small-arms fire and blasted their way into the city.

Port Said, however, didn't surrender easily. "Egyptians opened up from windows and side roads at some points with women and children around them," recalled James Robinson, "and the tanks blazed back with their Brownings and the Commandos with Brens from the top of their Buffaloes." Fighting raged through residential neighborhoods, government districts, even a cemetery. Machine guns, grenades, and bazookas did deadly work in this close quarter combat.

Eventually, weight of numbers and firepower told, and the Allies cleared the city. More fighting the next day extended their position; with Egyptian troops in full retreat, General Stockwell prepared to thrust further south to secure the Canal. Then, incredibly, he received orders from London and Paris to halt. Two days of bloodshed, which claimed 16 British and 10 French lives, along with dozens more wounded (and more than 500 Egyptian deaths) - all, it appeared, for nothing.

The Allied troops felt angry and betrayed by this sudden about-face. General Beaufre found it so ridiculous that he contemplated ignoring the order and continuing the offensive. General Stockwell contented himself with biting sarcasm. "We have now achieved the impossible," he wired London: "We're going both ways at once."

Ultimately, the superpowers tipped the balance. Nikita Khrushchev gloated that Nasser had "cut the lion's tail" and threatened nuclear attacks on the West. Eisenhower, furious at Eden for undercutting him as Soviet tanks crushed Hungary, applied more subtle tactics. America froze British assets and instituted sanctions that threatened to sink the British economy. Eden raged against Eisenhower's actions, but they exposed his impotence. Britain could no longer proceed without American support, and folded.

Now, even Britons who supported Suez abandoned Eden. Several members of Eden's government followed Anthony Nutting in resigning, with one branding the Prime Minister "a criminal madman." RAF Marshall Sir Dermot Boyle lamented that British troops "were being stopped when victory was…imminent." Even Winston Churchill criticized his former protege: "I am not sure I should have dared to start, but I am sure I should not have dared to stop."

The Prime Minister embodied England's newfound feebleness. In September, he had suffered a seizure resulting in hospitalisation, a prelude to further dissolution. As the invasion unfolded, Eden paced around his home, called friends and cabinet ministers at night, alternating amphetamines and sedatives at an alarming rate. One evening he called Guy Mollet, complaining to the French Premier that "the whole world reviles me." The long-suffering Clarissa Eden remarked on "the Suez Canal flowing through my drawing room."

Finally, under withering domestic criticism and mounting international pressure, he collapsed. J.P.W. Mallalieu, a Labour MP who supported the invasion, found Eden in a pitiable state. "[He] sprawled on the front bench, head back and mouth agape… The face was gray except where black-rimmed caverns surrounded the dying embers of his eyes. The whole personality seemed completely withdrawn."

Eventually, the United Nations intervened, gradually replacing British and French troops with a multinational peacekeeping force. This allowed the Allies to save face, but underscored their failure. After the last British troops departed in December, an Egyptian mob attacked the statue of Ferdinand de Lesseps at Port Said and destroyed it. A fitting exclamation point on the whole sorry affair.

Afterwards, Eden and Clarissa retreated to Jamaica, spending several weeks at Ian Fleming's Goldeneye estate. His career in shambles, Eden resigned in January 1957, turning the Premiership over to Harold Macmillan. Eden wrote several memoirs justifying his actions, but never restored his reputation. When he died in 1977, kind eulogists remembered his wartime diplomacy and opposing fascism over his imperial debacle.

Guy Mollet outlasted Eden only by a few months, resigning in June. Disgusted by the Crisis, France's military decided they could no longer leave government to politicians. In May 1958 they toppled the Fourth Republic and restored Charles De Gaulle to power. While De Gaulle exited Algeria on his own terms, his anti-British policies (especially excluding Britain from the Common Market) stemmed in part from lingering resentment over Suez.

Far from being knocked off his perch, Nasser's successful defiance enhanced his standing in the Middle East. At home, his regime continued to vacillate between economic development, social reforms and repression of political rivals. His pretensions at a pan-Arab empire resulted in a failed union with Syria, a muddled conflict in Yemen and the disastrous Six Day War with Israel. Still, when Nasser died in 1970 he remained the Arab world's greatest modern hero.

If Britain retained any illusions about its empire, Suez destroyed them. With Macmillan citing "the wind of change…blowing through this continent," Britain granted independence to its African colonies over the next decade. In the Middle East, nationalists murdered Iraq's royal family in 1958, Communists seized power in Yemen, Jordan turned towards the United States. Eisenhower soon proclaimed the Eisenhower Doctrine, committing Americans to an open-ended presence in the Middle East.

More than anything, Suez was an anachronism. Eden acted like nothing had changed since the era of Lord Cromer and General Gordon, when chastising third-world rulers through military force went unchallenged. Unfortunately, 1956 (the era of decolonisation and Cold War tensions) was an entirely different world. Refusing to recognise this, Eden initiated an unnecessary tragedy that shamed his country and destroyed him.

EDWARD III
THE FIFTY-YEAR KING

Edward III was the king of England for 50 years, during which time he turned the country into one of the most powerful military forces in Europe; initiated the beginning of the Hundred Years' War with France; made huge developments to the English Parliament and led the country through the devastating Black Death. Initially, a much-admired king whose main interests were warfare and the extension of the Kingdom of England, Edward III became unpopular in his later years as his military campaigns failed, the economy suffered, and his health deteriorated.

Edward III did not have a particularly stable upbringing. The first son of King Edward II, a notorious royal failure, Edward was used by his mother Isabella and her new lover Lord Mortimer to remove his father from the throne forcibly.

In 1325, King Charles IV of France demanded that King Edward II perform homage for the English Duchy of Aquitaine. Unwilling to leave England and ignorant to the plot that his wife Isabella and her exiled lover Mortimer were forming against him, Edward II sent his son Edward in his place. Isabella promptly had the young Edward engaged to Philippa of Hainault and, with the support of the French King, launched an invasion against England. King Edward II was forced to relinquish his throne and the new king, Edward III, was crowned in January 1327.

At first, Edward was a puppet in the administration of Mortimer, the de facto ruler of England. Mortimer and Isabella were instantly unpopular as they had signed a costly treaty with King Charles IV of France. A treaty that proved to be even more damaging than first thought as Charles died almost immediately, giving Edward a legitimate claim to the French throne that was now forfeited.

Edward was married to Philippa in January 1328. Despite that fact that Edward was only 15 at the time of the marriage and Philippa just 13, the couple managed to have a son within two years. Having suffered the indignity of being ruled by his mother's lover for long enough and as the proud new father of a legitimate heir, Edward took violent action against the unpopular and unsuccessful Mortimer. When a parliament was called at Nottingham Castle, Edward and a group of close friends dragged Mortimer from Isabella's bed in the middle of the night and executed him as an 'enemy of the state.'

KEY FACTS

- Edward III was born at Windsor Castle on 13 November 1312.
- He succeeded as King of England, Duke of Aquitaine and Overlord of Ireland on 20 January 1327 aged 14.
- Edward III married Philippa, daughter of the Count of Flanders in January 1328. The couple had 14 children together.
- The king died of a stroke on 21 June 1377 aged 64, having reigned for 50 years.

Edward took to the throne with gusto and immediately set out to prove himself as a worthy king by renewing the war against the Scots. But Scotland was already at war with itself. On one side was King David II and on the other the pretender Edward Balliol, a representative of 'The Disinherited' a group of English magnates who had lost land in Scotland due to the peace accord. Edward supported Balliol while King Philip VI of France supported King David II and gave him refuge. Philip confiscated Edward's title to Aquitaine, so Edward threw the match into the powder keg and made his claim to the French throne, starting what became the Hundred Years' War.

In 1339, King Edward III invaded France and laid claim to the throne. Victory over France would lead to the expansion of an already lucrative wool trade with Flanders and wine trade with Gascony as well as opportunities for feudal taxes and all-out plunder of French towns. The invasion was popular with the English public.

The first few years of the Hundred Years' War went brilliantly for Edward. In a significant naval battle in 1340, the English Navy destroyed almost the entire French fleet at Sluys. In 1342, Edward overran Brittany, and in 1346 he landed in Normandy and defeated the French King Philip VI at Crecy. At the same time, Queen Philippa was fighting independently in the north, defeating the Scots at Neville's Cross and capturing King David

The Battle of Crecy Froissart

II of Scotland.

Edward's costly war went on with no end in sight until it was forced to pause in 1348 while England fought an invisible enemy, the bubonic plague. The Black Death killed 1.5 million people in England alone over the next few years. One-third of the population of England died of the plague and what remained of the decimated population was neither able nor willing to fund a war overseas. Serious fighting did not begin again until the mid-1350s when Edward's oldest son, Edward, later known as the Black Prince, won the Battle of Poitiers and captured King John II, the youngest son of Philip VI.

This was to be the most glorious moment of Edward III's aggressive reign. At one time the King of Scots was held in the Tower of London, and the King of France was held in Windsor Castle. England owned a great deal of land in France, and the French central government had totally collapsed. However, the final push that would have seen Edward III crowned King of France never came, and in 1360, Edward renounced his claim to the throne and in return was awarded extended territory around Aquitaine and the bastion of Calais, now owning almost one-quarter of France.

Edward's attempt nine years later to claim his title as King of France proved to be too little too late, and the rest of his reign was a disaster, militarily and politically. All five of Edward's sons were granted ducal titles with a deed to English territory, and Edward created the Duchy of Cornwall to provide the heir to the throne with an income independent of the sovereign or the state.

By the mid-1360s, Edward was increasingly relying on his sons to manage his military efforts and state affairs. Lionel of Antwerp, the king's second surviving son, led a campaign in Ireland where he hoped to exert control over the autonomous Anglo-Irish lords in charge there. The venture was a disaster, and in April 1364, John II of France died in captivity in England having failed to raise his ransom, restarting the war with France. Edward's younger son, John of Gaunt, led a disastrous campaign in France that culminated in the 1375 Treaty of Bruges and leaving only Calais, Bordeaux and Bayonne and Brest in English hands.

Public opinion about King Edward III and his reign shifted dramatically. Previously seen as a chivalrous, victorious, and strong King, Edward was now seen as weak and was accused of leaving his duties in the hands of his advisors who were running England's economy into the ground. Following Queen Philippa's death in 1369, Edward took a mistress by the name of Alice Perrers who, in the mid-1370s, was thought to hold too much power over the weakened king and was banished from court by parliament.

Largely deserted by his family, Edward was alone with Alice Perrers when he died of a stroke in June 1377. So the story goes, Alice Perrers looked at Edward's prone body, stripped the rings from his royal fingers, and left.

Legacy Today

During his lifetime, King Edward III was an extremely popular king. Edward created the Order of the Garter, creating a sense of camaraderie amongst his peerage, a peerage that he purposefully expanded during his reign by creating many new earls and dukes. Edward's popularity extended out from the nobility to the lower classes thanks in part to his reputation as a fearless warrior. The people of England were united in their fear of a French invasion and turned to Edward, a war-hungry king, for reassurance. Edward III's reign saw key developments in the establishment of the English Parliament and a strong revival of the English language in literature and law. Only one thing has scarred the reputation of the chivalrous warrior king, and that is the length of his reign: Edward III won some of the most important battles of the Middle Ages but died with only three castles to show for them.

Film & TV

- "World Without End" (2012) TV series
- "Eduard III" (1961) TV movie
- "The Death of King Edward III" (1911)
- Further Research
- Ormrod, Mark (2013) "Edward III" (English

Edward III Coat of Arms

Monarchs Series) (The English Monarchs Series)
- Mortimer, Ian (2008) "The Perfect King: The Life of Edward III, Father of the English Nation"
- Bothwell, J. (2001). "The Age of Edward III".
- Waugh, S.L. (1991). "England in the Reign of Edward III".

Locations to Visit

- Edward III was born at Windsor Castle where visitors can see his famous round table.
- In York, visitors can see York Minster, where Edward's marriage to Queen Philippa of Hainault, York Abbey, where Edward kept his chancery and York Castle where Edward kept his Exchequer.
- Edward III is buried at Westminster Abbey

CHURCHILL'S CHARTWELL
Exploring Churchill's Beloved Home

By Jonathan Thomas

Winston Churchill is such a widely known figure that it's easy to build a picture of him based on his actions and his perceptions from history. But what was he like as a person? What was he like at home, in his most private spaces? I sought the answer to this question recently and had the opportunity to tour Chartwell behind the scenes and get an insight into the one British historical figure that I admire the most.

Chartwell was Churchill's beloved home. Coming from an aristocratic family, Churchill had always wanted a grand house. But being the son of a 'second son' who wasn't going to inherit the Marlborough fortune, Winston was not a wealthy man. So, he set his sights a little lower and settled on an old manor house in the Weald of Kent. The house was not particularly grand when they bought it, but for the rest of his life, Churchill would put his personal stamp on the place and now it's forever associated with him.

Churchill bought in 1922, for £5,000 (a handsome some even when you convert it into a modern currency). When he viewed the place, he fell in love with it and he bought it without asking Lady Churchill. Churchill being Churchill, he just did it on his own and Clementine was furious. In fact, the house was a source of contention throughout the rest of his life because of the upkeep. But Winston was a canny operator, he enlisted his children to fall in love with it first then brought Clemi to get her to love it. She relented and the family moved in. Chartwell caused constant financial problems and Churchill spent £18,000 doing it up. A perfect example of putting more money into something than it was worth. It didn't help that Churchill would be a difficult client and change his mind often.

Money problems plagued Churchill his whole life. At this point in British history, Members of Parliament were not paid so Churchill had to survive on the income from his writings. After a particularly good spell of writing articles, he was able to afford the sum needed to buy Chartwell. And then in Churchillian fashion, proceeded to spend way beyond his means to do the place up. During the Great Depression, Churchill lost a fortune and throughout the 1930s contemplated having to sell the place. But Churchill was never one to give up.

The whole house was reconfigured in some way to make it the perfect home for Churchill and his family. He bought the house for the views across the Weald of Kent so the spaces inside are laid out best to show his favorite views. He was inspired by the landscape as a political, a writer and as an Englishman. He wanted to make the most of it.

Churchill wanted to make the place a haven for his children and he had a habit of doing nice things for them - like putting in a treehouse. The entire Chartwell estate was an expression of his personality and love for his family.

The house is currently set up like it would have been in the '30s during Churchill's 'Wilderness years.' This was the period of time that he was out of power and considered a political outcast. He had lots of free time on his hands and he spent it sculpting the house and the landscape to his liking. These were his most prolific years in writing and it was a factory for his bestselling books. The National Trust, which currently owns and manages the house, wants the house to have a lived-in feel, a snapshot in time when Churchill was in his darkest place. Chartwell made him happy, and inspired him during World War II when his political career was resurrected.

Chartwell is currently undergoing changes to open it up a bit more and show more of how the family lived while they were there. They also want to highlight how Churchill worked along with the staff of people for whom Chartwell was a workplace (not just house staff but the secretaries needed to type his writing). They are also going to make some slight structural changes to return the house to how it was originally when Churchill lived there but also improve the flow for visitors.

Winston was an avid amateur painter and many of his paintings are on display throughout the house but they wouldn't have been when he lived there. He loved to paint and he painted more than 500 paintings in his lifetime. He would take his paints on his holidays and paint wherever they went - thus many of his paintings aren't of particularly 'English' scenes at all. He especially loved the light in southern France and many of his paintings are of French locales. On display in the house is the painting he submitted anonymously to the Royal Academy, which won a prize, which he was quite proud of. During his life, most of the paintings were banished to the studio.

In addition to the gifts and Churchill's artwork, there are some priceless works of art that Churchill

Churchill's Bedroom

Main Sitting Room

'We shape our buildings, and afterwards our buildings shape us' - Churchill

Winston's Favorite View

collected and was gifted. He was given a Monet by his publisher for giving them worldwide publishing rights. It's actually the only Monet in a National Trust property in Britain.

The house was a place to entertain and Chartwell had many visitors. The guest book - anyone who came to stay overnight got to sign it (day guests didn't sign) - features the signatures of the great and the good of the 20th century. He received many gifts from all over the world after the war and the notable pieces are on display throughout the house (many have been recently acquired by the National Trust as part of the fundraising drive project). A bit of trivia, they don't actually own Churchill's Nobel Prize but at the time of publication, they were close to securing the funding.

As a man of letters, Churchill had a massive library. There are in fact, 918 books in his library. Many are about great figures and events in British history. Many were used as sources for his writings. The National Trust want to explore who gave the books and the stories behind them as part of its new project. Many books were gifts from other world leaders and dignitaries.

Chartwell was a working home. Churchill employed eight secretaries in the house - it's how he managed to write so many books. Plans are in the works to restore the room where they did their typing and share the stories of the secretaries who worked there. When he would come home, he'd visit the room and sit down and read that the typists had been working on (and then bark orders at them on what to fix and what to do next).

After World War II, Churchill was broke when he was kicked out of office. He had very generous friends. They made improvements to the house for him - like adding an elevator for the aging leader. They also banded together to buy the house for him to improve his finances. It was then donated to the National Trust with the proviso that Churchill and his wife could live there until they died.

Churchill worked in the study, he liked to pace back and forth. He had to have the tassels removed from the rug because he kept tripping on it. He also had a standing desk, proving that the current trend for standing desks is not a new thing. The floorboards are meant to look like a ship's deck to evoke his favorite office - First Lord of the Admiralty. His private bedroom was just off the study. The bedroom is going to be opened to the public eventually. There were five fish tanks in the study during his time - he loved fish.

They did not entertain big parties at the house - that was done at their London house. Guests at Chartwell were usually personal guests. The house was an intimate environment because compared to something like Blenheim (where he was born) Chartwell is not a large house. This is reflected in the art-deco dining room which only seats up to 10 people. Incidentally the dining room doubled at a film room - they'd close the curtains and have the perfect room to show films.

Outside of the family, the most interesting inhabitant of the house is Jock the Cat. Or rather Jock VI. Churchill owned many pets throughout the life but near the end of his days he received an orange marmalade cat named Jock, a present from his former secretary Sir John 'Jock' Colville. It was decided that there must always be a Jock, orange marmalade cat living at Chartwell. The current occupant of the office is Jock VI who took over from his predecessor in 2014. The current Jock is a rescue who loves living at Chartwell, though he's prone to mischief. Apparently he likes to hide under Lady Churchill's bed, which makes him a naughty kitty as they're silk antiques.

But there's more to Chartwell than the house and those who inhabited it. Chartwell was an estate. And in Churchill's mind, he was going to create his own English Arcadia. When you see Chartwell's grounds today, you see it as Churchill intended. He sculpted every view, every garden feature, every building bears his stamp. He was not afraid to muck in - the brick walls in the kitchen garden were built brick by brick by Churchill himself, who laid so many bricks he gained membership into the bricklayers union.

Changing the landscape took his entire life and he was never really full satisfied with it. He laid out gardens. He dug ponds. He got a digger and dug lakes. He planted trees (many which were sadly destroyed by windstorms in the 1980s). He laid out a croquet lawn. One of his famous spots was the koi pond that modern day visitor's pass by on their way into the house. There's a chair there, and he loved to sit there and feed the fish while pondering the problems of the world. Inspired by his childhood growing up and visiting the stately homes of the British Aristocracy, Churchill wanted his own great

Grounds of Chartwell

Winston's Favorite Pondering Spot by the Coy Pond

Winston at his standing desk before they were cool.

gardens. His house may not have been grand, but he wanted it to sit perfectly in HIS landscape.

And it worked for him. Many of his most beautiful paintings are of the Chartwell estate.

After you've explored the house and the grounds. You must take the time to visit Churchill's Studio, which is also open to the public (and there are guided tours of this as well). Churchill was a politician, but he saw himself as a professional writer. Painting was his hobby, his most favorite past time; a a tool he used to battle his 'black dog' - bouts of depression. His studio showcases that - it's setup just as it was when he was painting. There are hundreds of paintings on display. The easel is setup, as if he just popped out for a cigar and will be back to paint shortly. He never took himself seriously as a painter. But he was surprisingly good at it. If one had to describe his style, it would be impressionistic. It's fascinating to think that a man who could speak and write with such fire and force, command armies of men, administer a global war, could manage the patience and gentleness required to paint sedate landscapes (though, admittedly, he only painted one during World War II). But that's what is so surprising about Churchill and his home.

You can't fit him into a box.

Today the house and the grounds are lovingly taken care of by the National Trust. They seek to maintain the house and the grounds as Churchill loved them but also in a way that educates visitors into the kind of man Churchill was. Stepping into his home feels very intimate. Because of the timed entry system, the house does not get too crowded so you can linger and explore room by room. Attendants are happy to answer questions. The National Trust has opened up to some guided tours in the later afternoons that will take you into rooms normally closed to the public (these must be booked in advance).

If you want to peer into Winston Churchill's very soul, then visit his beloved home. You will come away knowing the man in a much more intimate way and appreciate his achievements even more.

Thank you to the Royal Oak Foundation who arrange for me to have a special behind the scenes tour and for the staff at Chartwell for taking the time to show me around.

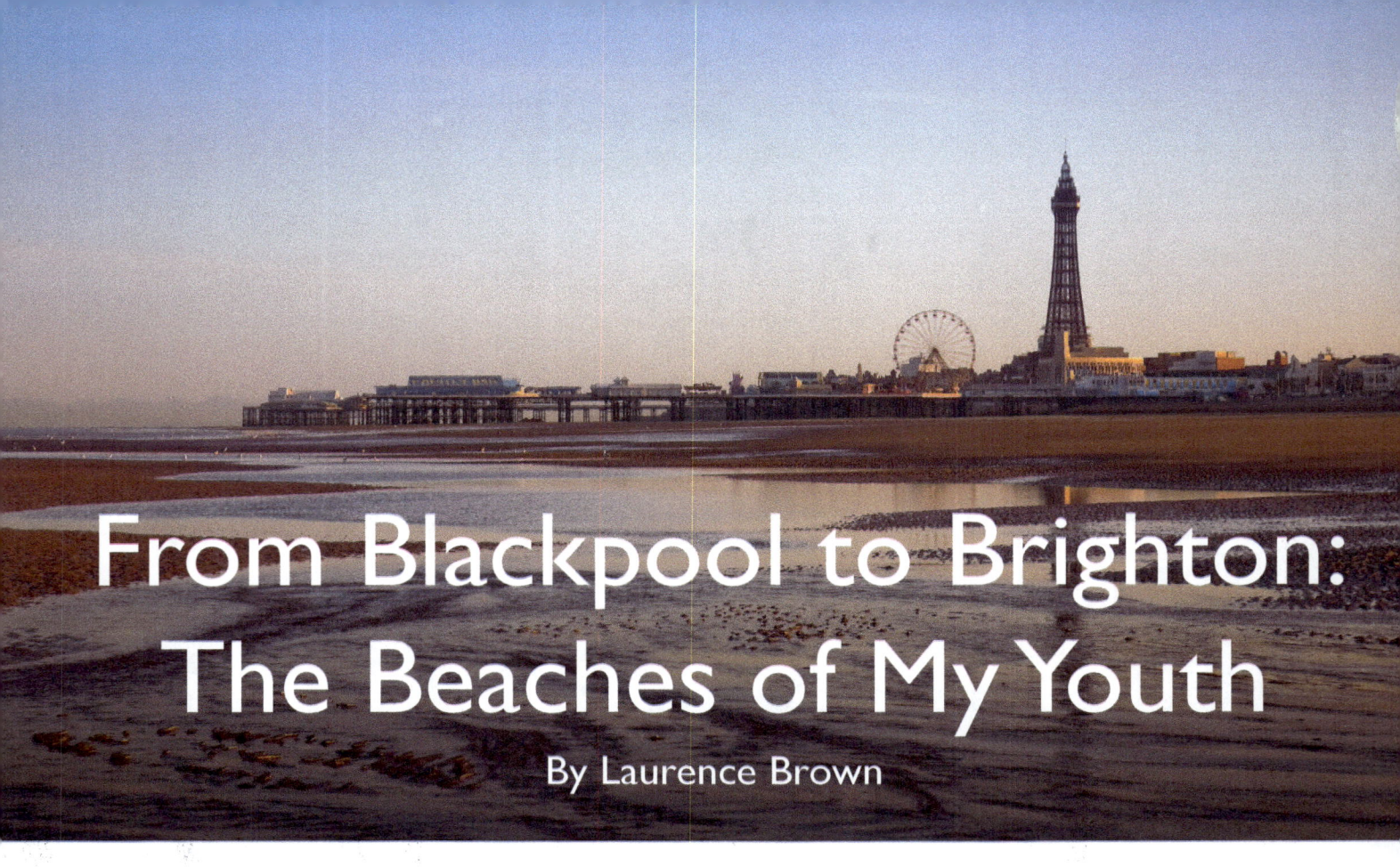

From Blackpool to Brighton: The Beaches of My Youth

By Laurence Brown

There's an old adage that happiness comes in waves. As someone who grew up a stone's throw from the sands of northeast England, I can agree with this unreservedly.

The beach in question was located along the gloomy bay of Cleethorpes, a town immediately adjoining Grimsby—the hometown of my childhood. In the daytime, Cleethorpes remained notable for its distinct lack of people. Sure, you might encounter the odd—sometimes frighteningly odd—individual walking (if not wielding) an Alsatian, but for the most part Cleethorpes did not favourably compare with the warmer beaches of the south coast.

That said, Cleethorpes was my first introduction to Britain's outer edge. And while it might have been low on homosapiens, it nonetheless made up for it with sentient beings of a different kind. Providing the soundtrack to the beach, and indeed all beaches I would encounter thereafter, were the seagulls.

Just as music has the power to transport you back in time, so too—for me, at least—can the

Photo - Above - Blackpool

ambience of nature. To this day, whenever those high-pitched squawks emerge from the skies above, I instantly—if momentarily—picture the Cleethorpes Pier, the seafront arcades, and the slew of used condoms adorning the boardwalk.

Seagulls, much like an attention-starved student at the back of the class, stand out in my mind merely because they were the loudest. But more on those vicious bastards later. You see, I could hardly recount the tales of my Cleethorpian youth without giving due mention to another creature who had shaped one of my earliest memories. And it wasn't a bird.

As best as I can remember, it had been a mild day on the seafront. My feet had given off a curious shade of brown; not from tanning, you understand, but from the sandy sludge that had engulfed them. My mum was in attendance. So too—I believe—my nanna. Neither had held my hand on this occasion. This is because all 10 of my tiny fingers were otherwise occupied with a bucket and spade.

You see, for every devastatingly cruel thing that has been said about Cleethorpes, one glorious fact remains: it is a formidable beach on which to build a sandcastle. This is because, and this might be viewed in equal measure a compliment and an indictment, the sand was almost entirely congealed.

No sooner had I finished scraping a moat around my three beautiful and imposing sandcastles than a visitor had made his way to the portcullis demanding to speak with the architect. That's a fancy way of saying that a sea creature had washed ashore and had invited me, or so I believed, to pick it up.

As I took it in my hand, my initial reaction was that this five-pointed mutli-cellular organism (I was a lexically advanced child) was not, in fact, real. After all, up to this point in life, every lifeform I'd ever known bore the distinction of having two eyes, two ears, a nose, a mouth, and a forehead. Upon first glance, this unusual inhabitant of Cleethorpes beach could boast none of those things and must, I surmised, have been some sort of failed art project concocted by an attention-starved student at the back of the class.

"That's a starfish," my mum revealed. "Its eyes are on the end of its pointy bits."

Indeed, it also transpired that its mouth—if you could call it that—was on its underside. Aside from that, it was unlike any creature I'd ever seen; it had no capacity to listen and didn't even possess a brain—a clear indication that the attention-starved student at the back of the class had designed it in his own image.

I might be making this up, but I feel strongly as if the beach typically boasted more starfish than people. Even so, my parents—in tandem with black-and-white photos from a bygone era—like to remind me that Cleethorpes was once a bustling place; that people used to come in droves to the beach and enjoy sticks of rock on the promenade.

But even if Cleethorpes has become a dusty shrine to a once-burgeoning past, it's got nothing—in this regard—on its more famous west coast counterpart: Blackpool.

With a renowned tower reminiscent of a certain Parisian structure of the Eiffel variety, Blackpool was once the tourism hotspot of the UK. For much of the 20th century, its beach could frequently boast more humans than grains of sand, though neither the Blackpool Information Centre nor the scientific community have confirmed this.

Facing the often-frigid Irish Sea, Blackpool first entered my life—from a visitor's standpoint—back in the early 1990s, when I was but a wee little nipper. In many ways, my young self had not deciphered the codes of the past as I was too busy enjoying those of the present. After all, the inherent tackiness of the seaside, with its array of candy floss (US: "cotton candy"), arcade machines, and sticks of rock, were the stuff of a child's dreams.

It was only when I returned some 15 years later, as an adult, that I became aware of the town's struggles. Indeed, they were hard to miss, given the numerous placards charting Blackpool's declining health during the 20th century.

In post-war Britain, beaches up and down the country enjoyed the fruits of a resurgent tourism industry. Britons in the thousands would take inexpensive holidays ("vacations" for American readers) to other parts of the country. Blackpool was among the largest beneficiaries.

But, as the cost of holidaying abroad became more affordable from the 1970s onward, more and more families gave up the Lancashire resort for Majorca and the like. The beach at Blackpool, once barely visible beneath the carpet of sun-soaked humans that enveloped it, became a lot less crowded.

That's not to say it doesn't still paint a fairly vibrant picture during the summer. Indeed, owing to the beach's relatively close proximity to the likes of Manchester and Liverpool, tourists and locals still occasionally pack up for a fun day out by the seaside.

The same, indeed, can be said for large portions of the south-west coast of England, a region that features heavily within the file folder of my brain known as "childhood."

Between what I believe was 1983-1993, my family and I had made the long (for England) 5-hour road trip from Grimsby to Devonshire on no fewer than three occasions.

The first of these occurred at a time when my prefered mode of "getting about" was a pushchair (US: "stroller") and when I referred to all four-legged animals as "dog." I hope you'll forgive me, then, if my recollection of this trip is a little hazy.

A little clearer in my mind is the holiday we took to Devon Cliffs in the late eighties.

It's difficult to explain—without doing the whole region a complete injustice—just how eye-catching the southwest coast really is. I could use the example set by the immaculate ITV series, "Broadchurch", but I'd hate for you to associate the

Cliffs of Devon

area with infanticide.

Perhaps the biggest compliment I can pay it is that the southwest—be it the county of Cornwall, Devon, Somerset, or Dorset—is not what most people picture when they think of England. Indeed, the majority of Americans with whom I've spoken on the subject seem to think that the country is made up exclusively of green fields and London; not the almost-Croatian cliffs that adorn the Jurassic Coast.

Indeed, one of the prevailing memories I have of Devon Cliffs is scratching—with the aid of a pebble—the words "Laurence Brown, 1988" into the titular red-brown facade of the resort. I often wonder, to this day, whether the engraving still exists or has succumbed to the effects of weathering. I'm almost certain it is the latter, especially given my failure to relocate it upon my next visit.

The year was 1993. I was at that age where life's finer details faced slightly greater odds of surviving the aging process. One of those finer details was that this second holiday in Devon definitely involved a caravan.

I should clarify to American readers that a caravan, in the British sense, is what you would call a "camper van" or a "travel trailer." Except this was not one we had towed ourselves but one that was static and part of the camping site. Caravan holidays of this sort were, and are, all the rage in this part of the world—so much so that Pauline Quirk's querulous character in the aforementioned "Broadchurch" lived in one. The novelty of holidaying in a caravan—with its built-in kitchen, fold-out bed, and miniature television—made it difficult to leave. This was punctuated further by the fact that I had brought with me a "Jurassic Park" coloring book and a copy of the UK magazine *Wrestling Big Shots*. Thankfully, the south coast offered plenty of incentives to put these down.

Ironically, one of those incentives was live wrestling. We had driven down to one of our old haunts, a coastal town—25 miles away—by the name of Teignmouth (the south coast is notable for containing roughly 14 billion place names ending in "mouth").

After arriving at the town, a charming community, it quickly became clear from all of the posters that a cheap WWF imitation was in our future. We were not wrong. The raucous 100-seater "stadium" (or cupboard, if you prefer) played host to an epic showdown between a maniacal masked villain by the name of El Monstruo (probably) and the English Pitbull (a not-so-subtle ode to WWF superstar and Lancashire-born British Bulldog).

For this newly-wrestling-obsessed little boy, it represented my first—and to-date only—live wrestling event. But more than that, it was an eye-opener into another, seldom-discussed side of coastal life: gimmicky entertainment—the kind that endearingly replaces the British Bulldog with the English Pitbull, Stonecold Steve Austin with Lukewarm Stephen Ostrich, and The Rock with The Pebble. And speaking of pebbles…

In Britain, beaches are not always made up of sand. If you want a concrete example of this, look no further than Brighton, where deck-chairs routinely mount the town's pebble beach. Although such a beach might prove an antidote to sunbathing, it does incentivise visitors to flock to the pier—and by visitors, I don't just mean humans.

In the skies above Brighton, the high-pitched squawks of a certain coastal bird can be heard for miles and miles. And on this day, as if not by coincidence, one such bird decided to swoop down at the precise moment my wife and I had emerged from an ice cream stand.

The seagull, skipping straight ahead to dessert, honed in on my wife's 99 Flake cone and snatched it from her hand before anyone knew what had happened. It was all over in an instant. And from that moment on, it was not merely their squawk that would transport me back to Cleethorpes, but their chav-like ability to pickpocket.

While we're on the subject of food, I could hardly conclude this story without talking about Britain's seaside cuisine.

You could travel from coast-to-coast, ticking off all the places I have mentioned, and still encounter the same tasty staples of the English beach.

No seaside resort would be complete without the existence of a well-to-do establishment that specialises in Britain's famous fish 'n' chips. Indeed, if you're lucky, this might be accompanied by a side-helping of mushy peas and almost certainly by a beautiful bottle of Sarson's Malt Vinegar.

As alluded to earlier, historically the 99 Flake had spearheaded Britain's list of seaside sweet-tooth items. However, reports in recent years indicate that

this soft-serve ice cream is on the wane, presumably because they were all stolen by seagulls. Thank goodness, then, for the consolation prize of the kid-friendly sticks of rock, whose similarity to peppermint candy canes might be appreciated by Americans. And if you're not interested in a sweet snack that will shatter your teeth beyond repair, candy floss has got you covered.

No one—I think it's fair to say—is under any illusion that British seaside cuisine comes recommended by your doctor. Indeed, in case you're doctor is unavailable for comment, I'd like to conclude things with a short piece I wrote for World Poetry Day. It is called "Winds of the English Coast".

"A seagull squawks from the windy shores,
Detached from drinking rabbles below,
Fish 'n' chips scattered across the floor,
Stench of seaweed stopping the airflow;
But the worst crimes came not from the sea,
Rather from a northern lad, from me
Like Friday night bottles it hit me;
I should have cut down on the beans."

Happiness does indeed come in waves.

THE SLANG PAGE
British Police Slang

After recently binge watching the entire run of "Endeavour", I heard lots of unusual words related to British policing. So, I thought it would be fun and useful to put together a list. I've tried to be comprehensive, if there's a word I left off, please leave it in the comments and I'll update the list later.

Bobby - Police Officer, so named because Sir Robert Peel set up the first proper police force in the UK - The Metropolitan Police.

Rozzer - Police Officer

Battenburg Markings - The markings on a British police car, also slang for the police as well.

The Bill - The police. It was originally a police show that ran from 1984-2010 and now it's proper slang for the police.

Bizzies - The police. Said to have been coined in Merseyside, as the police were always too "busy" to help citizens who reported low-level crimes such as house burglaries. An alternative origin is that the police are seen as "busybodies", i.e. they ask too many questions and meddle in the affairs of others.

Blues and Twos - British emergency vehicles have blue flashing lights and two-tone sirens.

Blueband - The Thin Blue Line.

WPC - Woman Police Constable, antiquated - ranks are now sexless.

Bluebottle - The police from Cockney Slang.

Booked - To be arrested.

Nicked - To be arrested.

Nick - A police station.

BTP - British Transport Police - police organisation responsible for policing the railways.

Candy cars - Slang term for police cars in the UK due to the livery being yellow and blue.

Chimps - UK slang term for Community Support Officers, acronym for "Completely Hopeless In Most Policing Situations"

Cop, Coppa, or Copper - A police officer.

Dibble - The name of fictional police officer in the cartoon Top Cat. "Dibble" has been adopted as a British-English derogatory slang term for police officer.

Filth - Normally "The Filth", UK, the police. Inspiration for the Irvine Welsh novel *Filth*.

Fuzz - As "the fuzz", used as slang for police officers; of unknown origin. The term was used in the title of "Hot Fuzz", a 2007 police-comedy film.

Grass - Cockney (English) rhyming slang for a police informant: Grasshopper = Copper.

Hobby Bobby - Another slang term for Community policeman.

Jam sandwich, or Jam Butty - Police traffic car, from the now largely obsolete historical colour-scheme – an overall white vehicle, with a longitudinal red, or red and yellow, stripe on each side. Still used for the metropolitan police in London. Silver cars with a red stripe down the side.

Old Bill - The Police

Paddy Wagon - A police van. So named in Liverpool, UK, as most of the policemen and prisoners were of Irish extraction.

Peeler - UK, archaic, although may have survived longer in Ireland than Britain, from Sir Robert Peel (see "Bobby").

The Sweeney - UK slang term for the Flying Squad of London's Metropolitan Police Service. From Cockney rhyming slang: "Sweeney Todd" = "Flying Squad". Also a classic TV show and recently a movie.

Metropolitan Police Service (MPS) - Formed in 1829 as a professional police force responsible for greater London and still in existence today.

The Met - Shorter version of Metropolitan Police Service.

Scotland Yard, New Scotland Yard, Newer Scotland Yard - The location of the original Met headquarters and became a metonym for the police in London. Eventually moved to 'New Scotland Yard.' It recently moved again but the name moved with it.

MI5 - Military Intelligence, Section 5 or the Security Service. Basically the domestic version of MI6 (the James Bond ones).

National Crime Agency - British equivalent to the FBI, formed from the remains of the Serious Organized Crime Agency.

ANGLOTOPIA
THE MAGAZINE FOR ANGLOPHILES
ISSUE #11   AUTUMN 2018

Letter from the Editors

As I type this, we're getting ready to leave on our biggest adventure in Britain yet - we're driving from Land's End in Cornwall 1,000 miles north to the top of Scotland at John O'Groats. This is a journey I have wanted to do my whole Anglophile life, and we're finally getting a chance to do it.

It's been a fun few months putting together the plans for this trip. From planning the route (and making sure we hit all the places we want to go) to picking hotels, there have been many spinning plates to this trip. This is just one of the wonderful things that this magazine makes possible. And starting next issue, you'll see articles that have come out of the adventure.

In other news, I'm writing a book. I can't talk too much about it at this stage, but I'm about halfway through writing the book I've always wanted to write about Britain. It answers the one question I get the most: Why do I love Britain so much? It turns out; it's not an easy question to answer. The book will explore my history as an Anglophile through the lens of 15 years of travel in the UK.

Autumn is one of our favorite times to travel to England. It lasts longer in Britain than it does in the USA so that you can get crisp autumn days well until into late November. There's nothing better than going down to a National Trust property like Stourhead and having a nice lunch and cuppa, then going for a walk in a beautiful autumnal landscape. London in the autumn is particularly exquisite as many new plays and exhibitions open this time of year. The place is also less crowded as tourists start to thin out. You get to enjoy England in a more natural and sedate pace.

We hope your journeys take you to Britain in the next year. Happy Travels!

Cheers,
Jonathan & Jackie
Publishers
Anglotopia

Table of Contents

On The Ullswater Steamer............................2
Brit Book Corner 12
Then & Now...14
The Life of a Queen....................................16
The Cricklade Cavalier................................20
Poem...24
Lost in the Pond...26
Great Britons: A.A. Milne 28
This English Life..32
The Mayflower...34
Notes from a Royal Wedding......................40
Mary I: Bloody Mary...................................48
Remembering The Few...............................52
Britain's Sentries of the Sea.........................56
Great British Icons: Land Rover...................60
Slang Page: British Police Slang...................64

About the Magazine

The Anglotopia Magazine is published quarterly by Anglotopia LLC, a USA registered Corporation. All contents copyrighted and may not be reproduced without permission.

Letters to the Editors may be addressed to:

Anglotopia LLC
1101 Cumberland Crossing #120
Valparaiso, IN 46383
USA

Photos: Cover: St Paul's Cathedral Nave, This Page: Windsor During Harry's Wedding, Back Cover: Garden at Snowshill Manor, Inside Back Cover: View of London from Highgate

ON THE ULLSWATER STEAMER

By Jonathan Thomas

I arrived at Pooley Bridge with about 30 minutes to spare. I figured that was plenty of time to catch the next steamer to Glenridding. I parked in the car park for Pooley Bridge as that's where the postcode that Ullswater Steamer's brochure provided sent me.

There was a hiccup when the machine in the car park wouldn't take my money. But it wouldn't take anyone's money. The machine was out of order, and this was a scenario I haven't encountered before in England. A young woman also trying to park simply said, "Just leave a note on your dashboard that the machine doesn't work."

That's what I did and as I walked away, I hoped that I didn't return a few hours later to a parking fine on my windscreen. I've prided myself in that the 10 years I've been driving in the UK as a tourist; I've never gotten a speeding ticket or traffic fine of any kind. I did not want this day to be the first time for that.

So, this is where clueless traveler comes in. I didn't know where to catch the Ullswater Steamer from Pooley Bridge. There was a sign in the car park with the sailing times. But there was no sign indicating where you catch the boat or which direction to walk. I walked towards the centre of the village and still, no signs there indicated anything. I looked across Pooley Bridge and saw people walking, but no sign indicating the boats were in that direction.

Finally, I saw lots of people coming down a drive.

That must be it, I thought. They must be streaming in from the lake.

I began to walk down the drive, and as I got to a turn, I began to wonder if I was heading to the wrong place.

"Is this it the way to the boat?" I asked some random English person walking past.

"No, mate," he said. "It's back over the bridge about 100 meters down the street.

"Thank you," I responded.

I backtracked to the bridge. I followed the pavement along the road. There were lots of people headed in the same direction, so I felt confident that I was heading in the right direction. I looked at my phone, and I was running out of time.

I walked, and I walked. Way more than 100 meters.

Where the bloody hell was this thing? I wondered, starting to sweat in the mid-afternoon heat.

Finally, I came around a curve in the street and saw the ticket office for the Ullswater Steamers and then eventually the boat came into view. And there was a crowd around it. Apparently, on this beautiful day, many people had the same idea as me.

My first thought was that there's no way I could get a spot on that boat with a decent view as it sailed along the lake. I went into panic mode. Should I chuck it in and cancel this? I'd already walked all this way. I was exhausted. I was hot. It would be cool on the boat. I could sit on the boat. For two hours.

I sighed and went into the ticket office and bought a return ticket (£15.95). I was very thirsty and they were out of water bottles. I was so hot, I was starting to feel slightly queasy, which is not something you want to feel when you're about to get on a boat for two hours. I was regretting my decision to skip lunch and just have cake at that National Trust property I'd visited previously. I purchased a soda and a bag of chips, hoping that eating something, anything, would tide me over for the boat ride.

I walked quickly along the long, white wooden dock. My ticket was checked and I stepped aboard. My plan was to record the journey using my GoPro, so I could share it later on. The best place to do this would be the front of the boat. So, I went downstairs and walked through the boat to get to the bow. Thankfully, there was still a space I could fit in. I set up my camera, attaching it to the railing on the hull.

We pulled away shortly thereafter, I ate my bag of chips and drank my soda, and I immediately felt better. It was hot, and the sun was beating down on the open deck. But once the boat turned around after clearing the dock and began to steam across the lake, we were treated to a cool breeze.

Ullswater is the longest of the Lakes, but it's only about 9 miles long (and at most 3/4 of a mile wide). The steamer takes the better part of an hour to make the entire journey. But despite this, the boat feels like it's going pretty fast. The bow was somewhat crowded as people jostled to get a view of the surrounding landscape and take pictures as we went along.

As with most travel experiences like this in

Britain, I was the youngest person on the boat. This always bothers me. It's a bit sad that there aren't more people my age out exploring and experience sublime things like this. Most people my age are cooped up in offices working. Another reminder of how truly lucky I am to be able to experience Britain on my own terms and write about it.

Ullswater Steamers have been plying the tourist trade on Ullswater for more than 150 years. All of their boats run on steam engines, some were built in the Victorian Age, some are newer. The boats run a regular schedule for 363 days of the year. It's something you can rely on. Many people take the boat for part of the way, then walk part of the way then get the boat again (they have tickets that accommodate this). The trip has no commentary (though if you download their mobile app, you can get commentary).

To be honest, there's not much to commentate on as the boat sails across the lake. There is nothing of real interest other than the beautiful landscapes. Ullswater is very undeveloped (and this is by design). There are no great houses along the lake, no large towns or buildings to look at. No, the landscape is the star and that's what you've paid £15.95 to look at.

My stomach settled once I had eaten my snack and rehydrated. As the journey progressed out deep into the water, the heat began to get worse. While there was a breeze as the boat steamed through the lake, the harsh midday sun was relentless. The front of the boat was a bit crowded and we all jostled for position to take pictures as we past particularly pretty parts of the landscape. No one was rude about it though, we were all there for the same reason - to capture a moment from something spectacular.

For most of the journey to Glenridding, I sat and soaked in the view, occasionally taking a picture if I saw something pretty. I also monitored the GoPro just to make sure it was doing its job. It was amazingly quiet out on the water, just the sound of the steam engine chuffing away. There were many others out enjoying the beautiful day on the lake. Quite a few sailboats and groups of people learning how to sail.

There were also groups of Boy Scouts on the shore, climbing cliffs and jumping off. I felt rather jealous. The most exciting thing I got to do as a Boy Scout was to go to a summer camp for a week. These Scouts got to jump into an Alpine-like lake.

I was sweating profusely and jumping in the lake sounded like a very good idea at that moment.

Then the boat came to a stop. We were approaching our stop at Howetown (what a remarkable name for a place). A sister ship was currently in the dock, so we had to wait our turn. As the breeze stopped because the boat was not moving, the heat started to accumulate. Jumping in the water began to look attractive. After a few moments, the sister ship got underway (heading towards Pooley Bridge where'd just come from). Our engine fired up again, this time slowly as we chuffed into the dock.

"You have to move!" barked one of the crew at me, so I hurriedly moved my GoPro setup because the crewman needed to access the ropes and cast on to the dock.

Several people got off, quite a few gone on.
Then the engine fired on again.

"Arms! Arms! Arms!" shouted the crewman at everyone in the front of the ship as we quickly moved backward along the dock. Fair enough. It could easily have chopped off a finger or dislocated an arm.

After Howetown, we rounded a mountain and the view changed to a new vista. I really could not believe that such a landscape was real let alone that I was there to see it in person. I've seen so many pictures of the Lake District. But none of that prepare you for actually seeing it in person. To visit the Lakes it to be in awe during your entire visit.

In no time at all, we arrived at Glenridding, the other main terminus for the Ullswater Steamers. Everyone got off the boat. The journey back would be in 15 minutes. Glenridding has a completely different vibe than Pooley Bridge, which felt a bit like a tourist trap. Glenridding was more sedate. The car park was full of cars and the beaches around the area were filled with sunbathers and people going for a swim.

I'd planned to GoPro the journey back, but my flash card was full. And your correspondent failed to bring a spare because he thought one was plenty. I thought perhaps that the gift shop on the dock would have one, but they didn't. The chap inside recommended going into the village, but I didn't have the time, and I didn't want to miss the boat back.

Well, I kind of did. I actually pondered just taking a taxi back to Pooley Bridge. I didn't relish

getting on the boat again. I'd 'done' it, I'd filmed it. Got plenty of pictures. I wasn't too keen on getting back on the boat with it being so hot.

"Ridiculous," I told myself. "At least do it because you paid for a return ticket."

Sod it.

I got back on the boat.

This time, though, I managed to get a seat under the shaded canopy. This would hopefully make for a much cooler ride back. At first, I sat against the funnel, but was surprised to feel how warm it was. Proof that the thing was actually run by a steam engine.

I relocated to a different spot, ate a snack and drank something I'd picked up in the dock gift shop. This journey would not be recorded by the GoPro. So, I did what was exceedingly difficult to do, I just sat there and took in the scenery as the boat got underway. I tried to practice some mindfulness tips and truly relish being in such a wonderful place. I did nothing on the boat ride back. My mind was quiet. I was at peace.

I was pleased to see that the boat takes a different route back to Pooley Bridge, along the Northern shore of the lake (it sometimes stops at the Aira Force National Trust park - but today would not). I was really surprised at how different the view was and how different the lake felt.

By this point, it was very late afternoon. The whole boat was snoozy. Even the rambunctious children were pretty sedate. The old English gentleman across from me, with a very friendly black lab on a leash, dozed off for most of the journey. One could not help but get a bit sleepy.

The journey reminded me of my honeymoon with Jackie. We'd decided to go to Lake Geneva, Wisconsin, a special place for us as we visited many times before we married. Despite having visited Lake Geneva so many times, we'd never done the steamer boats that ply that Pseudo-Alpine lake that's so popular with Chicago tourists. So, on our honeymoon, with not much else to do, we decided to do it. The journey was similar in length to my journey on Ullswater but it was cold and rainy (we got married in October). The commentary told us all about the rich people who lived (or had lived) in the mansions all along the lakeshore.

Most of the Ullswater lakeshore was either part of the National Park or owned by the National Trust. It was open for anyone to enjoy. There is, in fact, a footpath that goes around the entire lake (judging by the mountains surrounding, this could be quite strenuous).

But most of all, this journey made me miss Jackie, my usual travel partner in crime who was back home in Indiana and unable to join me on this trip. She would have loved the mountains and the sailboats whizzing across the lake.

The boat once again made a stop at Howetown and then resumed the journey back to Pooley Bridge. It felt as if the boat was going faster this time. I was grateful, despite enjoying the stunning views, I really didn't want to be on the boat anymore. And my regular camera battery had died (guess who didn't bring the spare battery - you'd think I was an amateur at this!).

Soon enough, the boat docked and we all shuffled off, beginning the long walk back to Pooley Bridge car park. I'd had a busy day before the boat ride and now I was properly knackered. When I returned to my car, exhausted from the voyage and the walk back to the car, I was pleased to see there wasn't a parking ticket on the windscreen. It felt like a minor victory worth celebrating.

I climbed in and called Jackie. I needed to talk to her. And I did for at least 30 minutes before the mountains around Ullswater cut off the signal.

Lake Geneva has been ruined for me. Ullswater is a 'proper lake.' I must come back to Ullswater, and next time with Jackie so we can rent a sailboat and spend a day on the water. Hopefully on a day that is not nearly as hot.

BRIT BOOK CORNER

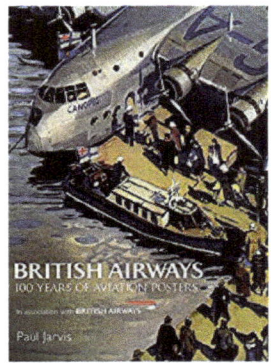

British Airways: 100 Years of Aviation Posters

This book is a tad bittersweet. Paul Jarvis was the longtime curator at British Airways's own museum at their headquarters and has wrote several books about the history of British Airways. His latest book about BA's aviation posters was published just days after he died. This new book from Amberley is a fascinating exploration of the design heritage present in the aviation posters used to sell flights from the beginnings of BA to the present day. It's easy to dismiss the posters as hollow advertisements. But these posters are works of art in their own right. The feel and standard set by these posters has influenced our perceptions of air travel since. It's an fascinaitng cultural exploration of aviation history (and the changed in design trends as time went on). My only complaint is that the format of the book could charitably be described as moderate, so you don't get to see a lot of details in some of the posters. There are many beautiful cutaways of great BA planes from the past and it's difficult to make out details because of the format of the book. Still, they're beautiful to look at and this will be a good addition to any AV geek library. Amberley $26.95

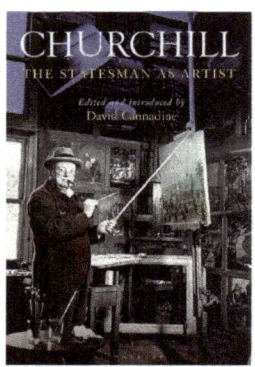

Churchill: The Statesman as Artist

In addition to being one of the greatest leaders of the 20th century, Winston Churchill was also an accomplished amateur painter. This new book from Bloomsbury is a guide to that aspect of his life. Edited by eminent historian David Cannadine, the book starts off with a long essay by Cannadine that summarises Churchill's painting 'career.' Then there are a series of essays, speeches and reviews, some by Churchill, some by others about Churchill's relationship with art. But the coup de grace of the book is the including of Churchill's own essay, "Painting as a Pastime", a manifesto on the important of hobbies and how painting works for him keeping the 'black dog' of depression at bay. It's a great little book on a not-so-widely-known aspect of Churchill's life. The editors have also included great color reproduction of some of his most well known paintings. Churchill was a man of many talents and facets and he did not take up painting until he was 40 years old. But as he did with most things in life, he took it up with enthusiasm and attempted to master it. The result is a catalog of more than 500 paintings, many now in museums all over the world. Another lasting memory of Churchill, physical objects that he touched that we can continue to enjoy to this day. Bloomsbury $30.00

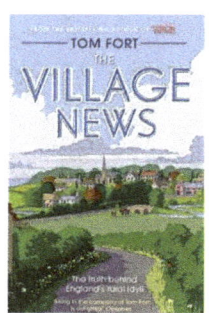

The Village News By Tom Fort

Tom Fort is currently one of Britain's best observational writers. His latest book is an excellent survey of the English village throughout history. It also explores the role the idea of the village has in British culture and lifestyle. The book does not shy away from the problems villages face in modern England. The idea that many people have in their heads of the English village doesn't actually exist and can't actually exist in modern times. But that doesn't stop people from dreaming about it. The book explores many famous villages in Britain in literature and film and provides context for why they are so famous. It's well researched and the author visits many of the places himself to give an accurate survey. I love Tom's books and can recommend them all (The Channel Shore and The A303 are my faves). A great read for those of us who dream of living in an English village. Simon & Schuster $15.99

THE FIVER
Five Fascinating British Biographies to Read
By John Rabon

As fascinating as it is to read about history, it can be just as fascinating to read about the people who made that history happen. Biographies and autobiographies offer us glimpses into the lives of people who changed the course of the United Kingdom. From periods of internal strife to all-out war and from the streets to the manor homes of the country, these people have their own great stories to tell. We've outlined five of our favorite British biographies for you to read that range from a servant to one of the UK's preeminent leaders.

Olaudah Equiano – The Interesting Narrative of the Life of Olaudah Equiano by Olaudah Equiano

Our first biography comes from a man who lived a truly interesting and tragic life. Olaudah Equiano was enslaved in West Africa and the Americas before buying his freedom and going on to a life that included being a sailor, slave trader, Arctic explorer, and abolitionist. Equiano's personal account was one of any texts during the abolition movement in Britain meant to relate the evils of slavery, and Equiano's story not only discusses the negative effects on the enslaved but also upon the slavers. Of course, since it is an autobiography from the 18th century, some readers may have a difficult time with the language, but it's a worthwhile read for the wealth of experience he acquired.

Princess Diana – Diana: Her True Story—In Her Own Words by Andrew Morton

Andrew Morton's book was quite a sensation when originally published in the early 1990s as it had one of the most in-depth and personal looks into Princess Diana's life. After her death, it came out that Diana herself had been the source of so much information that Morton used in the work. The book was later adapted into a mini-series of the same name that laid out all of the ugly sins from Diana and Charles's marriage. The 25th Anniversary edition offers even more material than the original not only from Diana but also her family and friends. If you are interested in Diana's life, you're unlikely to find a better book than this.

Russell Brand – My Booky Wook by Russell Brand

One of the most interesting and provocative comedians in British history, Russell Brand lays his life out for readers in this autobiography that discusses his career, relationships, and his successful fight against addiction. If you're interested in his stand-up, television, and film career, you'll certainly want to pick this up as his career so often intertwines with his personal life and will give you a real insight into how he thinks. For those not so interested in Mr. Brand, it is still a worthwhile tome that chronicles his personal demons and a life of excess that rivals that of Keith Richards.

Winston Churchill – The Last Lion by William Manchester and Paul Reid

Arguably the greatest Prime Minister in Britain's history, The Last Lion is a series of biographical works that chronicles Winston Churchill's life including his time in the army, as a reporter, the span of his political career, and the challenges of leading a nation through World War II and the rise of Communism. Volume 1: Visions of Glory covers the first 58 years of his life, Volume 2: Alone chronicles his fight against appeasement and preparations for War with Germany, and Volume 3: Defender of the Realm covers the period from his Premiership to his death in 1965.

Lady Nancy Astor – Rose: My Life in Service to Lady Astor by Rosina Harrison

Rosina Harrison began her service as a personal handmaiden to Lady Nancy Astor in 1928 and, as a result, her career with the Astor family was never a dull one. Known as much for her temperament as her time in politics, Lady Astor was as much a controversial figure as a historic one. The book offers an insight into one of the first women in Parliament and what she was like behind the scenes from one of the people who knew her best. Harrison paints an interesting portrait of a woman she was devoted to and good friends with but also isn't afraid to call out Lady Astor on her flaws.

THEN - House of Commons - 1808

The original British House of Commons was located in the Palace of Westminster and had been since it was formed in the early days of British politics. The chamber was separate from the House of Lords, but at this time it was not quite the 'senior' house that it is today. Britain was still very run by the landed interests. In fact, even in the commons, you had to be a landowner to stand for parliament. Many members were handpicked by the landowners of vast estates (in 'rotten boroughs'). Slowly though at the 19th century progressed, the House of Commons began to assert dominance as the voting franchise was increased. This change burned to the ground when the Palace of Westminster caught fire in 1834.

NOW - House of Commons - 2018

After the fire razed the Palace of Westminster (the ony bit that survived was Wesminster Hall), a contest was held for a new design for the Houses of Parliament. Sir Charles Barry and Augustus Pugin designed the new houses together in a neo-Gothic style to give the presentation of the new houses historical grounding (and today, they look very old despite being relatively new). However, the chamber picture above was not the one they designed. The Germans bombed the Houses of Parliament and the House of Commons was mostly destroyed. It was restored after the war but while adhering to Barry and Pugin's original designs, its chamber was modernised substantially. You can still see the bomb damage in the stonework when entering the chamber.

THE LIFE OF A QUEEN
THE CHILDHOOD OF QUEEN ELIZABETH II

Editor's Note: This is the first in an ongoing series about the entire life of Queen Elizabeth II. Each issue of this magazine will feature an article about every aspect of her life.

It might seem surprising to us today to think that Queen Elizabeth II hasn't always been Queen Elizabeth II; she is, after all, the longest-reigning British monarch in history, as well as the Western world's longest-serving leader. We sometimes picture her like the birth of Athena, springing from Zeus's head fully grown and in full battle regalia. But of course, she wasn't born queen or even heir to the throne. Her father was Albert, Duke of York, King George V's second son. It was Uncle David, momentarily (for 10 months, anyway) reigning as King Edward VIII, who was meant to be king.

Perhaps it was exactly because she was not meant to be a queen that she was able to have such a charmed, happy childhood. Elizabeth Alexandra Mary Windsor was born in London on 21 April 1926. Just as with Britain's royals today, her birth was met with a media firestorm, proving that even if she wasn't yet the "heiress presumptive," she was still not just a normal little girl. In fact, her future first Prime Minister Winston Churchill visited the family in Scotland at Balmoral when Elizabeth was just two years old and was completely taken by her charm. He called her "a character" and someone with "an air of authority." [1]

Even before her father took the throne in 1936 when Elizabeth was just age 10, young Lilibet, as she was called, had developed quite a personality. She was said to be shy and humble, yet clever, astute, witty, precise, and cheerful. In 1927, when Elizabeth was still just a toddler, her parents went on a royal tour of New Zealand and Australia, leaving their daughter with King George V and Queen Mary (and presumably a host of nannies and staff). Her grandmother, Queen Mary, called her "a joy." Lilibet had already stolen her grandparents' hearts. Her grandfather, King George V, who was rather harsh with his own sons, was crazy about Lilibet. She clearly was just as crazy about him, calling him Grandpa England. With the birth of little sister Margaret in 1930, four years after Elizabeth, the family was complete and happy.

Margaret and Elizabeth seemed to be a good complement to each other. While Elizabeth was dignified and standoffish, Margaret was lively and fun, often playing practical jokes on the staff (picture the von Trapp children putting frogs in Frauline Maria's pockets) while Elizabeth watched and giggled. In public occasions, Elizabeth was clearly already the older sister more ready for monarchy, at one point telling Margaret before an outing, "If you see someone with a silly hat, Margaret, you must not point at it and laugh."[2] And yet they were good friends and had a lot of fun together. Of course, there were not a lot of other options, since they did not leave to go to school or make friends with outsiders. One of Lilibet's favorite playmates was her Uncle David, in the years before his abdication when the whole relationship went sour. He often came to play in the family's after-supper games; he even gave the young princess her first copy of Winnie-the-Pooh, which was published the same year as her birth. Elizabeth's father, and soon the rest of their little family, called each other "we four," and had a strong bond of friendship and fun, probably realizing that they were really the only ones who know what it was like to be a family like they were. The press loved them.

Besides parlor games with the family, Lilibet loved her horses. She started riding at age three and took to it immediately, a love she has kept throughout her life. It was her father who taught her all about breeding and racing; she loved to ride and explore the stables with him at their estate in Norfolk—Sandringham—and at Hampton Court and Balmoral. When she wasn't outside with the horses, she was often inside with her pile of toy ponies, brushing their hair and arranging them on the stairs, sometimes even pretending to be a pony herself and refusing to answer those around her: "I couldn't answer you as a pony."[3] It was also her father who gave her her first Welsh Corgi, what was to become her signature breed. They named the dog Duke of York, calling him "Dookie" (again with the nicknames); after that, she was never without at least one dog, sometimes many underfoot. She even took her dog Susan on her honeymoon with Prince Philip.

In 1932, the family brought in a lively Scottish nanny, Marion Crawford, affectionately known as Crawfie (this family likes their nicknames). In an effort to introduce the young princesses to life outside the "glass curtain," as she called it, Crawfie would take the girls into town on the bus and the tube in the years before the abdication. After the

abdication, when it became clear that Elizabeth was not going to do as much traipsing around London, Crawfie arranged for a troop of Girl Guides (think British Girl Scouts) to meet at Buckingham Palace as a way to help Elizabeth make friends and have a normal (or normal-ish) childhood. This was not your average group of Girl Guides, of course, no Eastenders in the mix, but 20 girls of about Margaret and Elizabeth's ages carefully chosen from their relatives, of which there were so many, and local aristocrats. Still, the young princesses got to run around exploring the 40 acres of gardens at the palace, making campfires and learning outdoor skills. Crawfie and her young charges were very fond of each other, and they were together for years. However, in 1949 the nanny wrote a (very sweet, kindly, completely innocuous) memoir of her time with Elizabeth and Margaret, and the family cut her out completely for such a show of disloyalty, prompting the Queen Mother to cry, "We can only think that our late and completely trusted governess has gone off her head." 4

Before Crawfie's abrupt departure from the family, she also acted as tutor to the two girls. In the years before King George VI's succession, Elizabeth's education was fairly relaxed. She was expected to learn language and history, but no math or government to speak of. Crawfie remembers the first book she read with Lilibet and Margaret—"Peter Pan in Kensington Gardens", an appropriate choice as it was written and took place just down the street. Marion Crawford was also expected to teach her manners and penmanship, as well, skills that would be useful to a life of royalty but nothing to prepare her for the monarchy. Elizabeth's mother, Elizabeth Duchess of York, had taught Lilibet to read herself, often reading aloud to her. It was the Duchess of York who encouraged a light education, often interrupting her studying hours for little outings, and one day bringing home a stack of 18 P.G. Wodehouse novels, hardly heavy reading. Still, it was also the Duchess of York who taught Lilibet religion. Lilibet grew up with a strong Christian faith, learning her Psalms and reading the Book of Common Prayer with her mother. This turned out to be a great asset later on when she became head of the Church of England, hardly something her mother could have expected as they were saying their prayers together before bed.

The Windsors were a dutiful family, instilling

that sense of duty in Elizabeth from a young age. Queen Mary was particularly stiff-upper-lip about royal duties, teaching Lilibet how to walk and sit up straight so as not to embarrass herself—traditional royal family skills. Lilibet learned the useful skill of keeping a diary from her mother. When complimented on her daily writings in later years, the Queen said, "It's not really a diary-like Queen Victoria's . . . or as detailed as that. It's quite small." She called it just a habit, "like scrubbing your teeth."5 Despite her humility about it, we can imagine that one day beyond her death, those daily entries will be quite enlightening to the rest of us. The Duchess of York, by now Queen Elizabeth herself, was also a great example to Lilibet of how to treat other people, a characteristic that Lilibet has hung onto throughout her life and reign. Her mother told her, "if you find something or somebody a bore, the fault lies in you."6 Now there's a quality more of us could use in our modern lives, and those who know Queen Elizabeth II often comment on how interested she is in people, relating to them in a way that might seem surprising considering her sheltered upbringing. The family also tried to teach Lilibet and Margaret frugality and money management, giving the girls an allowance of five shillings a week—a somewhat comical idea to us today, considering Lilibet already had a yearly allowance of 6,000 pounds, and where was she really going to spend her weekly allowance anyway?

Young Elizabeth's easy, simplified education changed dramatically in 1936 when her father reluctantly took the throne, and she became the heiress presumptive ("presumptive" just in case her parents had a son, but of course they didn't). Suddenly Elizabeth needed to learn all sorts of new things—maybe not math, which was never her strong suit, but government and more history and languages, to be sure. To that end, in 1939 the family brought in Sir Henry Marten, vice-provost of nearby Eton College (nearby when they were at Windsor, that is, but they were in Windsor quite often, causing the queen to call Windsor her home). Marten was very knowledgeable as a professor at Eton, we might think of him as stuffy and a bit of a bore, but for Lilibet, he was engaging and brought history alive. That was, of course, just what she needed in the years of royal tutelage she had ahead of her. Marten taught her the ins and outs of the British Constitution with some instruction in American history, as well. As Americans we consider our constitution to be fairly straightforward as a document that was, for the most part, written all in one go. The British Constitution, however, is more of a conglomeration of accumulated laws and precedents, not surprising considering their history is well more than 1,000 years older than that of the United States and has gone through numerous governmental and monarchical permutations. The King's private secretary, and later Elizabeth's, Tommy Lascelles instructed Marten to "hide nothing" about the constitution and how to navigate it. Marten clearly took this task to heart—Elizabeth's Prime Ministers were often impressed with her command of the Constitution and her knowledge of the workings of Parliament, they were perhaps even surprised by her detailed knowledge. Marten also taught her critical thinking and how to use her best judgment in assessing an argument, a skill that would benefit her throughout her reign.

Along with learning the intricacies of the British government, Elizabeth's family brought in a French tutor for the young princesses, a Belgian vicomtesse with the improbable name of Marie-Antoinette de Bellaigue. They called her Toni (again with the nicknames, but these names are all such a mouthful, who can blame them?). Lilibet learned to speak fluently, a great skill in her future as Queen, never needing an interpreter in France and her other francophone territories. Her family and advisers clearly had quite a lot of foresight and experience in choosing her education and her educators, her natural curiosity and intelligence helped her to adapt well to the education she suddenly found herself needing.

These formative years were, perhaps surprisingly, happy and loving for the future queen. While the Queen refuses to grant interviews, she talks very fondly of her childhood and her years as "we four." She still has in her near future a world war, a marriage, the death of her father, and her own reign. It seems like it would be almost impossible to prepare for all the things she would see in her life, yet she seemed perfectly positioned to take them all on with the consistency, discipline, wit, and intelligence she learned from the start.

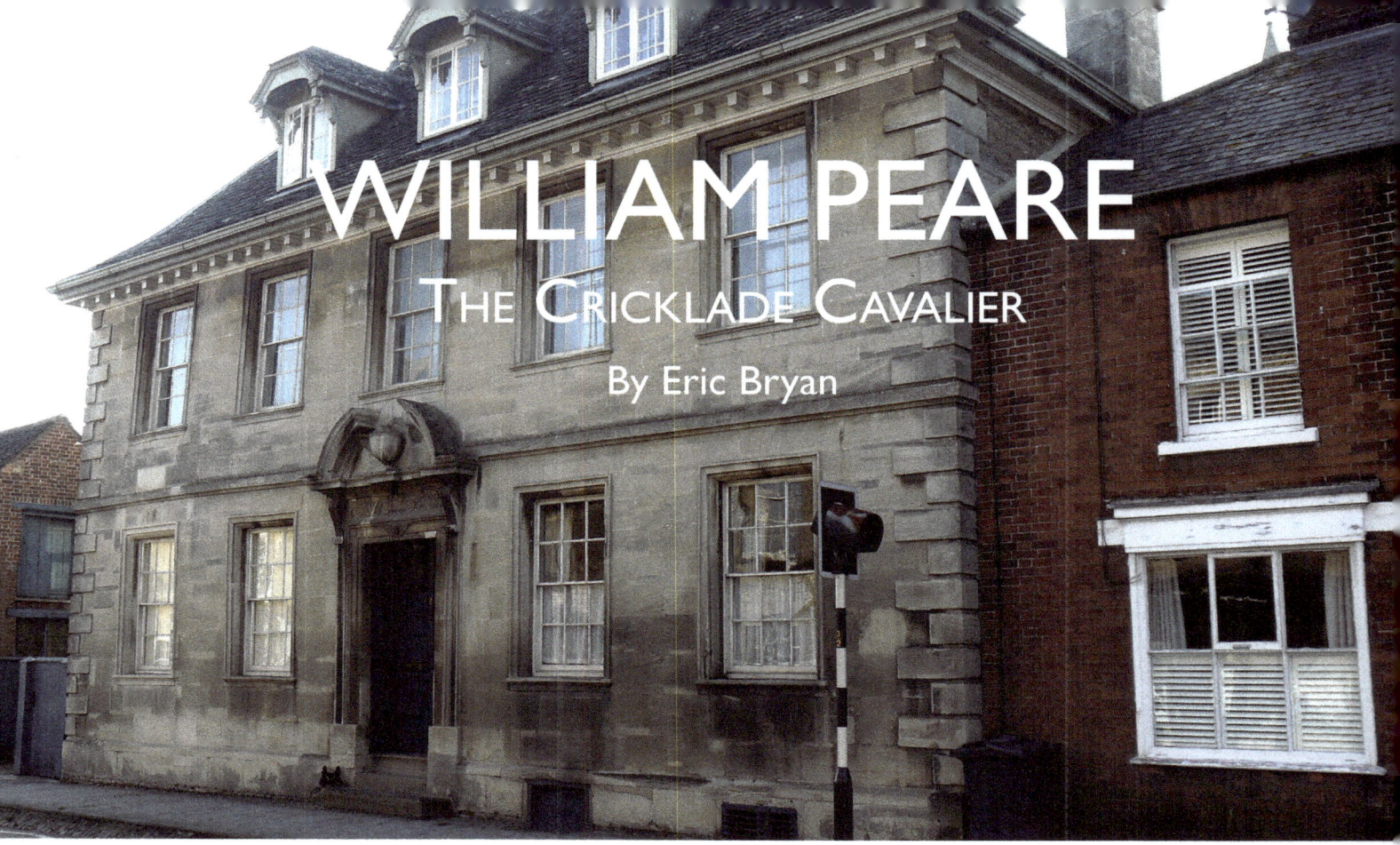

WILLIAM PEARE
THE CRICKLADE CAVALIER
By Eric Bryan

Highwaymen were active in Britain from the Elizabethan era into the early 19th century. Wiltshire's roads, lanes and byways were settings for some of the deeds of these 'knights of the road.' Several notable highwaymen and at least one alleged highwaywoman hailed from Wiltshire. One such was William Peare, whose career as a highwayman, though short, was nevertheless eventful, colorful, and tragically dramatic.

Peare was born in Cricklade circa 1760. (Peare's sister Mary was baptised on 13 May 1756 at St Mary's. Some have reported that Mary was William Peare's twin, but according to historical notes from the Friends of St Mary's Church, "the inscription in the register repudiates this.") In "The Highwaymen of Wiltshire; or a Narrative of the Adventurous Career and Untimely End of Divers Freebooters and Smugglers, in this and the Adjoining Counties" (1856) by James Waylen, the author described Peare as an "adventurer, of fashionable exterior, wearing a pig-tail, and riding a crack horse." Waylen reported him to have been 5 feet 10 inches tall, handsome, and popular. Peare initially went into business with his brother as a blacksmith.

Peare's first alleged crime occurred on 9 October 1780. The victim was a Mr. Jeffery, a grazier from Yateminster, Dorset. Peare ambushed Jeffery by a hare-warren near Salisbury. As Jeffrey rode by, Peare rushed from the cover of the warren and unhorsed the man. The robber's haul was £500 (about £84,550 today) in bank notes and £37 (approximately £6,250 now) in coin. A £60 (about £10,000) reward was issued for the apprehension of the robber.

The crime which made Peare's name notorious was the highway robbery of the Chippenham mail on 2 February 1782. Peare was caught for this offense and imprisoned in Gloucester Castle and Gaol. However, he made his escape on 19th April. A string of Wiltshire robberies and attempted robberies followed. Because of the repeated aggressive pattern of these holdups in which the brigand would fire a warning shot (sometimes directly into a carriage window) to cow his intended victims psychologically, it was believed that these crimes were all committed by the same bandit. On

Left: Cricklade High Street. Photo by Gary Haywood, Above: St Mary's Church, Cricklade. Photo by Poliphilo

8 February 1783, Peare held up a Salisbury diligence near St Thomas' bridge, first smashing the vehicle's windows then firing a warning shot. The passengers, a lady, and gentlemen handed over their valuables, and Peare cleaned out the carriage's tin receptacle for carrying small packages, its contents amounting to one parcel.

Sometimes Peare's strategy of attempting to frighten and overwhelm his prey with noise and bluster failed. Immediately following the robbery of the Salisbury coach, the highwayman pounced on another diligence at Stockbridge, which turned out to contain several military officers carrying a substantial sum of money. Peare smashed the barrel of his pistol through the window glass, wounding one man on the chin. When he saw that the carriage would be well defended by its passengers, Peare fired shots through both windows and galloped off.

On 20 February, Peare halted the Trowbridge coach in Marlborough forest. The vehicle carried a guard, but instead of being stationed on the outside of the coach this man was seated comfortably inside as Peare attacked. When the guard became aware of the holdup, he fired his blunderbuss through the glass of one window, but on the side of the coach opposite to where the highwayman sat astride his horse. Nevertheless, the blast unnerved Peare enough to enable the coach to rush off and reach Trowbridge safely.

Peare met his downfall due to his involvement in a scheme to burglarise the Stroudwater Bank in Gloucestershire by digging a tunnel from a neighbouring vacant building into the bank. Peare and a confederate dug the tunnel at night but worked by the flame of a torch or lamp, the light of which a passerby noticed late one night. The suspicious observer notified the owner of the bank, who secretly set himself up the following night on the premises along with armed officers. At about two o'clock in the morning, the men saw one of the stones in the floor shift, then lift, and one man climb up through the gap. The officers arrested the man, who was Peare's accomplice.

Peare, upon hearing the voices of the men in the bank, quickly retreated through the tunnel and into the night. His accomplice however informed on Peare, revealing that the highwayman might be

The old town cross in St Sampson's churchyard, Cricklade. Photo by Gary Haywood

discovered at Peare's father's house in Cricklade. There, Peare had hidden in a cavity between the wall and the outer tiles of the dwelling, hoping to evade detection. When he saw that he was finally discovered, Peare broke through the tiles and leaped into the garden, where he was apprehended. Peare's capture occurred on 14 May 1783 at 58/59 Cricklade High Street, beside the churchyard gate of St Mary's. Peare was again ensconced in Gloucester Castle and Gaol to await trial.

Peare had to wait for the Salisbury August Assizes when he was arraigned before the Hon John Heath and the Hon Sir Richard Perrhyn, the same judges who had presided over the trial of highwaywoman Mary Abraham, alias Mary Sandall (or Sandy). Heath was known for his severity in sentencing the convicted, and was quoted remarking, "there is no regeneration for felons in this life, and for their own sake, as well as for the sake of society, I think it is better to hang."

Peare was tried and sentenced to hang at Fisherton on 19 August 1783. He insisted to the end that he was innocent of the mail robbery, but admitted to being friends with highwaymen James Caldwell and Thomas Boulter. Peare referred to some watches buried in a cellar at Bristol and wanted to explain to the governor where he had found the banknote which was the evidence used to convict him at trial. (Peare was romantically connected to James Caldwell's sister-in-law, and James Waylen speculated that Peare slipped into the world of vice at the Ship Inn where he must have often met highwayman Thomas Boulter.)

The Salisbury Journal reported in columns dated 18 August 1783 that William Peare had been convicted of robbing the mail near Chippenham and that he would be executed at Fisherton gallows the following morning about 11 o'clock. The article continued: "and his body will then be enclosed in a suit of chains, ingeniously made by Mr. Wansborough and conveyed to Chippenham, and affixed to a gibbet erected near the spot where the robbery was committed." Would-be spectators, misunderstanding that Peare's execution was to take place at Green Lane, Chippenham congregated there – all 10,000 of them – in anticipation of the event.

On the morning of his execution, Peare prayed with his Ordinary and spent time with his girlfriend. Peare faced his execution bravely, finely decked out, sporting a white satin knot at his breast, and carrying a nosegay. Waylen wrote that Peare "advanced to the scaffold with great fortitude, and surveyed the dreadful apparatus of death with an unchanged countenance." Peare fussed over the adjustment of the noose around his neck, and asked the hangman, a man named Read, to do his job quickly and well. He bid the cart pull away from beneath his feet at his signal of a falling handkerchief. He dropped the handkerchief but held the nosegay in his other hand in a death grip until his body was taken down.

The gibbeting irons, called gemmaces, were made by whitesmith Mr. Wansborough. Thus enclosed, Peare's body was conveyed to Chippenham and hanged at Green Lane at the Chippenham to Marlborough Road crossroads. The following week the Salisbury Journal reported that Peare had been hanged at Fisherton on Tuesday the 19, and that "the remaining part of the sentence was completed on Wednesday, by hanging the body in Green Lane, near Chippenham, where it is now, a dreadful memento to youth, how they swerve from the paths of rectitude and transgress the laws of their country."

The body swung at the crossroads until Chippenham Fair in October, where several of Peare's Cricklade friends were spotted, and by the following day, the remains were gone. In paragraphs dated November 10 1783, the Journal related that Peare's corpse had been taken away during the night of 30th October. The rumor was that Peare's Cricklade friends and family had taken his mortal remains down in the night and buried them in St Mary's churchyard.

According to Waylen, Peare was but 23 at the time of his execution.

I WANDERED LONELY AS A CLOUD
By William Wordsworth - 1807

I wandered lonely as a cloud
That floats on high o'er vales and hills,
When all at once I saw a crowd,
A host, of golden daffodils;
Beside the lake, beneath the trees,
Fluttering and dancing in the breeze.

Continuous as the stars that shine
And twinkle on the milky way,
They stretched in never-ending line
Along the margin of a bay:
Ten thousand saw I at a glance,
Tossing their heads in sprightly dance.

The waves beside them danced; but they
Out-did the sparkling waves in glee:
A poet could not but be gay,
In such a jocund company:
I gazed—and gazed—but little thought
What wealth the show to me had brought:

For oft, when on my couch I lie
In vacant or in pensive mood,
They flash upon that inward eye
Which is the bliss of solitude;
And then my heart with pleasure fills,
And dances with the daffodils.

LOST IN THE POND
How the Rockies Make England's Lake District Look Positively Quaint
By Laurence Brown

Regular readers of Anglotopia Magazine might recall my retrospective account of the time I took a wrong turn at Lake Windermere in pursuit of William Wordsworth's house.

That day, my ambitions were stoked by the literature of England's past and the geological poetry of its present. All around were landmarks, both dainty and large, whose natural splendor influenced the writings of not only Wordsworth, but Coleridge and Southey.

But as all-encompassing as the Lake District may have seemed to my wide-eyed, 23-year-old self, I've come to find—in my 37th year—that it is positively quaint when mentioned in the same breath as the mountain ranges of my adoptive country, the United States of America.

Chief among those ranges, both in the sense of its enormity and its role in my recent travel exploits, are the Rocky Mountains.

Extending from northern Alberta, Canada, in the north down to New Mexico in the south, the Rockies cover a distance of roughly 3,000 miles.

Indeed, the Grand Canyon alone snakes its way through the state of Arizona at a distance roughly equal to that of Windermere to Brighton, and is so large, people have actually died of thirst after taking a wrong turn of their own, a fact that puts my Wordsworth expedition into humbling perspective.

But I'd be highly remiss to focus only on the area-differential between the two regions, particularly when a comparable difference naturally exists between the countries to which they belong.

Rather, what strikes me most is the breadth of topographic diversity up and down the Rockies, something to which I've had the good fortune of bearing witness - whether from 30,000 feet or from the foot of its endless row of mountains.

On a recent visit to Salt Lake City, Utah, I hiked to the top of Ensign Peak—a relatively straightforward climb—whose chief pay-off included not just a spectacular view of the city but the much higher mountains that surrounded it.

Those mountains, as well as hundreds more across the state, significantly dwarf England's tallest mountain, Scafell Pike. Indeed, the highest point along the Wasatch Range—Mount Nebo—stands at almost 12,000 feet, virtually four times that of the Lake District mountain.

And Mount Nebo is by no means the tallest peak in the Rockies. That distinction goes to Colorado's

Mount Elbert, which stands at a staggering 14,440 feet—or 10 Empire State Buildings stacked on top of each other.

In layman's terms, the Rocky Mountains don't merely cover significantly more land than the Lake District, but also more sky.

And speaking of sky, it is from the air that the full color palette of the Rockies comes into view. Back in June, I had the good fortune of flying from Dallas to Boise armed with both a wide angle lens and a window seat.

What I captured along the way was breathtaking. For hundreds of miles in any direction were mountains of red, green, and brown—many of which seemed to pierce a section of sky that not even Scotland's Ben Nevis could muster.

And the mountains were not the only geological wonder on display. It seemed that for every mound of rock pointing upward, there was a winding crevice doing the precise opposite. Canyons, albeit not necessarily those of the Grand variety, nonetheless wore themselves on the earth like a knife wound, a reminder—much like the mountains themselves—of Earth's dramatic geological past.

And, much like the Lake District, the Rockies are not left wanting for lakes. In fact, Grand Lake in Colorado boasts an area roughly 12 times that of Lake Windermere, while Utah's Great Salt Lake makes for an impressive visual feast—both from the air and the land. This is chiefly because the lake is divided into two colors—red and blue—either side of the railroad that cuts across it.

Just over 300 miles northeast of this sits Yellowstone National Park, where you'll find 60% of the world's hot springs and geysers, the former of which look eerily reminiscent of a supernova. And if that's not impressive enough for you, consider that under the park is a smoldering super volcano, the eventual eruption of which would cause unimaginable devastation to much of North America. A shuddering thought.

Such extremes also can be found within another highly important element of life in the Rockies: the climate.

A week before I touched down in Salt Lake City, the temperatures had hovered above 100 degrees Fahrenheit (37.77 degrees Celsius), accounting—perhaps—for the forest fires that had left a trail of smoke from Utah to Canada. Indeed, even the relatively cool temperatures I enjoyed were still pushing the mid-90s. Furthermore, the heat in Utah is decidedly of the dry variety, meaning that—even after six bottles of water—a relatively straightforward hike to the top of Ensign Peak nonetheless rendered me temporarily dehydrated.

Had I done the same hike in mid-January, I might well have done so in temperatures below freezing and almost certainly against the backdrop of snow.

Now that's not to say that similar winter weather is absent from the Lake District. After all, I have fond memories of witnessing the snowcaps of Scafell Pike, even as the foot of the mountain remained utterly untouched.

But in parts of the Rockies, snowfall can become so burdensome that people become rooted to their houses. For a fictional example of this, think of Stephen King's "The Shining", and particularly Stanley Kubrick's big screen adaptation of it, in which the Torrance family become stranded at the Overlook Hotel in Colorado.

In that very same state—particularly in the world-famous city of Aspen—winter skiing is a highly popular activity, underscoring just how much more snow Colorado receives compared to England's northwest, where skiing is a rare sight indeed.

I forgot to mention, by the way, that none of the above should undermine the splendor of the Lake District, a place to which I have long dreamed of retiring. It's just that, while I'm still relatively young, the promise of adventure, enormous heights, and the great expanse, is a promise worth pursuing—especially while I still have the strength. Perhaps one day I'll renew my search for Wordsworth's house—by then I'll be fully prepared.

Laurence is a British writer and humorist who lives in the United States. He also hosts the popular web series, "Lost in the Pond" on YouTube. He has an infuriating habit of taking America to task by pointing out how things are done in the UK. He really needs to stop this behavio(u)r. It's anti-American.

GREAT BRITONS: A.A. MILNE
THE CREATOR OF WINNIE THE POOH

A. A. Milne was an English author who began his career as a humorist, novelist, and playwright, but who saw his early successes eclipsed by his success as a children's author. He created the characters Christopher Robin and Winnie-the-Pooh from his own son and his stuffed bear. Their exploration of Ashdown Forest, beside the farm they lived in, became the inspiration for books of their adventures, written in a child-like style. He saw active service in both World Wars, and knew many of the major literary figures of early 20th century England. His sale in the 1930s of the rights to his characters to an American agent led to their commercialisation, and their development into a major marketing phenomenon.

KEY FACTS

- Born 1882 – died 1956
- Creator of Winnie-the-Pooh
- Became estranged from his son Christopher Robin
- Saw his more serious literary career extinguished by his success with children's books

While no one would ever ask, "Winnie-the-Who?", many people today might have trouble recognising the name A. A. Milne. Creators can be eclipsed by their creations, and Milne himself regretted that of all his work, it was his, "trifles for the young" that became his legacy. Milne's nostalgic vision was a product of those brittle years between the 'War to End All Wars,' that destroyed the halcyon days of Edwardian England, and the encroaching darkness of the total war and genocide of World War II. Those brief decades were his formative years.

Alan Alexander Milne was born in 1882, and he grew up the south London neighborhood of Kilburn. He lived in Henley House, a small 'public school' run by his father, meaning it was a private, fee-paying establishment. Milne was a pupil, and when he was seven, H. G. Wells was briefly the school's science teacher. His father John Vine Milne had been born in Jamaica – it was a British colony at the time – and his mother was Sarah Marie Heginbotham, from Derbyshire. Milne moved on to the prestigious Westminster School, and from there to Trinity College, Cambridge, graduating in Mathematics in 1903. His literary interests were apparent, however, as he edited and wrote for *The Granta*, a student magazine that was a literary outlet for several other future famous writers. R. C. Lehmann was an earlier Granta editor who had moved on to become a major contributor to the influential humorous and satirical magazine, Punch. After his graduation, Milne was soon also contributing regularly, and he became assistant editor to the magazine in 1906.

Milne mingled in literary circles, playing cricket, for example, in an amateur team called the 'Allahakbarries,' founded by J. M. Barrie (creator of Peter Pan). Other players included Arthur Conan Doyle, Rudyard Kipling, P. G. Wodehouse, G. K. Chesterton, and Jerome K. Jerome, to name just a few. The conversation was undoubtedly better than the playing.

In 1913, Milne married Dorothy de Sélincourt, known as "Daphne." After the outbreak of World War I, he joined the army as an officer in the Royal Warwickshire Regiment. Injured at the Battle of the Somme, he was sent back to England, where he wrote propaganda for military intelligence with MI7. Daphne had a son, Christopher Robin Milne, in 1920.

In the years bracketing WWI, Milne built a successful literary career, writing 18 plays and four novels. He also wrote four scripts for the early British film industry, all made into films by Minerva Films, owned by the actor Leslie Howard. Milne complained that whatever he wrote, his editors thought he should be writing something else. Despite Milne's own high regard for these works, they have faded into near-oblivion, overtaken by the result of his buying Cotchford Farm, in Hartfield, East Sussex, in 1925. Milne, Daphne, and Christopher Robin began an idyllic life there, with Milne wandering the surrounding countryside with Christopher, joining his son in the magical discovery of the world by young children during their early years of innocence.

Cotchfold Farm is on the edge of Ashdown Forest, an area of heathland and woods that had been a hunting forest since the Norman Conquest of England. Part of it is called Five Hundred Acre Wood, which became Hundred Acre Wood in

Milne's fictional creations. Christopher's stuffed bear, named Winnie after a Canadian black bear and ex-military mascot that lived in London Zoo, also famously figures in the stories. The 'Pooh' part was the name of a local swan. Piglet, Eeyore, Kanga, Roo, and Tigger were all stuffed toys belonging to Christopher, while Rabbit and Owl are fictional.

Pooh, still unnamed, first appeared in a poem, "Teddy Bear," published in Punch in February 1924. "When We Were Very Young", a book of children's poems, including "Teddy Bear", appeared later the same year. The named Pooh first appeared in a story called, "The Wrong Sort of Bees", which saw the light on Christmas Eve, 1925, in the London Evening News. "Winnie-the-Pooh" was published in 1926 and "The House at Pooh Corner" in 1928. A collection of nursery rhymes, "Now We Are Six", was published in 1927. All the original editions were illustrated by E. H. Shepard.

In 1922, Milne had published a detective novel, "The Red House Mystery", which had met with some acclaim. He was well-known both in England and America as a successful playwright. After the publication and immediate success of the Pooh books he still wrote for Punch, and he also wrote a still-performed stage adaption of Kenneth Grahame's novel "The Wind in the Willows", called "Toad of Toad Hall". In the aftermath of WWI, he removed the chapter called 'Piper at the Gates of Dawn,' which recounts a search for a lost son, from the play. Too many members of the audience would have lost sons in the war.

In 1934, as tensions in Europe increased, Milne wrote a condemnation of war called "Peace with Honour." By 1940, his position had shifted, and he wrote "War with Honour," to support the efforts of a country now at war – just 20 years after the last time. During WWII, he served as a Captain in the Home Guard, a division of the military responsible for home defense.

At a personal level too, the idyll of Cotchfold Farm had been shattered, although he continued to live there for the rest of his life. The success of the Pooh books had made his all-too-flesh-and-blood son a celebrity, and this was a role that Christopher Robin did not enjoy. He became estranged from his parents and felt used by his father. He is quoted as having said, "We'll see how father likes it when I write poems about HIM!" Christopher Robin moved further away from his parents when he married his cousin Lesley de Sélincourt, something legally permitted in the UK. Her father and Christopher's mother were estranged, and they had not spoken for 30 years, so this was hardly a move to unite the family.

Critical reviews were rare, but the adult Christopher Robin might have sympathized with the words of 'Constant Reader,' a weekly column in the New Yorker written by Dorothy Parker – Tonstant Weader twowed up.

In 1952, Milne suffered a stroke. That, and the surgery it required left him an invalid and he became disheartened with life, probably entering a period of depression. He died a few years later, in January 1956, aged 74. As for Winnie-the-Pooh, in the 1930s Milne had sold merchandising, television, and recording rights to Stephen Slesinger, an American pioneer of the rights licensing industry. When Slesinger died, his widow, in turn, sold many of the rights to the Disney Corporation, leading to today's massive commercialisation of Milne's original simple characters.

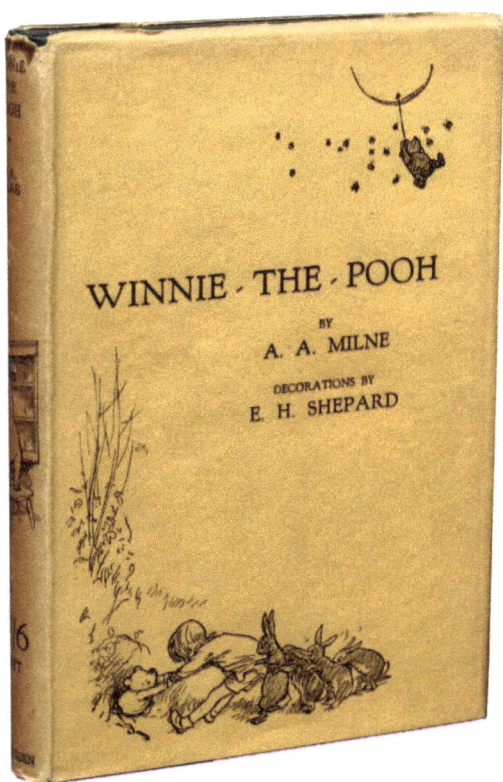

Sites to Visit

- A. A. Milne was cremated. The site of his ashes is unknown.
- Henley House was destroyed by a German rocket in WWII. The area is now a housing estate. There is a plaque on the wall at Mortimer Place, Remsted House, NW6, marking its location.
- Cotchfold Farm, Hartfield, East Sussex, where all the Winnie-the-Pooh books were written, still stands. It was owned for a time by Brian Jones, a member of the band the Rolling Stones. Jones drowned in the swimming pool there in 1969. The Grade-II listed building is currently on the market for £1.9 million. Hartfield village store does a thriving trade in memorabilia.
- A memorial plaque was placed in Ashdown Forest, in 1979, dedicated to Milne and Shepard. The 6,000-acre forest is always open.
- The real stuffed toys which became the characters in the Winnie-the-Pooh stories can be seen at the Main Branch of the New York Public Library, 5th Avenue at 42nd Street.
- The original book manuscripts are held at Trinity College, Cambridge.
- A star was placed on the Hollywood Hall of Fame for Winnie-the-Pooh in 2006.

Further Research

- Goodbye Christopher Robin (2017) is a film about Milne's creation of Winnie-the-Pooh, and his relationship with Christopher Robin.
- Goodbye Christopher Robin: A. A. Milne and the Making of Winnie-the-Pooh (1990), by Ann Thwaite is the biography on which the film was based.
- The Extraordinary Life of A. A. Milne (2017), by Nadia Cohen.
- In Which Milne's Life Is Told: A Biography of Winnie the Pooh Author A.A. Milne (2013), by Paul Brody
- The Natural World of Winnie-the-Pooh: A Walk Through the Forest that Inspired the Hundred Acre Wood (2015), by Kathryn Aalto, is a guide to the wildlife of Ashdown Forest, and a valuable resource for retracing the events of the books in their original locations.

THIS ENGLISH LIFE

The Echoing Green
By Erin Moore

It's midsummer 2018, and my daughter Anne and I are having a Talk, sotto voce, in the back of a taxi on a Tuesday night. It is a talk about how, when a London cabbie asks you whether you are following the World Cup, it is acceptable to say "no," but you must never follow it up with, "But I hope France wins."

We are a sporty family—we run, we lift weights, we play squash and tennis, and our son is on a little football team—but we don't watch any of it on TV, and we are usually out of the loop when it comes to professional sports. This summer, there was no excuse for it. It wasn't just that we lacked appropriate small talk; we were embarrassing ourselves. You could not live in England and remain agnostic about football during this World Cup. England had not made it to a Final since 1966, but this summer it seemed they were in with a chance, and no one could stop talking about it. We would have done well to keep our big traps shut, but we couldn't resist.

Later on the night of the Talk, I was in another taxi headed home. Colombia and England were playing. The driver was riveted to the match on the radio, but I couldn't understand what I was hearing (what was a penalty?). Suddenly the pubs and restaurants around us erupted in cheers, and the dummy in the backseat said, "Wow, England's really doing well tonight!" Turned out we were driving through a Columbian neighborhood.

Lying in bed reading a bit later, I heard the pub across the street go nuts. The cheering went on for a good 10 minutes. Car horns were honking in the street. People hugged. Presumably at least some of them were English people. It was like a mini VE Day out there. I turned to my husband and said, "Phew! That's over then. England won, now we can move on to the next thing." But it turned out that they had only made it to the quarterfinals. Hearing how much it meant to the crowd outside, I started to turn into someone who cared—if only a little, and only for their sakes—about the World Cup "Coming Home."

But the fact that I was on a yoga retreat in the US—meditation, sharing circles, the whole nine—and entirely unaware when England lost their semifinal match against Croatia, says everything about how much I cared. There weren't any English football fans around, but I heard about the loss from a lone and very excited Croatian in the kitchen early the next morning. I jumped up and down with her briefly, feeling super disloyal, and then went back to being a football agnostic. You know the ending, of course: My kid got her wish. We were standing in our kitchen at home with not one, but two, French people (also football agnostics) when it happened. No cheers from the pub across the street. And now we can move on to the next thing.

For our family, that was Anne's 8th birthday party. Anne's birthday is in late August when most of her friends are away, so instead of a big party during the school year, we decided to have a very small party for those few still in town in late July. Our friends in London come from many nations, and we have lots of different ideas about raising our children, but one thing we all seem to have in common is nostalgia for the backyard birthday parties of our 70s (-ish) youth. We played analog games, ate homemade cakes, and ran around like feral lunatics on a sugar high. There were no rented venues, no entertainers, no sound systems, no bubble machines, no fancy party bags and low expectations. It was (say it with us!) just so simple and honest. A more innocent time. And the unspoken subtext: it was all so much less work for our parents than it is for us.

No one in London has enough space to host an entire school class at home, so we resort to parties that would have given our parents the vapors (actually, still do). My kids have been to some absolute blowouts over the years. They have been invited to children's parties with ice cream trucks, live mermaids, pony rides, private film screenings, manicure stations, candy factories, flowing champagne (grownups only), discos, hula lessons, cooking classes, trampolines, catwalks, pirate ships, artists-in-residence, chocolate fountains, petting zoos, and indoor playgrounds. Anyone from my daughter's class reading this is going to be thinking, "Wait! Who had the chocolate fountain?" Guys, I can't remember, but for sure someone did.

Given only six or so kids to entertain, this year I was finally going to put my foot down: enough was enough. Anne's party would be a time machine back to my own childhood, with an English twist. Surprisingly (maybe unsurprisingly), Anne was all for it.

First of all, it would be outside in the sunshine in a garden. Instead of banners, we'd hang bunting. Instead of pin-the-tail, it would be pass-the-parcel. We'd play musical statues instead of musical chairs. Instead of hot dogs and pizza, there would be homemade tea sandwiches and scones with jam and cream and three-tier trays of cookies, only these kids call them biscuits. Anne wanted a rainbow cake and a firework candle. I had four days to plan, and I started where any sensible parent would have: on Amazon Prime.

By the time I had ordered a trestle table, a tablecloth, multiple three-tier trays (the reviews warned that at least one was likely to arrive broken), 16 boxes of American candy for pass-the-parcel, hula hoops for party favors, 2-liter thermoses for the coffee and tea, a pink tent for the kids to lark about in, bunting and other assorted necessities, a fully stocked venue was starting to look like the easy way out. (Confession: I did go ahead and get a bubble machine. Kids just love those things.)

When the one non-homemade food item—the cake—turned out not to be at the shop where I'd ordered it, but at another branch of the bakery an hour's drive away through rush-hour traffic, my dominant thought was, "I didn't sign up for this." Up at 6 am making tea sandwiches for a party whose guest list now topped 30, I knew it was far too late to reconsider my options. But here is one option I did reconsider: I'll never again imagine that my parents had it easy hosting those "simple" backyard birthday parties.

Anne's party was a great success, and a joy to plan and host. Nevertheless, by the time we had made and procured the food; loaded and unloaded the car; set up and taken down the tent, the bunting, the table; supervised the games; chatted amiably and over-caffeinated everyone in sight, all the adults involved were 7pm-on-Christmas-Day-level tired. I'd do it all again, though, for the thrill of watching my kids and their friends run around like feral lunatics on a sugar high without once having to shush them.

By the time you read this, the nights will be drawing in, and summer will be on the wane. But what a summer it's been—one for the record books. London's hottest in 42 years, with temperatures topping 80 degrees most days, and practically no rain in June and July. Most Americans wouldn't class these temperatures as a heat wave, but then again most Americans have air conditioning in their homes and offices. In a typical English summer, my American summer wardrobe of sleeveless tops, shorts, and sandals does not make an appearance, and people around me have notional thought bubbles over their heads most of the time saying things like, "I wonder how warm it is in Cannes right now?" or "Is it pathetic to eat ice cream in a driving rain?"

This year, we finally got the weather we'd been pining for, out loud, every summer since 1976. Complaining about the weather felt wrong, like ingratitude, so before we complained about the weather we would always preface it—as if in abeyance to the weather gods—with "I'm not complaining because this is an amazing summer, but…" We had complicated feelings about our good fortune. We couldn't walk out of the house without layers of SPF50. Even under all that sunscreen, between the playground and the ice cream truck, we all got more sun than we intended. We'll regret it on our next visit to the dermatologist, but I forgot how amazing the sun feels on bare skin and how much easier it is to leave the house without coats and jackets and real shoes. It was actually hotter in London than it was in Cannes. Ice cream ceased to be optional; it was a human right. I enjoyed almost every minute of our beautiful heat wave because when we are wearing wool and turning the lights on by 5 pm, we will look back at this summer and think, "such, such were the joys." Even without the World Cup, we felt like winners.

Erin Moore is an American who has been living in London for 10 years. Her book, That's Not English: Britishisms, Americanisms and What Our English Says About Us, is available on amazon.com.

THE MAYFLOWER
THE ENGLISH SETTLEMENT OF NEW ENGLAND

On the 6th of September 1620, the *Mayflower* set sail from Plymouth, England, carrying a cargo of hopeful, intrepid English pilgrims, eager to start a new life on the other side of the Atlantic. This group of settlers were part of the very early British colonising missions to North America, but their particular story and singular identity has created an enduring foundational myth in the American psyche. The *Mayflower* pilgrims were in search of a new land in which they could establish a somewhat utopian society, fleeing religious persecution and corrupting, immoral forces at home in England. The 'New World' offered a new start, allowing them the freedom to forge a new society based on the principles of faith, and austerity. The trials and tribulations of the *Mayflower* pilgrims have evolved into the stuff of legends, particularly with respect to their dealings with the local indigenous groups in and around Cape Cod. The modern festival of Thanksgiving, which is based on a shared harvest feast with the Wampanoag tribe, exists as a powerful reminder of the precarious beginnings of British settlement in North America.

KEY DATES

- September 1607 - Migration of the Scrooby congregation to Leiden
- 5 August 1620 - The Mayflower and Speedwell set sail from Southampton
- 6 September 1620 - The Mayflower sets sail from Plymouth, England
- 11 November 1620 - The Mayflower lands at Provincetown Harbour, Cape Cod

KEY FIGURES

- Christopher Jones - Captain of the *Mayflower*
- William Brewster - Early leader of the pilgrim community in Plymouth
- Edward Winslow - Early leader of the pilgrim community in Plymouth
- Samoset - English-speaking member of the Patuxet tribe

English Pilgrims: In Search of a New Home

In the century following the Reformation, England witnessed a period of intense religious conflict, as successive monarchs adopted contradictory policies concerning the right and ability of individuals to worship according to their own conscience. In this period, religion was inherently political, and any rejection of the Church of England was construed as a rejection of the crown, the monarch being the head of the Church of England. Those Protestants (usually Puritans) who rejected the doctrines and practices of the Church of England were therefore in an exceptionally precarious position and risked being accused of treason.

In the early 17th century, groups of Protestants emerged in English society that believed that the Reformation of the Church of England had been ineffective, and the only way to pursue a righteous path of Christian worship was to separate from it. These so-called 'separatists' did not have (at this point) any particular Church title and were distinct from the majority of Puritans, who accepted the Church of England while believing it to be in need of further reform. The separatists found their position in England increasingly untenable after the accession of James the VI of Scotland to the English throne, and in the first years of the 17th century, a significant group coalesced around the manor house at Scrooby, in South Yorkshire.

The congregation at Scrooby was led by William Brewster, who had previously lived and worked in Holland. As persecutions of separatists and non-conformists intensified, the congregation decided in 1607 to move to Leiden, in Holland, where Brewster and other members of the congregation had connections. In Holland, the congregation was free to worship, but over the course of the following decade, a number of issues emerged that caused tension and concern within the community. First, there was concern that the pilgrims were losing their English identity and assimilating to Dutch society. Concurrent with this process was a perceived corruption of the pure religious ideals espoused by the Puritan community: as a bustling, industrial city,

The Mayflower, Below - Landfall

Leiden offered too many temptations for younger members, and it was becoming increasingly difficult to sustain the austere values and practices of the original congregation.

In addition to this, although the majority of the community was in a stable position, the prospects for work and reward in Leiden were limited by the labor and immigration laws, which kept the pilgrims in menial, low-paying jobs. The rising tensions between the Dutch and the Spanish also gave rise to fears that the permissive attitude to Puritanism that had prevailed in Holland might be about to come to an end. The future for the congregation was uncertain, and community leaders such as Edward Winslow argued forcefully that it was time to find an alternative home: a place where the pilgrims could start afresh and establish their community in an area without the threat of war, moral corruption and religious persecution.

North America appeared to offer an ideal solution, but it was not without considerable risks. The experiences of early settlers in Jamestown just a few years previously functioned as a salient reminder that any attempt to establish a colony in an inhospitable landscape amid hostile native peoples posed an enormous challenge. The journey itself would be arduous, and the threat of disease and starvation played heavily on the minds of the community leaders. Nevertheless, in 1619, Robert Cushman and John Carver opened negotiations with the London Company, with the intention of gaining permission for a new settlement at the mount of the Hudson River. The terms of the settlement would be similar to other early colonising missions: settlers would be under the jurisdiction of the London Company and were expected to provide labor for them for seven years after the foundation of the colony.

Finding Passage to the New World

Once the decision was made, the pilgrims leased a ship named the *Mayflower* that would transport them to America's east coast. The pilgrims in Leiden needed to get to England in order to join the *Mayflower* and to say a final farewell to their ancestral home. As a result, a smaller ship named the *Speedwell* was hired to take them to Southampton, from whence the two vessels would transport the pilgrims to the New World. The *Speedwell* would remain in the colony where it would be used for fishing and exploratory ventures. However, these plans suffered considerable setbacks when it became apparent that the *Speedwell* was not seaworthy. Considerable delays were incurred as the ship underwent repairs, and it was not until the 5th of August that the *Speedwell* and the *Mayflower* departed from Southampton. Even then, the ships were forced to turn back twice due to further problems with the *Speedwell*, until finally, it was decided to abandon the plan and put all of the pilgrims and supplies on to the already-crowded *Mayflower*.

Finally, on the 6th of September, the *Mayflower* departed from Plymouth. It carried 102 passengers, around one-half of which were Protestant separatists: the remainder were non-separatists and crewmen. The early part of the journey progressed fairly smoothly, but the delays in departure meant that the ship would hit the stormy season. As the weather worsened, the *Mayflower* was thrown off course. The pilgrims had been aiming for northern Virginia and the Hudson River, but finally, after 66 days at sea, Cape Cod was sighted on the 9th of November 1620. Poor weather forced them to land at this point instead of continuing south to the Hudson, and so the new colony would, in fact, be established beyond the jurisdiction of the Virginia Company.

For approximately six weeks, the pilgrims spent their time exploring the Cape, trying to decide upon a site for their new colony. On Christmas Day, 1620, they finally agreed upon a location, named it Plymouth, and started to build their new settlement. In part, the decision to relocate to Plymouth had been motivated by tense encounters with the indigenous population, particularly after the pilgrims had disturbed burial sites and looted several grain stores along the coast.

The Mayflower Compact

As soon as the pilgrims arrived at the Cape, they were anxious to establish a firm basis for the administration and governance of the new colony. The new location meant that they were outside of the jurisdiction of the Virginia Company, and the leaders of the community seized the opportunity to form their own system of governance and social organization. A group of 41 of the pilgrims and the other passengers on the ship agreed on terms and signed a contract, which they called the Mayflower Compact.

This agreement set a precedent for the creation of a 'civil body politick' that would be governed by an elected representative body and regulated according to just and equal laws. They swore allegiance to the English king, but their system of governance was an innovation. In effect, the signing of a civil covenant between peers of equal status would form the basis of secular government within America.

Surviving the Winter

The first winter proved to be a harsh wake-up call for the settlers. The majority lived on board the *Mayflower*, which remained in Plymouth until April of 1621 when it departed with a number of survivors and crew members. Half of the early settlers had died through malnutrition, starvation, and disease. The harsh winter and difficult terrain that they had encountered in the new world meant that cultivation and construction was a much more difficult feat than anticipated. For a time, it seemed that the colony would suffer the same inevitable fate of so many other attempted English settlements before them.

The survival of the community may be attributed to the local indigenous tribes, particularly the Wampanoag, who taught the settlers how to hunt, fish, and grow basic crops. A deal was brokered between the settlers and an English-speaking member of the Patuxet tribe named Samoset, who was living among the Wampanoag. He operated as an interpreter, providing assistance to the pilgrims, and developed strong relationships with a number of the key members of the colony. Samoset appears to have played a crucial role in brokering relations between the native tribes and the settlers, in particular in softening hostilities that had been caused by the settlers' disregard for the property, lands, and customs of indigenous communities. As a consequence, the pilgrims were able to successfully cultivate crops over the summer of 1621 and reap a significant harvest the following September. The harvest was celebrated with a three-day feast, involving both settlers and natives, which is still remembered in North America today during the Thanksgiving festival.

Legacy

The Mayflower Voyage and the early pilgrim colony at Cape Cod have taken on an iconic role in America's national story. The pilgrim settlers represent the earliest incarnation of the American Dream: European migrants seeking a better life, opportunity, and possibility across the Atlantic. The stereotypical image of the Pilgrim Fathers as models of industry, austerity, and hard work has fuelled a value system in America that endures to this day. In addition to this, the social and political organisation of the early pilgrims set a precedent for fair, equitable governance and democratic collective organisation based on secular principles. This precedent was followed in subsequent processes of colonisation and organisation: the move to the new world facilitated this experimentation with different forms of social organisation and governance, that would fundamentally impact upon the future democratic development of the United States of America.

Finally, the culmination of the *Mayflower* voyage is celebrated every year in the United States during the festival of Thanksgiving. This festival tends to paint a rosy picture of indigenous-immigrant relations, and arguably occults the violence and suppression of local populations by what was effectively a colonising force. In recent years, there has been a greater recognition of the complexities that surrounded the relations between settlers and indigenous populations, and a re-narration of the story of Thanksgiving that takes account of these complexities. The *Mayflower* Voyage and settlement remain, therefore, a key event in American history, and one that deserves our continued attention.

Sites to Visit

The *Mayflower* Steps and Museum, Plymouth, UK. This heritage museum traces the history of the *Mayflower* pilgrims as they left England for the New World. The museum also includes the *Mayflower* Trail, which takes visitors to the

Elizabethan Gardens and the preserved Merchant's House, in addition to the port.

Harwich, Essex, UK. This site on the Essex coast is the point at which the *Mayflower* ship was launched, and the hometown of Captain Christopher Jones. The current *Mayflower* Project supports the building of a replica of the *Mayflower* ship, which will sail for the United States in 2020 to commemorate the 400th anniversary of the voyage.

Plimoth Plantation, Plymouth, MA, United States. This living history museum recreates the original settlement of the *Mayflower* pilgrims and contains a number of exhibits and museums, including a replica of the *Mayflower* ship, an English mill, a craft center, and an English village.

Film, Literature, and TV

- Saints and Strangers. This two-part miniseries, made in 2015, tells the story of the *Mayflower* Voyage, the settlement on the east coast on the United States, and early encounters with indigenous American communities.
- Desperate Crossing: The Untold Story of the *Mayflower*. This 2006 documentary, made in conjunction with the Royal Shakespeare Company, re-enacts the *Mayflower* crossing closely based on original sources.
- The Pilgrims. This 2015 documentary challenges the myths and misconceptions about the early pilgrims and situates the *Mayflower* Voyage in its broader historical context.

Further Research

- Nathaniel Philbrick, Mayflower: A Voyage to War, (Harper Perennial, 2007). This book, from an acclaimed public historian, exposes the conflicts that emerged in the aftermath of the pilgrims' arrival in America, providing a dramatic and gripping narrative.
- Rebecca Fraser, The Mayflower: The Families, the Voyage, and the Founding of America, (St. Martin's Press, 2017). Rebecca Fraser charts the story of the Mayflower and the early pilgrims through the prism of one important pilgrim family: the Winslows.
- Nick Bunker, Making Haste From Babylon: The Mayflower Pilgrims and Their World, A New History, (Pimlico, 2011). This accessible history provides the broader context for the pilgrims' departure from England, exploring the historical conflicts and tensions that were then imported into the new settlements.

It was one perfect moment. It was a moment that it seemed like the whole world was watching. The doors opened, the trumpets sounded, and there was a woman, entering a church to marry the man she loved. It felt as if almost the whole world had stopped in silence to watch. I'm an approaching middle-aged Straight White American Man, and it brought me to tears. Who doesn't love weddings? But Royal Weddings? Those are something extra special. And I was there to see it all.

What really struck me was the silence. Granted, there was plenty going on in the church. I'm talking about the silence in Windsor. Minutes ago, there were cheering crowds. And then, silence. You could hear a pin drop in Windsor. Windsor paused. The world paused. Two lovers got married. And we all rejoiced.

Windsor was really the perfect place for a Royal Wedding. When it was announced that the wedding and festivities would take place in Windsor. I was dubious.

Surely not in tiny Windsor?

There was no way they could handle the crowds. They could, and they did.

The British know how to prepare for events like this, and they did it with aplomb. Windsor did the job beautifully. They managed the crowds perfectly. The down was resplendent in Union Jacks and patriotic decorations. And not just the 'official' decorations. Many private homes when out of their way to show their excitement for the day. As an American Anglophile, I was chuffed to bits to see the American flag just as much as the Union Jack. Brits really embraced Meghan's American-ness. It was truly lovely to see.

On the big day itself, there was a veritable panoply of characters out on the streets of Windsor. There were plenty of Americans, waving the stars & stripes from the behind the barriers. There were Brits in costume - from town criers to pretend soldiers. And then there were the Brits who looked like they were in costume, but actually, they were dressed normally (insert image of the country gentleman in a tweed cap. Some women were even in formal dress - I even saw a wedding dress or two. And then there were the hats - the glorious hats. If you can't wear a fabulous hat at a Royal Wedding, then what's the point?

But by far the best 'cosplayer' I saw in the crowds was the chap who was dressed as Mr. Bean. Tweed jacket, teddy bear, suitcase and all. I had to do a double take to make sure he wasn't actually Rowan Atkinson in character. He was a popular chap to get a picture with, and he seemed to be eating up the attention. And honestly, and this is rather uncharitable of me, if you look like Mr. Bean, you have to take the positive attention when you can get it!

For many people in Windsor that day, it was a day of work. Everyone had a bit part play to make the day great. Of course, there were the police keeping everyone safe. And I'm always amazed at events like this - the police are never intimidating, even when you see armed ones. There was medical personnel throughout the crowds in case anyone needed attention quickly. The street cleaners entertained crowds keeping the streets clean. Then there were the grafters.

And who were they? Well, no event like this would be complete without street sellers hawking flags, scarves, face masks and a kaleidoscope of other Royal Wedding-related tat. I don't use that word to criticise. These people play a critical role, and I bought a flag myself from them. They work their arses off on days like this, and they deserve any penny they earn. It's the hardest work you can do during an event like this. We can't forget the small army of food vendors who camped out along The Long Walk, offering the most critical ingredients to a Grand Royal Day Out: endless cups of tea and endless cones of chips (that's fries to you and me).

During the last Royal Wedding, I was really intrigued to see such a wide range of people who had come out to watch the wedding. I was pleased to see much of the same for Harry & Meghan's wedding. I was really surprised at how many Americans there were in the crowds. Typically when I'm in England, hearing an American accent (at least outside of London) causes me to pause and feel a pang of patriotism. I would say there were tens of thousands of Americans who made the journey to Windsor to watch their fellow countrywoman wed into the British Royal family.

Looking at the crowds, it was a wide range of peoples and races. It was really a testament to Britain's diversity, and the legacy of its Empire and now Commonwealth that so many different types of people were represented in the crowds. The British get a bad rap as being a people of closet

racists and xenophobes, and while every culture has a subsection of close-minded people, the British are an open and welcoming people. If you don't believe me, just look at the pictures of the crowds from the day. Britain is diverse, and in its current struggles, it will take great strength from that. The wedding itself was a massive symbol of how much 'conservative' Britain has changed in the last 30 or so years. In the days of Princess Diana, it would have been unthinkable for a member of the British Royal Family to marry an American, let alone someone of a different race (and previously divorced and not Anglican!). The fact the event happened at all is a testament to how much Britain has changed for the better. And most people just didn't bloody care, and that's the way it should be (and the ones who did care and shared their racist views, were easily drowned out by how positive everyone was about it).

My experience at this wedding was much different than when I came to see Will & Kate get married back in 2011. Then, I got up before dawn and made my way to The Mall to get a spot right outside Buckingham Palace, then proceeded to stand there for a good 6 hours. It was brutal on my legs and my bladder. It was also a very hot day. And then when the crowds descended on the palace for the Wave and Flypast, it became a crush of hundreds of thousands people. It was both exhilarating and downright scary. I was so worried Windsor would turn into that, and I'm so glad it just didn't.

Instead of being on the streets, waiting with everyone for all the events to unfold, I spent the morning and afternoon in the ballroom at the Castle Hotel, hosted by the Foreign Press Association. This HQ for the foreign press provided fast WiFi, TV screens to watch, tea & biscuits and everything else reported would need to cover such a big occasion. Before I left for the trip, I was quite worried that being sequestered in the room all day would ruin the experience for me. I wouldn't be down on the streets with everyone else.

But, honestly, it didn't. I had a bloody great day. While I wanted to enjoy the day as a spectator, I was there to work. And the facilities provided by the FPA allowed me to work without interruption and do everything we planned to do on the day. The Castle Hotel was central enough, it's literally right across the street from Windsor Castle, that you still very much felt a part of events going on outside. You could hear the crowd cheer. You could hear their silence.

And when the big moment came, and it was time for the carriage procession to go by the hotel, I was able to pop outside, set up my cameras and actually get pictures and videos of the happy royal couple as they rode past. I didn't have to wake up ridiculously early, and I didn't have to deal with a massive crowd. It was the best of both worlds. I got to be there and experience the essential bits, and I was able to do it on my own terms.

It's hard to describe that feeling when they ride by. I felt it just the same when Will & Kate rode by me during their wedding. It's a massive thrill. The crowd is loud and cheering with anticipation. But then the crowd gets louder, but not all at once. They get louder in a wave. As the carriage passes people, the wave of sound follows them. The roar gets louder and louder as they approach to the point it's almost deafening. Then they clip-clop their way by and the roar recedes as they ride away. It's a huge feeling of excitement. Of shared experience. You've all just seen something wonderful.

And then it's all over.

Our world can be a terrible place. It's easy to get lost in all the bad political news and latest stories of violence all over the world and be depressed about it. Whether you hate the political situation in your country or elsewhere, a Royal Wedding is above all that. It's simply a happy event. Two beautiful young people are professing their love for each other for the whole world to see. And for one moment, we all stop to watch. For one moment, the world isn't such a terrible place. This is what it means to be human, to find small pockets of joy in life, even amongst absolute misery.

I felt only one thing as they rode by me on the carriage procession: absolute contentment. If I had my own state of nirvana, that would be it. In my mind, all was right with the world. But it's only a moment, and it's fleeting. I had to run back to the hotel to process my images and video. Once the headlines of the wedding recede, the bad news of the world slowly creeps back in, and the world returns to normal. Hoping that it can have another moment to pause and look out in wonder.

Once the festivities were over and I returned to the streets of Windsor, it was now late in the afternoon. The scene was massively changed. The crowds were gone from the main streets in Windsor. The campers had gone. Everyone with their silly hats had made their way back to Windsor's train stations to begin their long journeys home. Wedding-related ephemera littered the streets, blowing in the wind as cleaning crews started the long process of cleaning it all up.

Walking into the side streets, the day had turned into just another Saturday in Windsor, England. The sun was shining, casting a late afternoon golden glow on Windsor's Medieval and Georgian buildings. The weather was warm, and the sky was clear of clouds. People were out shopping on the high street. Eating food in the restaurants. Arguing with spouses. Arguing with children. A few hours about it was Britain at its finest, on show for the world. Now, it was Britain as it always is, which to me, is a much more interesting show. Airplanes, abnormally diverted away from Windsor during the wedding, returned to the flights above the city.

When I came back into Windsor the next day, a Sunday, to catch the train to Oxford, it was a completely changed place. If you weren't aware already, it was not clear that there was a Royal Wedding the previous day. All the street barriers were gone. The mess was cleaned up. The only crowds present were the regular tourists on a day trip to Windsor. It was all rather surreal.

It showed how fleeting this one event was. As someone who is part of the generation that grew up with William and Harry, watching both of them get married was a seminal event, not just in my life but in British history. Harry's wedding was the last royal wedding for at least 20-30 years (and I mean in the immediate direct line of succession, there will be smaller Royal Do's, but they won't have this kind of importance). By the time there is another Royal Wedding, I will be in my 50s or 60s, and my own children will be getting married (hopefully). It was genuinely fulfilling and special to be a part of two major events, even in my own small way. There will be other major Royal Events in the coming years (and I hate to say it, a Coronation, long away may that be), but for weddings, this was it.

And what a way to go out. As I sat in my flat, exhausted from a long day, and watched the Royal Couple drive away in their electric Jaguar to their party at Frogmore House into the sunset, I thought how lovely it had all been and to have been there.

May their marriage be long and happy.

MARY I
Bloody Mary and her short reign

Mary I began her life as a much-cherished and respected Tudor princess but during her adolescence was rejected by her father, King Henry VIII, declared illegitimate and isolated from the royal court. A devout Catholic, Mary took the throne from the pretender Lady Jane Grey after just nine days and began a campaign to restore Catholicism to England and undo the transformation to the Church of England her father King Henry VIII has begun. The method Mary chose was extreme persecution, and during her reign she had approximately 300 Protestants burned at the stake. Mary I ended her life as first Queen Regent of England, much-reviled and much-deserving of the sobriquet Bloody Mary.

The only child of Henry VIII and his first wife, Catherine of Aragon, to survive childhood, Mary was doted on by her parents and enjoyed a lavish and loving childhood. Mary was extremely well-educated and by the age of nine could read and write Latin and also studied French, Spanish, music, and dance. All was not well with Mary's parents, however, and realizing that Catherine of Aragon was unable to provide him with a male heir, Henry VIII had Mary, and Catherine sent to Ludlow Castle in Wales where she held her own court.

Eager to secure the continuation of the Tudor dynasty with a male heir and, perhaps, already in love with Anne Boleyn, Henry VIII appealed to Pope Clement VII to have his marriage to Catherine annulled. The Pope refused, and yet Henry VIII married Anne Boleyn in 1533, who was already pregnant with his child. In May 1533 the Archbishop of Canterbury, Thomas Cranmer, declared Henry and Catherine's marriage void, Henry broke with the Roman Catholic Church altogether and declared himself the Supreme Head of the Church of England. Mary became Lady Mary, and her newborn sister, Elizabeth took her position in the line of succession.

It is thought that Mary was treated badly by her father during the next few years during which time she was persecuted by Anne Boleyn and was frequently ill. Little did Anne Boleyn know that her own daughter Elizabeth would suffer the same fate as Mary in the years to come. Despite the fact that her mother was gravely ill, Mary was not permitted to visit Catherine, and in 1536, Catherine died leaving Mary inconsolable.

Following her mother's death, Mary

KEY FACTS

- Mary I was born on the 18th of February 1516 at Greenwich Palace.
- The first child of Henry VIII, Mary I succeeded as Queen of England Ireland on 19 July, 1553, following the disastrous nine-day reign of Lady Jane Grey
- Mary I was married on 25 July 1554 to Philip of Spain, son of Holy Roman Emperor Charles V, and later King Philip II of Spain.
- Mary died at St. James Palace on the 17 November 1558 of cancer having reigned just five years.

was encouraged by her Catholic advisers to acknowledge her mother's divorce and made an oath of loyalty to her father as the Supreme Head of the English Church. In the years that followed, Henry VIII worked his way through his next five wives with Mary enjoying a fairly stable place at her father's court. In 1543, Henry married his sixth wife, Catherine Parr, who convinced him to bring his family back together and return Mary and Elizabeth to the line of succession after Edward.

When Mary's half-brother Edward VI, a partisan Protestant came to the throne, Mary was harassed for her religious beliefs, but her response to these hardships and ill-treatment was to cling ever more fiercely to her Catholic faith. Edward died aged just 15, and following a disastrous attempt by the Duke of Northumberland to maintain a Protestant England by planting Lady Jane Grey on the throne, Mary finally claimed her throne. Having proven her popularity, Mary rode into London on the 3rd of August 1553 with her sister Elizabeth in tow. Her accession took place on the 1st of October 1553 at Westminster Abbey.

At first, Mary's reforms were relatively mild although she did slowly begin to restore Catholicism in England by re-introducing Mass, reinstating deprived Bishops and expelling married members of the clergy. Next, Mary reinstated old heresy laws that declared that anyone who practiced or believed in a religion different from that of the sovereign was committing treason. Finally, at the

Philip Ii of Spain

age of 37, Mary made it known that she intended to marry Philip of Spain, eldest son, and heir of Holy Roman Emperor Charles V. She hoped that the union would produce a child who would become her Catholic heir, effectively removing Elizabeth from direct succession. This decision was very unpopular both with parliament and the public and a revolt began.

Thanks to the reinstated heresy laws Mary was able to legally have any member of the aristocracy who challenged her beheaded and around 300 Protestant 'heretics' burned at the stake. The first executions took place in early February and included prominent Protestants John Rogers, Laurence Saunders and the Archbishop of Canterbury who was forced to watch fellow clergymen Bishop Ridley, and Bishop Latimer burned at the stake before he himself succumbed to the same fate. Even Mary's new husband Philip of Spain warned against these atrocities despite the fact that he was doing a very similar thing in the Netherlands at the same time.

The marriage of Mary and Philip was childless, and Mary suffered two 'false pregnancies' in 1555 and 1557 during which time she showed symptoms of pregnancy without actually being pregnant. Philip left England after just 13 months of marriage and returned only once in order to convince Mary to send England to war with France, an expedition that led to the loss of Calais after a tenure of 211 years. England received no share in the Spanish monopolies in New World trade and Mary's popularity continued to plummet as the burning of Protestants at the stake became even more frequent.

In ill health and finally accepting that she would never have a child, Mary withdrew to St James' Palace where she died during an influenza epidemic on 17 November 1558. It is thought that Mary may have suffered from ovarian or uterine cancer and it is this cancer that may have killed her. Mary was interred in Westminster Abbey on 14 December 1558 in a tomb she would eventually share with her sister, Elizabeth.

Legacy Today

Her posthumous sobriquet, Bloody Mary, says much about Queen Mary I's legacy. The first woman to claim the throne of England, Mary was a popular queen during the early years of her reign and was loyally supported by the Roman Catholic's of England. Mary has been seen as a bloodthirsty tyrant throughout most of history thanks in part to writings published in the years following her death that became popular with English Protestants. Mary's unpopularity wasn't only due to the horrendous executions carried out in her name, a mixture of failed crops, military failure in France and her failure to produce an heir combined to turn the public against her. Now, viewed through a more scholarly historical lens, Mary is seen as a bloody queen, but a queen who began the economic reforms, military growth and expansion of the British Empire that made the Elizabethan era glorious.

Mary's Coat of Arms - Combined with Philip's

Film & TV

- The Other Boleyn Girl (2008)
- The Tudors (2007) TV series
- The Virgin Queen (2005) TV series
- Elizabeth (1998)
- Lady Jane (1986)
- Elizabeth R (1971) TV series
- Marie Tudor (1966)
- Pearls of the Crown (1937).
- Tudor Rose (1936)
- Marie Tudor (1917)

Further Research

- Edwards, John (2011) Mary I: England's Catholic Queen
- Whitelock, Anna (2010) Mary Tudor: England's First Queen
- Duffy, Eamon (2009). Fires of Faith: Catholic England Under Mary Tudor
- Ridley, Jasper (2001). Bloody Mary's Martyrs: The Story of England's Terror
- Tittler, Robert (1991). The Reign of Mary I
- Loades, David M. (1989) Mary Tudor: A Life
- Erickson, Carolly (1978). Bloody Mary: The Life of Mary Tudor
- Prescott, H. F. M. (1952). Mary Tudor: The Spanish Tudor

Locations to Visit

- Mary and King Philip II took their honeymoon at Hampton Court Palace in London.
- For a time Mary held her own court at Ludlow Castle in Shropshire.
- Mary also lived in both Hatfield House in Hertfordshire with her half-sister Elizabeth and Hunsdon House in Hertfordshire following her mother's death.
- The Palace of Beaulieu in Boreham, Essex was granted to Mary I upon Henry VIII's death, as stated in his will. The property is now used as a private school.
- Mary assembled a military force and launched her attack on Lady Jane Grey's supporters from Framlingham Castle, Suffolk.
- Mary died at St James's Palace in London and is buried in Westminster Abbey

REMEMBERING THE FEW
Top 10 Places to Visit for Battle of Britain History
By John Rabon

The first military campaign fought entirely by air forces, the Battle of Britain took place from 10 July to 31 October, 1940. Nazi Germany's Luftwaffe had been seen as a nigh-invulnerable force, and they were the vanguard of a planned Nazi invasion force. As the Luftwaffe wore down Britain's ability to defend itself, it would make the island nation all that more vulnerable to a land attack. However, the advent of several technologies and British resolve thwarted Hitler's plans. There are many places across the country to visit related to the battle from monuments to museums. We've outlined our 10 favorites below, but you can let us know your own in the comments.

Spitfire and Hurricane Memorial Museum

Speaking of technology that helped win the battle, the Spitfire and Hurricane Museum in Kent is dedicated to the two planes that helped turn the tide against the Luftwaffe. In addition to the perfectly preserved planes in its collection, the museum has a number of other artifacts dedicated to the Battle of Britain and the rest of WWII. It's also based at a former RAF base (now Kent International Airport).

Churchill War Rooms

Part of the Imperial War Museum, the Churchill War Rooms are the place from which the Prime Minister directed Britain's response to the Blitz and the Battle of Britain as bombs fell around them. Tickets are required for entry, but once inside, you can witness how the war was fought at the highest levels and how people lived when forced to remain underground during the conflict.

Kent Battle of Britain Museum

While you're checking out the fighter planes in Kent, you may as well head over to the Kent Battle of Britain Museum. It's located over the former RAF Station at Hawkinge, the closest RAF facility to Nazi-occupied France and it boasts the largest collection of Battle of Britain artifacts anywhere in the UK. While the Spitfire and Hurricane Museum may have the best intact planes, its sister museum

has artifacts recovered from crash sites, a terrible reminder of the cost of freedom.

Aldwych Tube Station Tour

Now disused, Aldwych Tube Station is one of the best-preserved former London Underground Stations. Ceasing use in 1940, the government turned it into one of many air raid shelters that were active during the London Blitz and the Battle of Britain. Several companies provide tours of the station whether you're interested in the history of its use as a filming location.

Bentley Priory Museum

This Grade II listed mansion house was RAF Headquarters Fighter Command during the Battle of Britain, and so is a must-visit for any historian. The majority of the museum's exhibits are split into three categories: The One, dedicated to Air Chief Marshall Sir Hugh Dowding; The Few, focused on the aircrews; and The Many, that features those men and women serving on the ground. There's also a significant amount to the museum dedicated to the house itself that is also worthy of your time.

Bawdsey Radar

Radar was a new technology in World War II that allowed Britain to have advance warning of impending Germany attacks. Bawdsey Manor was the location of the UK's first radar station from 1936-1939 and was where the technology was developed until everything moved at the outbreak of the war and afterward became one of many radar stations that kept Britain alert. The museum has not only exhibits dedicated to the history of radar technology but also interactive exhibits for more hands-on learning.

Imperial War Museum, Duxford

Another RAF fighter station turned museum, IWM Duxford has one of the largest collections of aircraft of all British military museums. Further, having

been a fighter station, it has dedicated exhibits to the Battle of Britain and the Air Defense of Britain. There's also an American Air Museum featuring planes used by the United States both during and after the war as well as regular airshows where you can see greats like the Spitfire and Hurricane fly again.

Battle of Britain Bunker, Uxbridge

On the western outskirts of London, the Battle of Britain Bunker in Uxbridge offers another perspective on waging the war underground. Utilized by No. 11 Group Fighter Command during the war, it was another place that Churchill and British leaders used to make decisive moves to win the Battle of Britain and later plan the D-Day invasion of France.

RAF Museum London

The site of RAF Museum London was also once a fighter station and is especially proud of having the most extensive collection of Battle of Britain aircraft anywhere in the country. This not only includes the legendary Spitfire and Hurricane but many lesser-known craft as well. The museum also plays host to a number of German aircraft that participated in the battle, which is another thing that sets it apart from other museums.

Battle of Britain Memorial, Capel-le-Ferne

Also known as The National Monument to the Few, the Battle of Britain Memorial in Capel-le-Ferne is dedicated to the aircrews who flew in the battle and especially to those who lost their lives in defense of the nation. There isn't a museum as such, but there are plenty of interactive exhibits to help you understand what it was like for the pilots who flew. If making a tour of important Battle of Britain sites, you'll want to make this your last as a fitting tribute to those who served.

BRITAIN'S SENTRIES OF THE SEA

The Royal National Lifeboat Institution was founded in 1824 to provide a coordinated system of stations around the coastline of the British Isles to rescue sailors from ships in peril. With 237 stations manned by volunteers, the Institution relies on endowments and donations through collection boxes for its activities. More than 140,000 lives have been saved since the Institution was founded by Sir William Hillary, who lived on the Isle of Man. The Institution has Queen Elizabeth II as its current patron and has been instrumental in the development of lifeboats and safety vests to protect both professional and amateur sailors from the hazards of the sea

Since men first took to sea in boats, shipwrecks have been a regular and tragic hazard. Major shipwrecks, with significant losses of life, became more common in the 19th century when shipping was the primary method for transporting goods and people over substantial distances. One notoriously dangerous place off the coast of England is the Isle of Man. This island lies between the east coast of England and Ireland, in the Irish Sea and is surrounded by hidden reefs that are a potential graveyard for ships.

In the early years of the 19th century, the Isle of Man was home to Sir William Hillary, a minor noble who had managed to squander the large fortune he had inherited. Consequently, he was on the island to avoid his creditors, as well as the family of his irate first wife. Born a Quaker, but now not a practicing one, it may nevertheless have been his Quaker sensibilities that affected him when, on the night of the 14th of December, 1822, the Royal Navy ship *HMS Racehorse* foundered on rocky reefs off the southeast coast of the island. Five intrepid local men from Castletown, then the capital, made four trips to the wreck to rescue sailors, but in the end, six men from the ship and three of the rescuers drowned.

Accounts vary as to whether Sir William actually took part in the rescue, or just heard accounts of it, but he was moved by the experience and decided to establish an organisation that would provide rescue services, not only on the Isle of Man but across Britain. In February of the following year, he published a pamphlet entitled An Appeal To The British Navy On The Humanity And Policy Of Forming A National Institution For The Preservation Of Lives And Property From Shipwreck. Pamphleteering was a common way of drawing attention to an issue at the time – print a booklet that could be distributed widely to develop interest in a cause. In making his appeal, he presented persuasive arguments based on using the latest tools available to rescue sailors.

For distressed ships to signal for help, he suggested the use of rockets, recently developed by the inventor and military rocket pioneer, Sir William Congreve. To pull ships away from being blown on to reefs he proposed the two-string kite system for which Charles Dansey has won a medal from the Royal School of Artillery, just the year before. Kites were also used to carry lines to shore, but William Hillary favored for that the much more practical and successful Manby Mortar, a small cannon that fired a line from the shore, invented by George William Manby in 1808. Hillary also wanted to take advantage of the flag code recently developed for merchant shipping by the sailor and novelist, Captain Frederick Marryat. Marryat's Code (precursor of the International Code of Signals) was the standard system used throughout most of the 19th century.

Despite this list of innovations, Hillary's appeal fell on deaf ears at the Admiralty. Undeterred, he decided to seek private support. A meeting was held on the 4th of March, 1824, at The Tavern, on Bishopsgate Street in London. Besides Sir William, Thomas Wilson, MP for the City of London and George Hibbert, ship owner and chairman of the West Indies Dock Company were there. The West Indies Dock (today the site of Canary Wharf) was London's major merchant-shipping port, so Hibbert's interest in marine safety had a practical

KEY FACTS

- Founded in 1824 by Sir William Hillary from the Isle of Man
- Operates 237 stations around the coast of the British Isles
- Carried out countless rescues of sailors in peril
- Played a part in the WWII evacuation from Dunkirk

1974 postage stamp marking the RNLI's 150th anniversary of the rescue of Daunt Lightship's crew by Ballycotton lifeboat RNLB Mary Stanford

aspect. Today Hibbert's image is tarnished by his support for slavery.

The three men agreed to form the National Institution for the Preservation of Life from Shipwreck. King George IV agreed to be a patron, and the society received a Royal Charter in 1860. In 1854 the name was changed to the Royal National Lifeboat Institution. There were already existing lifeboats around the coast of the British Isles by that time, typically manned by volunteers drawn from local sailors. There were believed to be 39 such boats in 1824, but within one year the RNLI had added 13 more. It actively encouraged and assisted in the establishment of more stations, until by 1909 there were 280 RNLI boats, and only 17 independent boats, around the coast.

Of course to rescue sailors lifeboats are needed, able to operate in rough seas, and the first ship specially designed for this was an 'unimmergible' boat, designed and patented by Lionel Lukin in 1785. He modeled his ship on some earlier French designs, and it had airtight compartments that kept it afloat even when completely full of water. Even though he was directly encouraged by King George IV, he too, like Hillary later, found his approaches to the Admiralty received no response. His work floundered when he entrusted his boat to a captain in Ramsgate for testing, but the captain found it much more useful for smuggling than for rescuing sailors. The first functioning lifeboat using his design was built in 1786 and used at Bamburg Castle, Sharpe, Northumberland. In 1851 Algernon Percy, 4th Duke of Northumberland offered a prize of 100 guineas and attracted 280 entries for a lifeboat competition. The winning design was by James Beeching of Yarmouth, for his 'self-righting' boat.

The Conister Shoals and St Mary's Isle lie off the harbor of Douglas on the Isle of Man. This was another 'hot spot' for shipwrecks, and although Hillary may not have been there for the wreck of *HMS Racehorse*, when he saw the packet-steamer St George being washed onto the Shoals on the stormy night of the 19th of November, 1830, he raced to the docks, put together a volunteer crew and set out in a lifeboat to rescue the ship. The lifeboat was almost swamped, and the 60-year-old Sir William was washed overboard, but eventually, after a great effort, the crew of 22 and all the 18 on the lifeboat made it safely back into Douglas Harbour. In all, Sir William is credited with being personally involved in saving 300 lives at sea.

In its early years the Institution depended on private philanthropy, and when appeals by Sir William for government support were rejected as being 'a departure from the principle of private benevolence,' the Institution went through a period of some decline. It was only when the Duke of Northumberland stepped in as President at the same time as he became First Lord of the Admiralty, that funding from the Privy Council for Trade was secured. Although this annual support of £2,000 only lasted for 15 years, it was during that time that the Institution was able to establish itself on a firm footing based on endowments and donations. It has continued to support itself in that way, and the familiar collection boxes in shops can be seen all across the country, especially in coastal areas.

During WWI, volunteer boats of the RNLI carried out numerous rescues, although the single largest rescue was in 1907 when multiple crews from stations in Cornwall spend 16 hours rescuing 456 passengers from the ocean liner *SS Suevic*. During WWII, lifeboats of the RNLI took part in the evacuation of soldiers from Dunkirk in 1940, as well as rescuing many downed pilots during the Battle of Britain.

The RNLI has a system of Gold, Silver and Bronze medals awarded to its members for bravery in rescues. The youngest recipient was Frederick Carter, who was 11 years old at the time. Grace Darling was the daughter of a lighthouse keeper who rowed the boat she and her father used to rescue nine people from the SS Forfarshire in 1838. She was praised for her heroism and awarded an RNLI Silver Medal for gallantry.

Sites to Visit

The RNLI Headquarters is on West Quay Road, in Poole, Dorset. It houses historical archives in its library, as well as a model lifeboat collection and other memorabilia. There is also a shop, but visits to the archives are by appointment only.

The RNLI Historic Lifeboat Collection is at The Historic Dockyard, Chatham, in Kent. It is open

Punch cartoon celebrating the RNLI on the occasion of Queen Victoria conveying her appreciation in saving the crew and passengers of the steamship Eider, 1892.

every day from 10 am to 6 pm from February to the end of October.

There are several RNLI Lifeboat Stations museums, including the stations at Salcombe, Devon; Eastbourne, East Sussex; Whitby, Yorkshire; and Cromer, Norfolk.

The Grace Darling Museum is on Radcliffe Road in Bamburgh, Northumberland.

A large number of the 237 RNLI Lifeboat Stations around the coast have open days during the summer months. A number are in historic buildings.

Visitors to the Isle of Man will find a memorial to the 1830 rescue of the St George, in the sunken garden on Loch Promenade, Douglas. The Tower of Refuge, looking like a castle, was built by Sir William Hillary in 1832 on Conister Rock, in Douglas Bay, so that sailors who were shipwrecked there could take refuge until they could be rescued. The Tower was stocked with water and provisions.

GREAT BRITISH ICONS: LAND ROVER

By David Goodfellow

From the grouse moors of Scotland to the African savanna and the Australian outback, nothing said 'off-road freedom' like the Land Rover. Inspired by the US Army Jeep, and designed for farmers, the first basic Land Rover, painted in army-surplus green, was revealed at the Amsterdam Motor Show in 1948. The Rover company was born in Coventry, as a bicycle brand, created by John Farley, a gardener's son. In the early boom days of the British car industry Rover had only limited success, until it created the Land Rover. It found favor not only among farmers and the landed gentry, but even more so overseas, where for a while it totally dominated the market for four-wheel-drive in Australia, Africa, and the Middle East. In the chaos resulting from the creation of British Leyland, Rover lost its dominance, never to return, although the Land Rover continued to innovate and improve, reaching its functional zenith with the Land Rover Defender, produced from 1983 to 2016. Unable to comply with contemporary safety regulations it ceased production, but it may soon be reborn.

It seems like a long jump from a conventional bicycle to a four-wheel-drive off-road vehicle, but both came from the same company, which began in 1877 as Starley & Sutton Co. The genes for inventiveness seem to run in families, and the Starley family were well supplied. James Farley was the son of a farmer, with a knack for fixing things. He was working as a gardener, but when he startled his employer by improving an early sewing machine, he was quickly given a job by the manufacturer, the Coventry Sewing Machine Company. When his nephew John turned up one day with an early French bicycle, the business decided to start making bicycles too, and Coventry soon became the center for a new British industry. James Starley perfected the chain drive and developed the differential gear, which makes motor cars possible, regulating the speed of the paired wheels as they go around curves.

Nephew John was no slacker in inventions either, and he started Starley & Sutton Co. with a fellow enthusiast for bicycles. They adopted the brand-name 'Rover' for their machines, and in 1885 produced the first 'modern' bicycle. Previously the Penny-farthing style was normal, with a large front wheel and a much smaller rear wheel. Starley's bike, called the Rover Safety Bike, had wheels about the same size, and rear-wheel drive from pedals and a chain, and it looked pretty much like a modern bike. In the late 1980s, the company changed its name to the Rover Cycle Company Ltd. In 1901 Starley died, only 46 years old, and under the new director, Harry Smyth (or Smith), they began to build motorcycles.

Starley himself had brought over a French Peugeot motorcycle to test, and by the end of 1902 Rover released their first motorbike, the 3.5HP Rover Imperial. A year later they were manufacturing cars, in the rapidly-expanding and fluid Coventry motor car industry, alongside names like Armstrong-Siddeley, Humber, Wolseley, and Standard. The company had limited success, although it kept going through WWI and into the 1920s. After a major capital reduction – always a sign of an ailing company – new management was brought in. This was Frank Searle, who became Managing Director in 1928. Searle had already made a name for himself with Daimler, at that time a British company, in buses and with aircraft at Imperial Airways, and under his direction, the company began to improve. After a major re-structuring Searle left in 1931, and despite losses during the early years of the Depression, the company began to thrive, and make profits. During WWII Rover built engines and airframes for the government, and also built experimental cars using gas turbine and diesel engines. They began to build a reputation for quality cars rivaling Rolls-Royce and Daimler, with cars like the Rover 12 Sports Tourer.

In the end, their signature vehicle was not to be a luxury model, but a working car, suited to farms and hunting, and so favored by the landed gentry. It began in 1947 in the mind of Maurice Wilks, chief designer at Rover, who had been brought in

KEY FACTS

- Based on the US Army Jeep
- The first British 4x4 vehicle
- Widely used globally for off-road driving
- Went through many model changes, culminating in the Defender (which was discontinued recently).

from the Hillman Motor Company by his brother Spencer, managing director of Rover since 1932. Maurice had an American war-surplus Jeep at his farm in Anglesey, Wales, and he and his brother were inspired by this to develop a four-wheel-drive utility vehicle for farmers – the Land Rover. After building several prototypes on Jeep chassis, the new vehicle was launched at the 1948 Amsterdam Motor Show.

The iconic green color was a product of post-war rationing, which continued in the UK into the 1950s. The only paint available was military surplus aircraft cockpit paint, so that was it – khaki green. The first models – Series I – were very basic, and even the canvas roof was an 'extra.' The modest engine produced just 56HP, and the four-wheel-drive operated by pulling on a ring in the driver's footwell. A more luxurious 7-seater station wagon version was soon offered, with a body built by Tickford, a coachbuilder going back to the 1820s. Series I was produced until 1957, with continuous improvements added during that decade, including a larger engine and a longer wheelbase.

Series II, released in 1958, had more style, the result of the eye of Rover's Chief Stylist David Bache. It looked less like a Jeep and more 'British,' with discrete curves and a neater frame. The engine, which would remain standard until the mid-80s, was a petrol engine delivering 72HP. Due to the vagaries of taxation laws, the 12-seater station wagon was cheap, since it was classified as a mini-bus. This made it very popular as a country vehicle, ideal for a shooting expedition with men, guns, dogs, and whisky or gin.

The Series II continued until 1961 when the Series IIA was introduced. The main difference was a diesel engine, but what stood out was the headlight position, in the square wheel wings. This vehicle became the 'Land Rover' of the popular imagination, seen in adventure documentaries, and on the African plains in films like 'Born Free.'

In 1967, Rover was acquired by the Leyland Motor Corporation, a holding company owning by that time numerous once-independent manufacturers. This was all part of a misguided attempt by the British government to create a car giant to rival Ford and Chrysler. By 1977, England was a net importer of cars, and the end result was the destruction of the British car industry, but that is another story.

Rover continued to operate quasi-independently, reaching a total production of almost 600,000 Land Rovers by 1968, 20 years after that first prototype. 70% of these were exported, and by 1969 production of the Series IIA peaked, at 60,000 a year. In Australia, Africa, and the Middle East, Land Rover dominated the four-wheel-drive market, capturing as much as 90% of the business. At home, the military became a large buyer of vehicles, often modified for military use. Land Rovers were used during the Korean War and the Suez Crisis.

Series III was a very similar car, with minor changes, but it became the most common, with 440,000 produced between 1971 and 1985. But the good times never last, and during the 1970s the problems of British Leyland began to impact Rover, especially in its vital export markets. Long waiting lists, inferior quality and a loss of image led to its replacement in the Australian, African and Middle East Markets by Japanese equivalents, and by 1983 the Toyota Land Cruiser was the biggest-selling four-wheel-drive vehicle in Australia.

In 1983 a new model was introduced, variously called the Land Rover 110, Land Rover 90, or Land Rover 127, depending on the length of the wheelbase. Although very similar in appearance to the Series III, these vehicles had spring suspension for a smoother ride, an improved four-wheel-drive system, a modernized interior, and increasingly stronger engines. This new car turned around British and European sales, but it failed to reverse the decline in the overseas market. In 1990 the vehicle was re-named the Land Rover Defender. The biggest improvement in this vehicle was the engine – the turbodiesel 200TDi. This 107HP engine gave the Land Rover, for the first time, road cruising ability, and greater towing ability, both with reasonable fuel economy.

During this period Rover itself went through numerous business changes. In 1986 British Leyland became the 'Rover Group.' In 1988 the Rover Group became a private part of British Aerospace. In 1994 it was taken over by the German carmaker BMW, who, in 2000, broke it up, selling Land Rover to Ford Motors for £1.8 billion. In 2008 Ford sold Land Rover (and Jaguar) to the Indian car companies Tata Motors and Mahindra & Mahindra Ltd. During all this time Land Rovers continued to roll off the production lines, along with the more luxurious Range Rover, Discovery, and

other models.

In the end, it was increased concerns over safety, and the introduction of new regulations, that ended the Land Rover. To meet these, particularly air-bag requirements, needed a complete re-modeling of the vehicle, so at least temporarily, the last Land Rover Defender came off the line on the morning of Friday, the 29th of January 2016. A replacement is possible as early as 2019.

Sites to Visit

- Land Rover Classic Experiences offers the opportunity to drive vintage Land Rovers on the Eastnor Estate, in Herefordshire.
- Vintage Land Rovers are part of the Classics Work Tour, at Prologis Park Ryton, Oxford Road, Ryton-on-Dunsmore, Coventry.
- The production facilities at the Solihull plant can be visited: The Jaguar Visitor Centre, Jaguar Land Rover, Solihull, Lode Lane, Solihull, West Midlands

Further Research

- Land Rover: The Story of the Car that Conquered the World, by Ben Fogle
- Land Rover: 65 Years of the 4 x 4 Workhorse, by James Taylor
- Land Rover: Simply the Best, by Martin Hodder
- Land-Rover Series I, II & III: Guide to Purchase & D.I.Y. Restoration, by Lindsay Porter
- Land Rover Defender, by Mike Gould
- Land Rover 90 - 110 - Defender Workshop Manual 1983-1995, by Brooklands Books Ltd

THE SLANG PAGE
British Motoring Terms

AA – abbr – The British Automobile Association, whom you call when your car breaks down.
A Road - n - A main road, usually a dual-carriageway.
Average Speed Camera - n - A hated speeding cameara that averages out your speed during your entire time during a specific stretch of road. Don't exceed the average speed!
B Road - n - A minor road, usually off an A Road, sometimes a single track. We would call them the 'backroads.'
Bollard – n – Metal post that usually indicates a place one should not drive into.
Bonnet – n – The hood of a car.
Boot – n – The car's trunk, opposite of the bonnet.
Camper van – n – Recreational vehicle.
Car boot sale – n – Swap meet or flea market where people sell items from the back of their car.
Car park – n – Parking lot or parking garage.
Caravan – n – Another term for Recreational Vehicle.
Caravan Park – n – Campsite for recreational vehicles and trailers
Cat's eyes – n – Reflectors located on the road in the center line.
Central Reservation – n – The median between two opposite sides of a road.
Chelsea Tractor - n - A derogatory term for the fancy SUV's that rich people drive in the nice parts of London (that often never see the countryside).
Damper – n – The shock absorber on a car.
Dual carriageway – n – A divided highway a step down from a motorway.
Estate car – n – A station wagon.
Gear lever – n – The stick shift in a manual car.
Give Way - v - Yield
Golf buggy – n – Golf cart.
GPS - n - A turn-by-turn navigation system. Often directions will tell you not to trust GPS.
Handbrake – n – Parking/ Emergency brake in a car.
Hard shoulder – n – Shoulder on the side of the road that's paved.
High street – n – Main street.
Hire car – n – A rental car.
Indicator – n – Turning signal in a car.
Kerb – n – A curb.
Kerb crawler – n – A person who solicits street prostitutes.
L-plates – n – Special license plates you're required to have on your car while learning to drive in the UK.
Lay-by – n – Rest area along the highways.
Lorry – adj – A semi or heavy goods truck.
Manual gearbox – n – A manual transmission on a car. Simply known as a manual.
Motor – n – An antiquated term for an automobile.
Motorbike - n - A motorcycle.
Motorway – n – The equivalent would be an interstate highway.
Nearside – n – The side of the car that's closest to the curb.
Number plate – n – License plate.
Pavement – n – The sidewalk.
Pelican crossing – n – A type of crosswalk on British streets.
Puncture – n – Flat tire.
Registration – n – A car's license plate.
Roundabout – n – A traffic circle.
Saloon – n – Standard 4 door family sedan car.
Services - n - Rest areas where you can get fuel and usually eat (there's often a hotel too).
Single Track Lane - n - A type of road where there is only one lane, with occasional turn-off for people to get by.
Sleeping policemen – n – A speed bump in the road.
Slip-road – n – An exit on/off ramp on a highway.
Soft-Shoulder – n – Roadside shoulder that's made of gravel.
Tarmac – n – A paved road.
Traffic Light – n – Stoplight
Trailer tent – n – A pop-up camper.
Undercarriage – n – The underside of your car.
Verge – n – Shoulder on the side of the road.
Wave - v - The Wave is often just a lifted finger from the other driver when you let them pass.
Windscreen – n – Windshield.
Wing – n – Car fender.
Zebra crossing – n – Pedestrian crossings on roads.

ANGLOTOPIA
THE MAGAZINE FOR ANGLOPHILES
ISSUE #12 WINTER/CHRISTMAS 2018

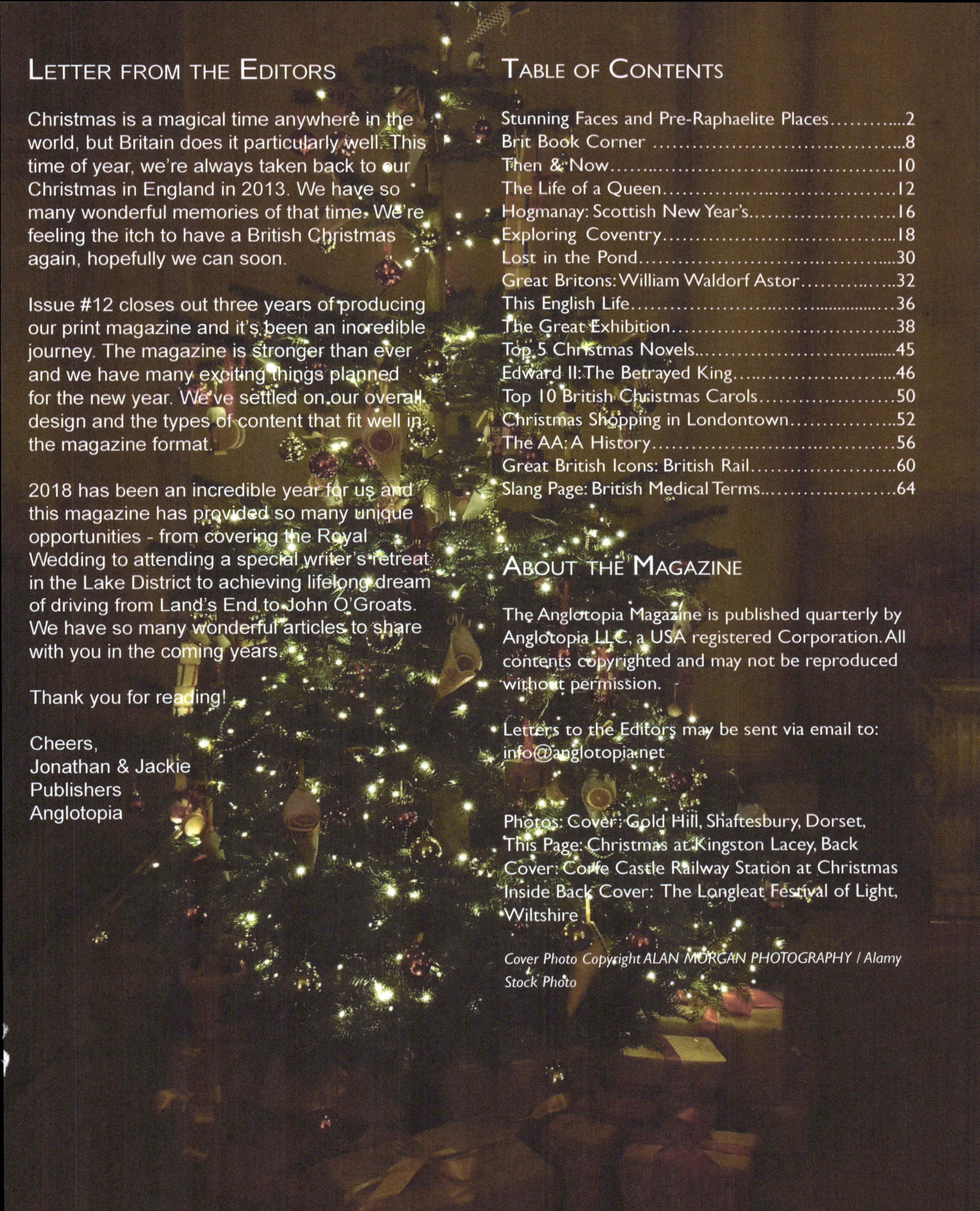

Letter from the Editors

Christmas is a magical time anywhere in the world, but Britain does it particularly well. This time of year, we're always taken back to our Christmas in England in 2013. We have so many wonderful memories of that time. We're feeling the itch to have a British Christmas again, hopefully we can soon.

Issue #12 closes out three years of producing our print magazine and it's been an incredible journey. The magazine is stronger than ever and we have many exciting things planned for the new year. We've settled on our overall design and the types of content that fit well in the magazine format.

2018 has been an incredible year for us and this magazine has provided so many unique opportunities - from covering the Royal Wedding to attending a special writer's retreat in the Lake District to achieving lifelong dream of driving from Land's End to John O'Groats. We have so many wonderful articles to share with you in the coming years.

Thank you for reading!

Cheers,
Jonathan & Jackie
Publishers
Anglotopia

Table of Contents

Stunning Faces and Pre-Raphaelite Places..............2
Brit Book Corner 8
Then & Now..10
The Life of a Queen..12
Hogmanay: Scottish New Year's...........................16
Exploring Coventry..18
Lost in the Pond...30
Great Britons: William Waldorf Astor..................32
This English Life...36
The Great Exhibition..38
Top 5 Christmas Novels.......................................45
Edward II: The Betrayed King...............................46
Top 10 British Christmas Carols..........................50
Christmas Shopping in Londontown....................52
The AA: A History..56
Great British Icons: British Rail............................60
Slang Page: British Medical Terms......................64

About the Magazine

The Anglotopia Magazine is published quarterly by Anglotopia LLC, a USA registered Corporation. All contents copyrighted and may not be reproduced without permission.

Letters to the Editors may be sent via email to: info@anglotopia.net

Photos: Cover: Gold Hill, Shaftesbury, Dorset, This Page: Christmas at Kingston Lacey, Back Cover: Corfe Castle Railway Station at Christmas Inside Back Cover: The Longleat Festival of Light, Wiltshire

Cover Photo Copyright ALAN MORGAN PHOTOGRAPHY / Alamy Stock Photo

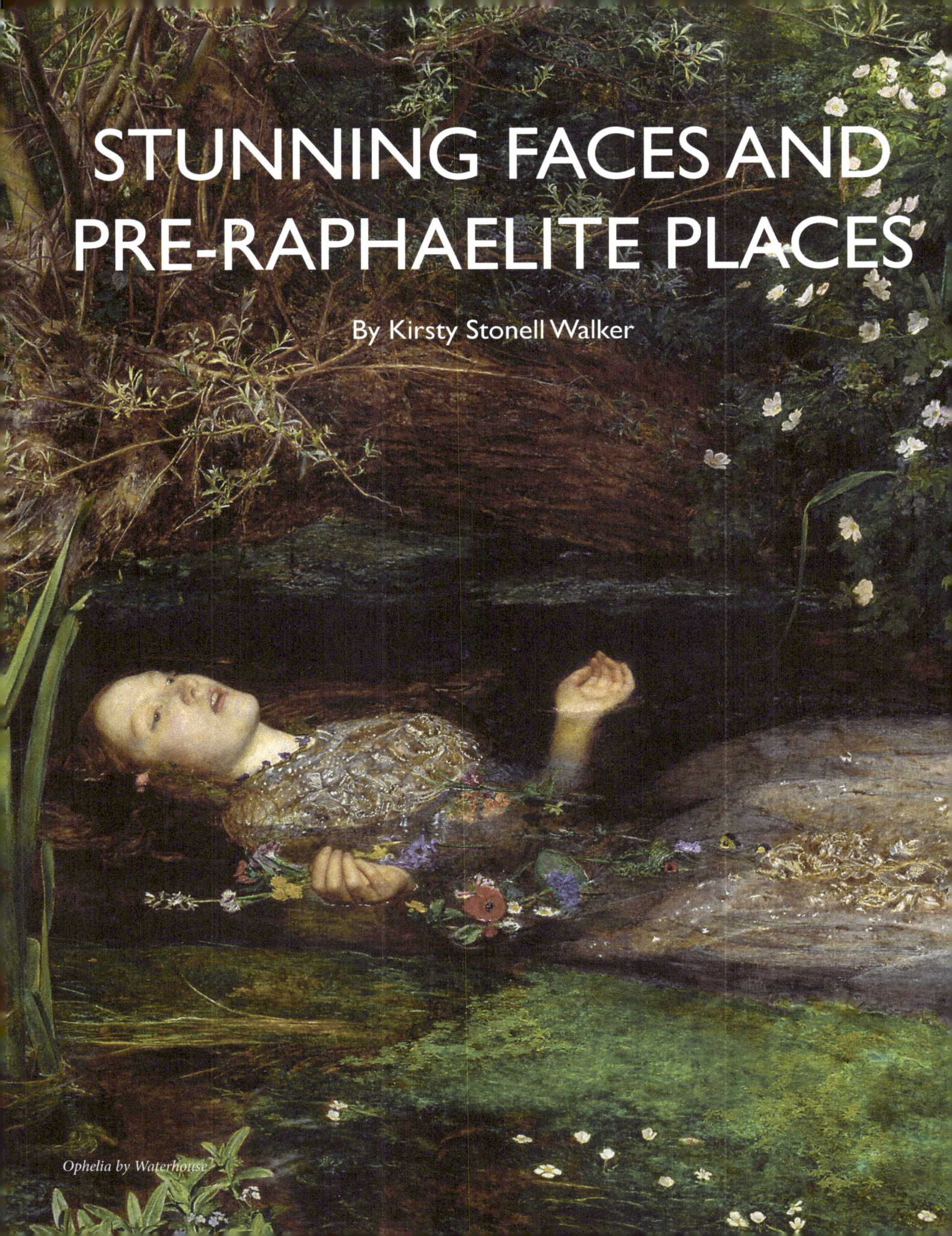

STUNNING FACES AND PRE-RAPHAELITE PLACES

By Kirsty Stonell Walker

Ophelia by Waterhouse

There has been renewed interest in the art of the Pre-Raphaelites over the last few years including some high profile exhibitions currently touring America. The paintings of this group of nineteenth-century young art rebels, who valued truth to nature in their highly detailed, vividly color paintings, inspire a fascination in the artists themselves: Dante Gabriel Rossetti, the Italian romantic, John Everett Millais, the child prodigy, and William Holman Hunt, the religious maniac, gave voice to a movement of art that drew in artists for almost a century. In an attempt to take art back to a time before Raphael, these 'Pre-Raphaelite' artists found the faces for their truth in working-class women they christened 'Stunners.' Their ability to not only find beauty in ordinary women but to exalt these women to positions of queens, goddesses and heroines of literature caused early critics such as Charles Dickens to ridicule them, but slowly they changed the face of beauty.

Before the Pre-Raphaelites, the standards of female beauty had much to do with the image of small, dark-haired Queen Victoria. Women were praised for being slight and almost frail, with smooth, tightly bound dark hair. The women of Pre-Raphaelite art had loose copper hair or a wild abundance of curls of frizz, dressed in loose flowing gowns. Scandalously, the names of these models became known alongside those of the artists. Elizabeth Siddal, artist and poet as well as model and mistress to Dante Gabriel Rossetti, is now well-known to gallery-going art lovers, especially as the face of John Everett Millais' Ophelia (1851). Others such as Jane Morris and Fanny Cornforth are the subjects of researchers who want to know more about the muses behind such stunning paintings. Their lives tell us much about the position of women in such a bohemian slice of an otherwise rigid society, and it is possible to walk in their footsteps and visit their homes and haunts. The following are three pilgrimages with stories of love and loss, beauty and sadness that are as inspiring to the modern visitor as they were to the artists over a century and a half ago.

Starting in London, it is possible to visit a great many sites of Pre-Raphaelite interest in England. Despite the Second World War bombings and the post-War 'redevelopment,' key buildings can still be visited so you can experience standing in the place of a Victorian supermodel. The alleyway where Elizabeth Siddal was discovered by a friend of the Pre-Raphaelites, Walter Deverell, working in Mrs. Tozier's hat shop can be visited at 3 Cranbourne Street, north of Leicester Square. Similarly, in Red Lion Square, where Rossetti, Edward Burne-Jones, and William Morris lived, it is almost possible to feel the spirit of 'Red Lion Mary,' the young artists' patient housekeeper, forever putting up with their antics whiles appearing in some of their early sketches. Elizabeth Siddal's grave is something of a Mecca for Pre-Raphaelite lovers, within the Rossetti family plot at Highgate Cemetery. She is buried beside her poet sister-in-law Christina Rossetti, but not her erstwhile husband, Dante Gabriel Rossetti. After he arranged for her to be disinterred to retrieve a book of poems he had romantically buried with her, he swore he would never be buried beside Elizabeth for fear she would crawl into his coffin to take her posthumous revenge.

On a far more cheery note, a short walk in Chelsea reveals two great romances in the Pre-Raphaelite story. Starting at 59 Cheyne Walk in 'Prospect Place' where William Holman Hunt had his studio, you can see the Cross Keys public house. It was here in the early 1850s that Hunt, desperate to discover his own 'stunner' to inspire his art, saw barmaid Annie Miller and fell in love. Annie was the strong-willed and independent daughter of a Chelsea Pensioner (retired soldier) left to support her sister, Harriet. She jumped at the chance to model for Hunt, which was considerably easier and safer work than the pub. Hunt fell in love with her and promised to marry her if she took lessons to learn to be a lady. Whilst envisaging My Fair Lady but with a happy ending, Hunt didn't take into account Annie's feelings and the romance was not destined to end well. Annie and Hunt parted ways, and Annie moved to the south coast to have a long and happy life, well away from Pre-Raphaelite artists.

Walking along Cheyne Walk, you will reach number 16, also known as the Queen's House or more commonly Tudor House, the home of Dante Gabriel Rossetti from 1863 until his death. He had been living 14 Chatham Place, Blackfriars (now sadly demolished), but after his wife's tragic death from an overdose of laudanum, he could not bear to remain there and moved to Chelsea. It was in the wide back garden there that he had a wild menagerie of animals, from peacocks to wombats,

Kelmscott Manor

William Morris

The Lady of Shalott by Waterhouse

and chasing them around was his lover, Fanny Cornforth. Fanny had been a country girl from Sussex, who had come to London seeking better fortune. She met Rossetti at a public celebration for the return of Florence Nightingale from the Crimean War, and the artist was instantly besotted with her long wild hair and no-nonsense approach to love and life. She was not so popular with Rossetti's friends who found her loud and common, but Rossetti remained fond of her until the end of his life. To keep her close, Rossetti rented a house for her which can be found at 36 Royal Avenue, a short walk from Tudor House. From here it might well have been possible to see or even access the back garden of Tudor House, and Rossetti, who suffered mental health and addiction issues for the last decades of his life must have been comforted to have her close at hand.

If like Annie Miller, you wish to escape London, many Pre-Raphaelite places can be found along the south coast of England. Rossetti died in a bungalow in Birchington-on-Sea, far to the east, and his Celtic cross gravestone, designed by friend Ford Madox Brown, was visited by his friends and models in his lonely Kentish corner of England. Traveling west, you will find Rossetti in happier times. Hastings is the town where, in 1860, Rossetti rushed to the sick bed of Elizabeth Siddal, fearing she was about to die. He swore that he would marry her if she recovered and as soon as she had strength enough, he carried her to St Clement's Church close to the High Street house where they spent their honeymoon. For a brief time the couple were blissfully happy by the seaside, and despite the events of the two years that followed, it is possible in the narrow streets and pretty houses to see the charm and romance of this seaside town.

Traveling still further west along the main south coast road, you will pass other homes of Pre-Raphaelite women. Annie Miller married the cousin of Lord Ranelagh, Captain Thomas Thomson, and lived happily at Shoreham-by-Sea, where she is buried in an unmarked grave in the cemetery there. Fanny Cornforth's origins can be discovered in Steyning, just outside of Brighton, where she was known as plain Sarah Cox, the daughter of a

Clockwise from Top Left: 36 Royal Avenue, Holman Hunt Studio, North End House Rottingdean, The Cross Keys Public House

blacksmith. Far removed from the poverty and illness of Fanny's village home is Rottingdean, a delightful village which was home to the Burne-Jones family. Margaret Burne-Jones married in the aptly-named St Margaret of Antioch church where there is a St Margaret window, designed by her father, the artist, and designer Edward Burne-Jones. The family home, North End House can be seen across the village green, where Georgiana Burne-Jones protested the Boer War by hanging a banner from her windows. A woman of strong opinions, Georgiana was never afraid of standing up for what she believed in, not only in national politics but also locally, as a parish councilor.

If you are after a more traditional and poetic side of Pre-Raphaelite women's lives, then walking in the footsteps of Jane Morris is your best bet. From her humble beginnings in Oxford to the bittersweet homes of her marriage, it is possible to follow Jane through her rags to riches life to a greater extent than any other woman in the Pre-Raphaelite movement. St Helen's Passage is the address of Jane's family home in Oxford, a narrow corridor filled with slum homes of the poor workers of the city, now marked with a blue plaque. Tall, ungainly Jane was not expected to do well in life, but she was thrust into the spotlight by the Pre-Raphaelite artists who found her stature and unusual looks to be exactly what they wanted for their vision of a romantic, Medieval England. The designer William Morris fell deeply in love with Jane and married her, despite the difference in their social standing. He built the Red House for her, a grand Arts and Craft home now preserved by the National Trust in Bexleyheath, just south of London.

As the Morris family grew, they sought out a summer home, away from the noise and pollution of London and looked west to Kelmscott Manor in Gloucestershire. Kelmscott not only provided a healthy family home for the Morris's two young daughters, but also an illicit romantic hideaway for Jane and her lover Dante Gabriel Rossetti, William

St Margaret's Church

Morris's best friend. Morris accepted his wife's infidelity and gave the couple the time and space to conduct their affair, traveling to Iceland during the summer months. Kelmscott remained with the Morris family, even after the death of William Morris in 1896 and then Jane in 1914. One of Jane's last acts was to buy the manor house for her two daughters to live in. A final love story happened at Kelmscott in the years after the First World War when an outspoken, boisterous Land Girl came to work for May. Miss Mary Lobb stayed by May Morris's side until her death in 1938 and brought much-needed joy and laughter to the manor. She died of a broken heart less than a year after May.

The joy of visiting the homes and haunts of the Pre-Raphaelite women is that it illuminates the lives of the women that we would otherwise only experience through the eyes of the artists. By visiting the humble homes of Jane and Fanny shows you how far they came in their life-journeys, all the way to the walls of national art galleries. Georgiana's traditional home is at odds with her political stand against the war. Annie's flight from London to the peace of the south coast shows you the impact the Pre-Raphaelite circle had on the lives of both the artists and their models. By walking in their footsteps, it is possible to appreciate the models not just as beautiful faces on a canvas but as real women whose homes and haunts were witness to their lives, loves, joys and tears.

Pre-Raphaelite Girl Gang will introduce readers of all ages to the remarkable women of the Pre-Raphaelite art movement which began in the second half of the nineteenth century and continued through the early part of the twentieth. From models to artists, these women all contributed something personal and incredible towards the most beautiful and imaginative art movement in the world.

BRIT BOOK CORNER

A Royal Christmas - Royal Trust Collection

Many of the Christmas traditions that are celebrated around the world originated with royalty around the world. It was Prince Albert and Queen Victoria that had the first Christmas that we would recognize today. This is the first book ever published about Royal Christmases put out by The Royal Trust Collection. This book feels luxurious, relevant to its subject matter. The book starts with Queen Charlotte's first Christmas as Queen all the way to the current Queen, Elizabeth II, highlighting favorite Christmas memories, and traditions of the Royal Family. The book is beautifully illustrated and has numerous pictures, making it the perfect book to sit on a coffee table during the holidays. By far, one of my most favorite chapters was on Christmas Menus; it was interesting to see how tastes changed over the years. There was also a very informative chapter on the history of the Christmas Address, the message given by the monarch each year on Christmas day. This book is a wonderful treasure for royal fans and fans of Christmas too. This 140-page book is so beautifully done, that it is a treasure in itself and would make a beautiful Christmas gift. Royal Trust Collection $24.95

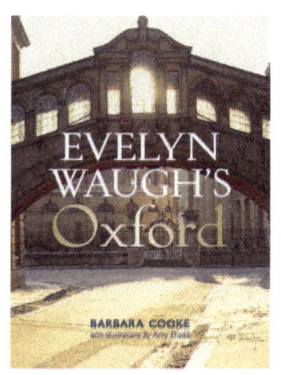

Evelyn Waugh's Oxford by Barbara Cooke

Brideshead Revisited is one of my most favorite British books and British dramas as well. So it was with great excitement that I received a copy of Evelyn Waugh's Oxford. Oxford played a huge role in Waugh's life, and as a consequence, it also played a significant role in his writing. This handy little book is a guide to all those connections. The author, Barbara Cooke, does a great job at providing lots of background of Waugh's actual experiences in Oxford and how they related to the books he wrote. The first half of the book is an exploration of Waugh's life and relationship to the city while the latter half focuses on specific places and how they relate to his works. I must confess that I've only read two of Waugh's works, so many of the references were lost on me simply because I haven't read all his books. But my one major takeaway from reading about his catalog of works is that I now really want to read them all. The book is short and informative - I highly recommend it even for casual Waugh fans. If you like Brideshead Revisited and Oxford, you will find this book interesting. Bodleian Library $35.00

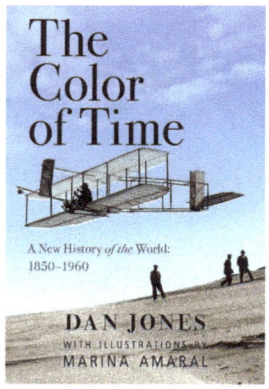

The Color of Time by Dan Jones and Marina Amaral

While this book is not strictly British related, it's a pretty awesome book with lots of British stuff in it (and one of the authors is British). The Color of Time takes iconic black and white pictures and colorizes them in a natural way, providing a new way to look at some amazing history. Highly recommend for any History buff! Some of the pictures inside are just amazing and once color was added to them - it really brings historical figures and events alive for you. About the book: "It spans more than one hundred years of world history from the reign of Queen Victoria and the American Civil War to the Cuban Missile Crisis and the beginning of the Space Age. It charts the rise and fall of empires, the achievements of science, industrial developments, the arts, the tragedies of war, the politics of peace, and the lives of men and women who made history. This illustrated narrative is a collaboration between a gifted Brazilian artist and a New York Times bestselling British historian. Marina Amaral has created two hundred stunning images, using rare photographs as the basis for her full-color digital renditions. Dan Jones has written a narrative that anchors each image in its context and weaves them into a vivid account of the world that we live in today." Pegasus Books $39.95

The Knowledge - By Robert Lordan

London Cabbies are among the best cab drivers in the world, if not the best. Their skill is not by accident or chance; it is through hard work and something called The Knowledge. All London Taxi cab drivers must learn "The Knowledge" a six-mile radius around Charing Cross Train Station, is the memorization of every bit of roadway in this circle. Sometimes it can take years to accomplish and complete "the knowledge." Lordan, a London taxi cab driver, gives some insight into what this feat takes and how hopeful drivers go about learning one of the busiest and most complex cities in the world. Each chapter is broken down into "runs" as the cabbies call them, or segments of the map. Each chapter has a hand-drawn illustration, pointing out unique London landmarks, tucked into side-streets and alleyways. At the back of the book, there is also a wonderful selection of "cabbie slang." This small black book is well organized and the perfect primer for anyone wanting to test their skill and learn more about what it takes to cut it as a London taxi cab driver. Quercus Publishing $19.99

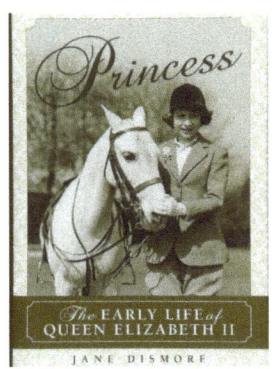

Princess- By Jane Dismore

Princess by Jane Dismore is a detailed and unique look into the early life of Elizabeth II. While there have been many wonderful books written about the Queen's life, this book is special in that it really delves deep into a specific time in her life, her early years until she became the Queen in 1952. The book starts with Elizabeth's sense of duty coming into fruition at ten as her Father, became the King of England. From there the book chronicles the Queen's teen years, what it was like to grow up as a Princess. It also goes into detail about the first time The Queen met Prince Phillip at the age of thirteen. This comprehensive look at The Queen's remarkable life also covers her time during WWII, as she worked as a mechanic. It goes on to look at her early marriage with Phillip. This book was well researched an made a great companion to Netflix's show The Crown. Dismore took her time and lovingly did her research to put this beautiful book together. There is also a nice selection of photographs that chronicle and add to the richness of this book. This book is a sure hit with Royal Fans! Lyons Press $26.95

Beside the Seaside by John Heywood

An interesting book on the history of Yorkshire's seaside resorts. A very granular book but also a good survey of English seaside holidays in general. This short book is an excellent view on British seaside culture through history. This book will appeal particularly to those with a connection to Yorkshire, as that is the focus of the book. About the book: "Almost all of us have happy memories of excursions and holidays spent beside the sea. For many, these will have included the Yorkshire coast which runs unbroken for more than one hundred miles between the two great rivers, the Tees and the Humber. Within those boundaries are the popular seaside resorts of Whitby, Scarborough, Filey, and Bridlington as well as numerous smaller and quieter but equally well-loved destinations. How did the love affair with the area start and how did it develop? Over the years, all the ingredients for the perfect holiday are there - the spas, the sea and sunbathing, board and lodgings, entertainment and just as importantly, the journeys there and back. "Beside the Seaside" takes a detailed but entertaining look back at the history of these resorts over the last four hundred years and asks, "what does the future hold?" Packed with information, this book is fully illustrated with photographs, old and new, together with paintings and etchings. Coupled with the thoughts and memories of tourists and travelers from the 17th century through to the present time, it gives a fascinating insight into how our ancestors would have spent their time at the coast." Pen & Sword Books $29.95

THEN - Victorian Christmas Tree

The romanticized image of Christmas was a trend started by Victoria and Albert during her reign. It was an effort to paint the portrait of the perfect Victorian family. The Christmas Tree, a tradition started in Albert's Germanic homeland was incorporated into the Royal Family's Christmas, which set a trend in wider society, creating one of the most enduring Christmas traditions in the Western Christian World. The tree was much the same then as it is today - except live burning candles were used to light the tree - a considerable fire hazard.

NOW - Anglotopia's British Christmas Tree

The modern British Christmas tree hasn't changed much since Victoria's age - except that they now use safe lighting that doesn't catch fire! Ornaments are still placed on the tree and presents are still nestled underneath the branches for children to open on Christmas day. We had the pleasure of experiencing a British Christmas in 2013 and this was the tree provided by the kind friends who owned the cottage we stayed in. While it was very different from the tree we were used to back home, it was very British and we loved it to bits.

THE LIFE OF A QUEEN
Life of a Princess in Wartime

When World War II started in September 1939, King George VI was still a new king with a young family; Winston Churchill was gearing up to bolster his nation in enduring the long war ("Never surrender!"); and the future Queen Elizabeth was just thirteen years old. Those years of war turned out to be some of her most formative years, teaching her more than she would ever have learned in peacetime, working harder than she thought possible, meeting people she would not have met otherwise, and facing grief and turmoil right alongside her country.

The war years must have seemed very uncertain for young Elizabeth. Sure, she was unlikely to lose everything she owned like some people in London, but when your family is dedicated to service to your country and your country's future is at stake, and your parents are in the thick of the danger, Lilibet had a lot to be concerned about. With the start of the war, the King and Queen were urged to send the two princesses off to Canada to keep them safe. This was not an unreasonable request—Hitler and his armies immediately proved aggressive and ruthless, kids all over Great Britain were being evacuated to safer locations. But the Queen Mother was insistent that she would not be separated from her daughters or her husband, and since George VI wouldn't budge from London, they were all staying in the country.

When war broke out, the family was in Balmoral for their summer holiday, although the King and Queen soon returned to London. It was in the Highlands of Scotland that young Elizabeth got her first glimpse of wartime deprivations. In what was probably her first service in wartime, Lilibet helped her mother host tea for women and children displaced by the war. This would prove to be a recurring theme for the future Queen during the war—as a young teenager herself she seemed the perfect one to minister to the children left behind or sent away.

In 1939 the family kept to their tradition of spending Christmas at the royal estate in Norfolk, Sandringham. But after that initial popping around the countryside, the family settled into what would be their home for the duration of the war. Elizabeth and Margaret would spend almost all of their war years just outside the city, in Windsor, while their parents would stay at Buckingham Palace a few miles away in London. Being a royal residence of considerable size, Windsor Castle was seen as a target for the German forces because Windsor was quickly fortified, fitted with barbed wire, anti-aircraft guns, bomb shelters, and black-out curtains. Fearing a land invasion, King George even removed the gems from the Imperial Crown and buried them in a cookie tin under one of the entrances to Windsor Castle, as well as removing the priceless artwork from the walls and sending it off to a more secluded and secure estate.

Lilibet did her share of protecting Margaret, as well, remarking, "I don't think people should talk about battle and things in front of Margaret. We don't want to upset her." Lilibet clearly knew there was something to be worried about, especially after they spent their first night in the bomb shelter at Windsor. Crawfie, their beloved nanny and governess, describes it this way: "The shelter was in one of the dungeons, not a particularly inviting place anyway. There lingered about it always the memory of others who had probably been incarcerated there and left some of their unhappiness behind them. The atmosphere was gloomy, and there were beetles." They would spend many nights down there, although after that first time the staff did a little more clearing out the doom and gloom, making it seem a bit homier and less beetle-y.

Continuing her outreach to the children displaced by war, Elizabeth gave her first radio broadcast in 1940 on the BBC program Children's Hour, addressed to children evacuated overseas. At just age 14, she very sweetly and confidently reassures the children listening, giving them hope and comfort, speaking of "victory" and "when peace comes." In the end, we even hear little Margaret wish everyone "good night, children." The future Queen seems warm and sympathetic; something people will compliment her on for years to come.

Life at Windsor during the war wasn't always quite so heavy, however. Crawfie was there with them and wanted to bring some fun and distraction into the home. She arranged pantomimes for the young princesses to act in, partly as entertainment and diversion for them and the staff, and partly as a fundraiser for the Queen's war efforts. Crawfie also decided to continue the Girl Guides on the estate at Windsor, but this time with local girls (traveling was difficult and dangerous, they couldn't bring in their own crowd of young nobility). This was maybe the first time that Lilibet mixed with the children from the village, it was probably a refreshing surprise—they didn't curtsy, and they even dared call her Lilibet.

Besides the barbed wire and other measures taken to protect the young princesses, the Grenadier Guards were placed at Windsor for protection. Lilibet acted as hostess to these soldiers, getting to know them and including them in their activities. At age 16, young Elizabeth was named an honorary colonel in the Grenadier Guards. This protection did not immune her to the grief and suffering of war, though. Just as in other places the country, hot water was rationed at Windsor, the windows were blown out, and she got to know some of the guards protecting her who later fought and died overseas. Her mother wrote, "Lilibet meets young Grenadiers at Windsor, and then they get killed. It is horrid for someone so young." The young Elizabeth, sadly, got very good at sending letters to the guards' families, offering her heartfelt condolences and sympathies.

The young princesses became even more acquainted with grief when they lost a member of their own family. Their uncle, Prince George, Duke of Kent, the King's younger brother, was serving with the Royal Air Force during the war. In 1942 his plane crashed in Scotland on the way home from a mission. He was the first member of the royal family to die in battle in 500 years. The Windsors were mourning along with the rest of the country.

Lilibet was also worried about her parents in London. London during the Blitz was facing nightly bombing raids by the Luftwaffe; the destruction was awful and terrifying. Still, today if you walk down Exhibition Road you can see the chunks taken out of the side of the Victoria and Albert Museum, left as a reminder of Londoners' tenacity, suffering, and eventual victory. Buckingham Palace was hit by Luftwaffe bombs nine times during the war. The second bomb destroyed the chapel in the Palace and nearly killed the King and Queen. The King and Queen were sympathetic to the plight of their citizens; they wanted to stay with them and give them hope and reassurance. They went out among war-ravaged London and beyond, visiting hospitals, evacuated children, and troops, raising money for the wool fund and metal drives, the Queen was just as visible as the King. Their efforts did not go unnoticed; they were hugely popular during the war, people saw them as brave and steadfast, serving their country in deeds just as they'd done in word.

With everything young Elizabeth was seeing and experiencing during the war, Lilibet wanted to do more to serve. Initially, her parents said it was just too dangerous for her, but they finally relented, and at age 18, in 1945, Elizabeth joined the Women's Auxiliary Territorial Service, the women's branch of the Army. She trained at the Mechanical Transport Training Centre with eleven other young women, most of whom were a few years older than she was, first learning to drive, then learning to change spark plugs, repair an engine, change a wheel, and drive a large army truck through heavy London traffic. She wore an olive drab uniform like everyone else and was called Second Subaltern Elizabeth Alexandra Mary Windsor. She said of the experience, "I've never worked so hard in my life. Everything I learnt was brand new to me." After a promotion five months later, she finished her service in the ATS as a junior commander. While she was never required to get a driver's license (she still doesn't have one, who would you even get to give the Queen her driving test?), this automotive experience started a lifelong love of driving and taught her skills that she is still proud of. Her short time in the ATS was the only time she felt like she could compare herself to other citizens and see how she stacked up, to interact freely with women her age. We have to imagine that she must have tried very hard to prove herself not just as a member of the royal family but as a member of the British public serving during wartime.

Young Elizabeth had few official royal duties until the war was nearing its end. In 1944, she was made Counsellor of State, a position which gave her power to act as a delegate for her father when he was unavailable, either because he was out of the country or, as often during wartime, was kept from traveling to where events were happening. It was during this time, and at just age 18, that Elizabeth signed a reprieve for a death sentence, causing her to wonder what brought the prisoner to such a state and what circumstances he must find himself in. It is a very empathetic and thoughtful response for someone so young and makes us think that she had grown, learned, and seen quite a lot during the war years. That same year she also visited

miners in Wales with her parents, launched her own battleship, gave public speeches, and attended her first official dinner at Buckingham Palace.

Finally, the war was over. Victory in Europe was celebrated on 8 May 1945, and Elizabeth and Margaret were as excited as the rest of the country. That evening she made a public appearance on the balcony at Buckingham Palace with her family to the cheers and tears of the crowds outside, then she and Margaret and a small crew of chaperones, among them Crawfie and Toni the French tutor as well as a few of the King's men, slipped out into the crowds. In her uniform so she wouldn't be recognized, she rode the buses, celebrated in the streets, and drank in the pubs, returning back to the palace in time to cheer on her parents again, but this time with the rest of the throng outside the palace gates. She and Margaret did the same thing the next night, enjoying the freedom of anonymity and justly feeling like she earned the celebrations along with the rest of the public, only sneaking back into the palace at 3:00 in the morning to make her companions sandwiches in the kitchens of the palace.

King George VI became a very prominent and visible supporter of his citizens and his wartime Prime Minister Winston Churchill, visiting troops on the front lines and making public speeches urging the British people to stay calm and carry on. Most of us are familiar with his 1939 address to the nation as the war starts (if nothing else, from *The King's Speech*, and if not, go watch it immediately, you won't be sorry). In this moving speech, he acknowledges that for most of his people this is the second war they will go through and that there will be dark days ahead but that they must stand firm and stand together. Yet even while he maintained a comforting presence for his people, he had a careful plan in place to remove Elizabeth and Margaret from Windsor or Buckingham Palace should the Germans invade London, with armored cars and dedicated guards at the ready. Thankfully, that was never necessary. Elizabeth saw her parents' bravery and service and the adoration the people had for them. Their dedication became a great lesson for her as she became monarch a few years later. Her own war service also brought her the experiences she would need as head of the armed forces.

Indeed, she is the only female member of the royal family to have served in the armed forces, and the only living head of state who served in World War II—she could not have realized at the time what a meaningful and impressive accomplishment that would be throughout her many years of leadership.

HOGMANAY
Your Guide to Scottish New Year's
By John Rabon

In Scotland, Christmas isn't the most important holiday on the calendar. That honor goes to Hogmanay, or Scotland's version of New Year's Eve. Multiple traditions take place during the day, including the giving of gifts, the singing of the classic New Year's song "Auld Lang Syne," and numerous local traditions such as bonfires, fireworks, and special feasts. Hundreds of years old, the holiday actually goes back to the Norse and today is celebrated in different ways throughout Scotland. We've managed to find ten interesting facts about this very Scottish take on New Year's Eve, and maybe next year you'll consider doing something a bit different to finish out the year.

Etymology

No one seems to be quite sure where the name "Hogmanay" comes from. The first time someone ventured a guest was 1693 in the Scotch Presbyterian Eloquence, as a corruption of the Greek phrase "agia mina" meaning "holy month." Other suggestions include the word coming to the Middle Scots from the French, Gaelic, or a common Norse root word. The holiday itself has origins in the Gaelic celebrations of Samhain as well as Norse celebrations of Yule and the winter solstice so that it could give the latter explanations some credibility.

Is This a Good Idea?

Part of New Year's Day celebrations in Edinburgh include jumping into the freezing waters of the Firth of Forth, often in fancy dress. Known as the "Loony Dook," it began in 1986 as a joke cure for a New Year's hangover and thirty years later draws thousands of participants and onlookers.

An Extra Day to Sleep It Off

In addition to January 1st, January 2nd is also a national holiday in Scotland just in case you need one more day to get over that hangover (or the hypothermia from the Loony Dook). The rest of the UK has to go back to work on the 2nd.

Getting Your Footing in the Door

One common Hogmanay tradition is "First Footing." It is said that the first person who comes across the threshold after the New Year brings a piece of coal for the fire as good luck. It's also believed that dark-haired person coming across your door will bring good luck, while someone fairer-hared will bring bad. As part of the custom, some brunette friend may be asked to leave just before midnight so that they can come back in and bring the good luck with them.

First Before the English

Scotland actually adopted January 1 as New Year's Day in 1600 when it switched from the Julian calendar to the Gregorian calendar. England wouldn't do this until 1752. Under the Julian calendar, the new year began on March 25th.

Establishing Prominence

One of the reasons that Hogmanay is considered more important than Christmas in Scotland is due to the Scottish Presbyterian Church. Following the Reformation, the Presbyterian church considered Christmas to be a Catholic holiday and ceased Christmas celebrations for about 400 years. This meant most Scots spent Christmas as another day, maybe save a special church service. Without Christmas to celebrate, Hogmanay became a much bigger holiday.

Tricking You Into Cleaning House

One Hogmanay tradition celebrated in many Scottish homes is called "Redding the House," which basically involves doing a complete cleaning of the house to get ready for the New Year. Sweeping the ashes was part of the tradition, and some people would even read into the ashes the way a fortune teller reads tea leaves. After the cleaning, someone would go from room to room carrying a smoking juniper branch to chase out evil spirits.

It's a Record

The Guinness Book of World Records has listed "Auld Lang Syne" as the world's most-sung melody, even more than "Happy Birthday." Poet Robert Burns actually transcribed the lyrics from an older Scottish folk song, and it was later paired with the music to create the traditional song we know so well. Radio play in American starting in 1929 helped to popularize the song on this side of the Atlantic and contributed to it becoming a tradition worldwide.

It's Another Record

Hogmanay celebrations in Edinburgh actually established another record in 2000 when 1,914 people danced Strip the Willow at "Night Afore Fiesta," making it the single-largest country-dance.

Enough About Edinburgh

Glasgow has some pretty big Hogmanay celebrations as well. The Hogmanay concert in George Square draws roughly 30,000 celebrants per year.

EXPLORING COVENTRY
Your Complete Guide to This Jewel of the Midlands

By Laura Porter

Coventry Cathedral Ruins and new Cathedral

When it was suggested I should write a feature about somewhere in The Midlands, I could have kept it simple and gone to Birmingham. But I opted for the less obvious choice of Coventry (and not only so I could say I was 'sent to Coventry'!)

If you've heard anything about the city, it's most likely the damage caused during the Blitz in 1940. I was told 'You won't find any old buildings there' so I wanted to prove the naysayers wrong. What I actually found was a city growing in both size and pride. The mix of old and new buildings and the amount of construction work going on brought lots of comparisons to London for me.

And that pride is well-placed as Coventry has won the accolade of UK City of Culture 2021.

UK CITY OF CULTURE 2021

In late 2017, Coventry was announced as the third city to hold this title. The judges unanimously agreed that awarding Coventry would have the most significant impact on the rest of the UK. It is a young, diverse, modern city which is reimagining the role culture can play in bringing people together.

Coventry is a city of peace and reconciliation, a city of innovation and invention, and a true city of culture from music, the arts, heritage and more.

While the locals love their city, they don't sing it loudly enough yet so civic pride is going to have to grow over the next few years. What they have here is good, and well worth visiting, but Coventry has to compete with Birmingham and 'Shakespeare-land' in nearby Stratford-upon-Avon, plus Kenilworth, Warwick and Royal Leamington Spa too.

LOCATION

In The Midlands, Coventry is England's ninth largest city and is about 100 miles north-west of London. It's really easy to reach by train from London, and the journey takes around an hour.

THE BLITZ

Before we go any further, we need to acknowledge the major devastation caused by WWII bombing on Coventry city center.

On the evening of 14 November 1940, more than 500 German planes rained bombs onto the city in a bid to destroy its munitions factories. It was the most concentrated air raid of the Second World War, and hundreds died. Two-thirds of the city center was destroyed and, yes, the city lost its medieval cathedral. Its ruins are now an iconic reminder.

After the war ended, Coventry worked hard to build a city of peace. It was first twinned with Stalingrad (now called Volgograd), in Russia, then later with Dresden, in Germany, two cities which also know the horrors of war (allied troops dropped more bombs on Dresden than fell on Coventry). The new Coventry Cathedral, built alongside the ruins of its predecessor, is a world center for reconciliation, and Coventry is now twinned with 26 cities around the world.

While the 1960s post-war city center is often maligned, it should be remembered that there had already been a lot of clearance in the 1930s in preparation for new town planning. And it is certainly not a 'concrete jungle' as I could hardly turn a corner without finding more heritage architecture.

LADY GODIVA

A well-known name associated with the city is Lady Godiva. Yes, she is the English noblewoman who rode naked on horseback through the city on market day, covered only by her long hair.

The legend dates back to the 11th century when this pious medieval streaker argued with her husband who wanted the people of Coventry to pay high taxes. He said, "You will have to ride naked through Coventry before I change my ways," so she called his bluff.

She is remembered in the city today with a 1949 statue in Broadgate and the entertaining Lady Godiva Clock. On the hour she rides out and is watched by a cheeky 'Peeping Tom' above. There's

Clockwise from Top Left: Coventry Cathedral door handle, Herbert Art Gallery & Museum, Coventry Transport Museum, Ford's Hospital

Old Coventry Cathedral

also the annual Godiva Festival – the UK's biggest free family music festival.

SENT TO COVENTRY

To ignore and alienate someone is to be sent to Coventry. But where does this phrase of derision come from?

The strongest theory is that it originates from the English Civil War in the 1640s when Parliamentarian supporters would take Royalist prisoners of war to Coventry, where they would be shunned by its inhabitants.

ARCHITECTURE

Aside from the heritage attractions, there is still plenty of medieval architecture in Coventry. So much that I'm surprised it isn't mentioned more often. It's worth noting that, in medieval times, Coventry was one of the largest cities in England. There are gatehouses from the city walls and medieval ruins that everyone just walks past because there is just so much to see here. The three spires, which have dominated the city skyline since the 14th century, are from the ruined cathedral, Christ Church (Greyfriars) – only the spire remains – and Holy Trinity Church – the only one still in use.

Some buildings are in use such as the former gatehouse to Cheylesmore Manor which is now the local Register Office (for recording births, deaths, and a wedding venue). Parts of the building dates to 1250 making this the oldest building in the country to hold that function. Edward, the Black Prince and Henry VI are among the royals who lived there. The refurbished 12th century Old Grammar School, that was the former Hospital of St John, is also in use as a wedding venue.

Next to Holy Trinity Church, Lychgate Cottages is a lovely timber-framed building and the only surviving part of St Mary's Priory. While these were used as church offices, there are now plans to turn them into holiday accommodation. There's a Wetherspoons pub connected on the left, but you can see the old church site in a garden to the right of the cottages.

And next to the old Cathedral and St Mary's Guildhall are more timber-framed cottages at 22 and 23 Bayley Lane built around 1500. The decorative woodwork is probably 17th century and the windows date from the 19th century. Do also look at the 20th-century red sandstone Council House around the corner and notice the elephant and castle above the entrance. Once you've spotted it, you'll start noticing elephants all across the city used as symbols of strength and loyalty.

To allow the post-war building of the city, a collection of medieval buildings were removed and rebuilt on Spon Street. Most are used as pubs, restaurants, takeaways, and hairdressers as far as I could see. While the street is a nice grouping of heritage buildings it could be improved by not having cars parks down both sides, and then having cafes and craft stores added. Carry on to Upper Spon Street, and there's The Weaver's House – a restored medieval working man's house and garden showing how John Clarke the weaver would have lived in 1540.

Although it was being renovated when I visited, it's worth looking out for Ford's Hospital. It's a row of almshouses endowed in 1509 by William Ford and built around a courtyard. You can't go into the courtyard but you can peer through the gate, and you may recognize the filming location in the Doctor Who story, The Shakespeare Code.

ATTRACTIONS

Coventry has a very walkable city centre, and there are Uber taxis available.

Coventry Cathedral

Coventry's medieval cathedral was lost during the WWII bombing, but the ruins can still be seen, along with St Michael's Tower. You can climb the 181 steep, spiral steps to get panoramic views across the city. But goodness my legs wobbled when I came down!

After the war, there was a design competition for a new cathedral. Out of 219 entries, only one wanted to keep the ruins. And so, Basil Spence became the architect for this iconic modern building that has a strong focus on reconciliation.

Unusually, it faces north-south rather than east-west. This was so the old and new cathedrals could be connected via a porch above St Michael's Lane. The huge glass screen at the entrance has alternate lines of saints and dancing angels. It took John Hutton two years to finish the 91 panels, and his ashes are interred just outside. The cathedral was 11 years in construction and opened in 1962. It is free to visit.

Behind the altar is a huge and austere tapestry of Christ in Glory by Graham Sutherland. It's nearly the size of a tennis court! If it's hard to grasp the scale, the figure standing between the feet, which looks tiny from the cathedral entrance, is actually 4ft 6in. Come to the front to look more closely, and you can then also take a seat in the Queen's chair. Designed by Anthony Blee, it was based on the comfy bar stools in the Canonbury Tavern in London.

The curved stained glass Baptistry window by John Piper is fabulous. In front of it is the Bethlehem font – that is a boulder hewn from a Bethlehem hillside. And opposite is The Chapel of Unity. Look closely on the 'fins' on this connecting structure as they have pieces of glass that were given as a gift from the Church of Germany.

Do admire the 4975 organ pipes that rise up in levels on both sides of the nave to reach the high, undulating diamond ceiling. And look down in the aisle to see old pennies embedded in the floor to keep the choir boys (and girls) in line.

A lovely little aside is that the tapestry kneeling cushions (hassocks) were completed as kits and many were done by the cast of My Fair Lady in London in their downtime at the theatre.

Don't miss the Jacob Epstein sculpture of St Michael and The Devil on the outside of the building. And look closely at the entrance door handle as it is Epstein's grand-daughter (and Lucian Freud's daughter), Ann Freud.

Cathedral Stained Glass

St. Mary's Guildhall

One of the many places where Mary, Queen of Scots, was held during her long imprisonment (for her own protection), St Mary's Guildhall in Coventry's Cathedral Quarter, has some fine medieval interiors and striking artworks. First built in the 1340s for the merchant guild of St Mary, it grew between 1394 and 1414 and was extensively embellished at the end of the 15th century.

The building served as the center of King Henry VI's court during the War of the Roses (1455-1485), and it is thought that Shakespeare staged plays here. George Eliot also featured the building in her writing.

The main attraction is the magnificent Great Hall, with a ceiling of carved angels and heraldic bosses. And dominating an entire wall is one of the rarest and most important tapestries in the country. The Coventry Tapestry was made in 1500-1510 and is particularly unusual because it is still in place for where it was made.

Open from March to October, entry is free and the Undercroft Café Is accessible from the courtyard on the cobbled Bayley Lane. Do look over the entrance to see the 14th-century wooden carved heads in the vaulted stone ceiling.

The Herbert Art Gallery and Museum

Another attraction in the area with free admission, The Herbert is the city museum on the ground floor and art gallery on the first floor. (Even the temporary exhibitions are free.) It's a good place to come on your first day as the Tourist Information Centre is in the lobby along with a really good gift shop too.

The museum opened in 1960 and is named after Sir Alfred Herbert, a Coventry industrialist and philanthropist. It had a multi-million-pound refurbishment in 2008 making it great for families.

> **LAURA'S COVENTRY TOP 10**
> 1. Coventry Cathedral
> 2. Coventry Transport Museum
> 3. Coventry Music Museum
> 4. Holy Trinity Church
> 5. St Mary's Guildhall
> 6. Lady Godiva clock
> 7. Fargo Village
> 8. Belgrade Theatre
> 9. Medieval architecture
> 10. Coombe Abbey

The museum tells the story of Coventry's history from Medieval times, through Victorian and onto the 20th century, and there's a whole gallery dedicated to the Lady Godiva story. As George Eliot (Mary Ann Evans) lived in Coventry during her formative twenties, the museum has on display her writing cabinet and desk. And with the bicentenary of her birth in 2019, more will be added.

There's a gallery dedicated to Peace and Reconciliation with John Piper's painting of the cathedral in ruins, and Matthew Picton's poignant burnt paper sculptures showing the extensive bombing in Coventry and Dresden.

Don't miss the What's in Store gallery with wonderfully random items from the museum's collections that wouldn't be on display otherwise. Stuffed animals, clocks, artworks and (my favorite find) a bingo machine from the Massey Ferguson social club at the agricultural equipment factory.

Coventry Transport Museum

Also in the city center, this is a huge modern museum and, again, it's free. The motor and cycle industries have shaped the last 150 years Coventry's history. The museum's current collection of vehicles is acknowledged as being one of the finest in the world, and the largest in public ownership, including the two fastest cars in the world. Don't miss the simulator where you can see what it feels like to achieve the land speed record (763 mph)!

Holy Trinity Church

This isn't just for transport enthusiasts as the exhibits range from the London black cab (as they have always been made in Coventry) to Queen Mary's Daimler and the earliest bicycles. It has the stories about the people in the industries for that human perspective too.

The museum is chronological so starts with bicycles – did you know a Penny Farthing had to be made to your leg length? – Before reaching the first cars in the late 19th century. I saw wooden frame cars covered only in leatherette that were popular after WWI for the low cost but not for safety. By the Blitz Experience, there's an armored car that looks like a tank, and I found out SS Cars was the pre-war name for Jaguar. The museum has Field Marshal Montgomery's iconic Victory car and George VI's car that collected Princess Elizabeth when she returned from her trip to Africa when her father died making her the new Queen (the car was used in the movie The King's Speech.)

The UK motor industry's inexorable rise and fall are very well told, and there's a magnificent model collection that all came from one man (and only half is on display). There's an excellent café onsite, and you can look out at the Whittle Arch and the statue of Sir Frank Whittle, inventor of the turbojet engine, who was born in Coventry.

If you do like transport, the Lanchester Interactive Library at Coventry University comes recommended and is only a 15-minute walk away. And the Midland Air Museum at Coventry Airport has a collection of military aircraft and is a 15-minute bus ride away.

Holy Trinity Church

Close to the cathedral, Holy Trinity dates back to the 12th century (although most were rebuilt during the 1300s). It's incredible it survived the Blitz – the only damage was the loss of two stained glass windows at the East and West ends, but this was the only building left standing on Broadgate (and the only large historic building in Coventry left intact after WWII). As this is a crown church, do look in the Marler's Chapel to see a section of the 1953

Bayley Lane in the Cathedral Quarter

gold coronation carpet.

Most visitors come to see the Coventry Doom painting of the Last Judgement – an impressive medieval painting created in the 1430s on the chancel wall. (There had been an earthquake in Coventry in 1426, and the townspeople believed it was God's wrath for their sins.) The painting was rediscovered in the 1830s but the varnish to preserve it turned black, so it was soon hidden again. In 2004 it was unveiled after nearly 20 years of conservation and restoration.

It's very high up so you may prefer to buy the guidebook to study in detail as it is a remarkable painting. Christ is in the center with the dead rising from graves on the left. Look closely, and you should spot the three Coventry alewives on the right, chained and being led to the mouth of Hell. These women represented the damnation of those who sold watered down beer. (It wasn't the weakened beer so much that was the problem as the fact the water was so contaminated which was why people drank beer instead.)

Coventry Music Museum

While the museum came from a need to recognize Coventry as the home of 2-Tone music – a fusion of ska and punk popular in the 70s and 80s – it actually covers the city's musical heritage from the Roman occupation to today.

It's a small, volunteer-run museum with a collection that's grown with donations from the band's themselves. The Specials, the Anglo-Caribbean originators of 2-tone music, obviously feature here but there's also The Enemy (Coventry's most recent famous group) and the Radiophonic Workshop goddess, Delia Derbyshire, who came up with the electronic arrangement of the Doctor Who theme music.

A surprise find is the Lennon Bench commemorating the 'Acorns for Peace' event on 15 June 1968 when John and Yoko planted two acorns at the cathedral garden. The acorns were moved and then stolen, so Lennon took back the original bench. In 2004 a replica bench was made for a play, and it was used when Yoko Ono revisited the city to plant oak trees. So Lennon hasn't sat on this actual bench, but Yoko has.

I'll admit, the 80s section brought back a lot of memories for me (when I was 13 years old, King was my favorite band.) And the bedroom of an 18-year-old 'rude boy' has so many clever details including posters, cigarette cards, and even an old crisps packet.

Most of the artifacts are in glass cabinets, but there's a strong sense of being part of something fun here as you can use props (inflatable guitars, wigs, etc.) for photo opportunities and there's a weekly top 5 chosen by visitors from the Wall of Hits. Then head downstairs to the music studio and make some noise before checking out the rest of the '2-Tone Village' as there's a café that serves 'skapuccinos,' a retro clothes shop, a memorabilia shop and a Caribbean restaurant.

The museum has been open for five years and is consistently the no.1 attraction in Coventry on TripAdvisor. It's open from Thursday to Sunday and is about a mile from the city center. As 2019 is the 40th anniversary of 2-tone, I'm sure this will remain popular.

EAT AND DRINK

There are a number of restaurants overlooking Broadgate, the pedestrianized shopping area. Bistrot Pierre has lovely modern French cuisine, and the Ramen at Wagamama is always good. Zizzi has Italian and Mediterranean dishes, and Nando's is all about the chicken. Cozy Club has an eclectic style in the food and decor that made for a funky, relaxed vibe, delicious meals with excellent service. And if you'd prefer the food brought to you, I saw lots of cycle deliveries from Deliveroo and Uber Eats from the city center restaurants.

Coventry has some great historic pubs and restaurants including the Golden Cross pub near the Cathedral and Turmeric Gold, a popular Indian restaurant on Spon Street. And if you're going to The Belgrade Theatre, there are decent restaurants in Belgrade Plaza.

I have to try afternoon tea wherever I go, and on this trip I found two to recommend. When you're in the city center, the Rising Café in the undercroft at the cathedral has afternoon tea for just £11 (or £19 for 2), and it's amazing! The café has a WWII vibe with music, bunting and mismatched crockery. The scones and cakes are made in-house, so this really showcases their talents. I wish I was nearer as I've been dreaming about their gorgeous heart-shaped mini chocolate brownie. The café is also a charity with 100% of its profits going to improving the lives of those suffering drug and alcohol addictions.

If you're looking for the country house hotel version, then Coombe Abbey Hotel is the place for you. Afternoon tea is served in the elegant garden room on the side of the 12th-century building. The abbey was surrendered to King Henry VIII during the dissolution of the monasteries, and the future Queen Elizabeth I even lived there as a child. There are Newby loose leaf teas, and I can confirm the scone separated in half perfectly. And if you feel you should be good and take a stroll afterward, then Coombe Abbey Park is right outside.

There's also afternoon tea available at the Castle Yard Tea Rooms and The Undercroft at St Mary's Guildhall. And you can even have Cocktails and Cakes at the Slug and Lettuce pub on Bayley Lane.

SHOPPING

As well as the post-war pedestrianized shopping area in the city center (the first to be built in the country) the place you really want to go shopping is FarGo Village, the creative quarter just 15 minutes walk away. This former industrial space is now really vibrant with small, independent shops, artists' studios, cafés, an entertainment space and a brewery with a tap room.

It really reminded me of Shoreditch in London, and they have events such as soul food and music nights.

Highlights here include the The Sgt Bilko's Vintage Emporium that specializes in vintage and modern film, stage and television memorabilia, and has The Phil Silvers Archival Museum inside. And

Tea Time

Lady Godiva Clock (and Peeping Tom)

don't miss the lovely Big Comfy Bookshop – a secondhand bookshop that has author visits, paper craft workshops and a decent café inside with relaxing armchairs.

SPORT

Both Wasps Rugby Club and Coventry City Football Club are based at the Ricoh Arena 32,609-seater stadium.

NIGHTLIFE

As well as the music shows at the Ricoh Arena, there's regular live music at The Tin Music and Arts Centre in the Canal Basin and The Empire on Far Gosford Street, co-run by Tom of The Enemy. The Kasbah nightclub has live music and club nights too.

The Belgrade Theatre was the UK's first civic theatre to open after WWII in 1958. It is one of the largest regional producing theatres and stages touring shows too. The Albany Theatre is an Art Deco theatre that stages in-house and professional touring dance, drama, music and comedy productions.

Don't be confused by the name as Warwick Arts Centre is actually in Coventry. It's on the Warwick University campus (yes, Warwick University is in Coventry) and has an excellent programme of music, comedy, dance and more.

ACCOMMODATION

There are the usual hotel names you would expect to find in a city (Hilton, Premier Inn, Holiday Inn, Travelodge, etc.). I stayed at the Ramada, and while it was next to the ring road it was clean and comfortable, and I slept well there.

I didn't find any boutique hotels, but there are some great AirBnB properties in the area.

Of course, you could treat yourself and stay at the opulent Coombe Abbey Hotel with its four-poster beds and that very good afternoon tea.

INSIDER TIP

The Herbert closes at 4pm, and most other attractions close by 5 pm so plan to eat early.

LOST IN THE POND
Ten Years Away from the British Christmas Season

By Laurence Brown

In 2008, roughly a month into my continuing American adventure, I was asked a question by my wife's grandma that had the profound effect of rendering me speechless. Without the slightest hint of irony, she polished off a slice of ham and inquired, "do you celebrate Christmas in England?" Until that very moment, I hadn't considered the possibility that English Yuletide might be an alien concept to others around the world.

The answer to her question, of course, was a resounding yes. Christmas and the monotheistic religion from whence it emerged has remained a part of English life—save for a brief, puritan-sponsored ban in the 17th century—for hundreds and hundreds of years. And for twenty-seven of those, from 1981 to 2007, the English Christmas season was an annual jollity enjoyed by yours truly.

To this day, I retain fond childhood memories of soundly defeating my brother in the annual Christmas cracker pull, even if my prize for doing so was a flimsy green hat and a paper-printed joke of the "dad" variety. For the uninitiated, a Christmas cracker is a brightly decorated twist of paper that sort of resembles an ultra-sized sweet-wrapper and is pulled apart by two opposing hands. Whichever hand is left with the biggest piece wins the prize.

Speaking of prizes, if I concentrate hard enough, I can still taste my mum's Christmas pudding (which may or may not have been pre-made), not to mention the custard that so artistically enveloped it.

I can still smell the splendid aroma of non-artificial Christmas trees—both those adorning the Grimsby market stall and those that came and went from the family living room.

I can still see the tinsel that snaked its way around said room and doubled as a prop from which to hang Christmas cards, a large percentage of which featured either an English robin or a wintry London scene.

I can still hear the sound of sleigh bells, produced—I later came to discover—by one of the family neighbors, whose chief aim was to instill in the young a belief that Father Christmas (British English for Santa) was on his way.

I can still touch the wrapping paper that friends and relatives (mainly just my mum, let's be honest) had used to conceal the He-Man action figures that would shortly bear the sad distinction of becoming my closest friends. Orko and I were inseparable for the better part of 1986.

Memories are a magnificent thing. But in the ten years, I've resided in the United States—which have included question time with grandma and Christmas in the Windy City—the traditions that so often accompanied English Yuletide have grown more and more distant.

Initially, of course, relinquishing such traditions in favor of their American counterparts was novel. For example, it was—and still is—a delightful signifier of the coming of Christmas to hear Feliz Navidad and I Saw Mommy Kissing Santa Claus.

Moreover, certain British staples, such as the aforementioned Christmas crackers, mince pies, and advent calendars—all notable by their absence during the early days of my American transplant—have since grown in popularity stateside. And it's not just the likes of World Market (or other internationals stores) that stock up on these; you can occasionally find them at Target and Walmart, too.

But as time wanders on I'm left to wonder when I will next experience a good old English Boxing Day—the day immediately following Christmas Day when all of the good films are shown, and a full a schedule of Premier League football graces out television sets. In the United States, not only is the term "Boxing Day" little known but also seldom practiced. If you're lucky, your employer might build December 26 into the company calendar, but—owing to the fact that Boxing Day is not a national holiday in the U.S. (it is in Canada)—your employer is not mandated to do so.

And what about Britain's Christmas soundtrack? While the likes of Wham's Last Christmas and Band Aid's Do They Know It's Christmas? were fortunate beneficiaries of what music scholars refer to as the second British Invasion of America, other hits weren't quite so lucky. Take, for example, Slade's Merry Xmas Everybody, a highly popular tune from 1973 that remains a rollicking symbol of British Christmas time. So, too, the song it beat to number one in that very year: I Wish It Could Be Christmas Everyday by Wizzard. Neither song, however, is likely to feature over Walmart's sound system.

Furthermore, the weather of British Christmas is something I've been giving a lot of thought to recently. When I pondered earlier the initial novelty of American Christmas, I ought to have included the bitterly cold winters of the Midwest. At first, it was oddly exciting to feel my eyeballs freeze over the moment I walked out into a crisp Indiana morning. But ten years living in the Midwest, including two in Chicago, have left me scarred. With average temperatures in the month of December a whole six or seven degrees lower than those of northern England, it's little wonder I long so ardently for British weather.

On a more personal note, I'm likely to receive an ear-full if I don't conclude this piece with reference to the very people who made British Christmas what it was: my family. Every year, like clockwork, our house would provide the intimate setting for a gathering that included me, my two brothers, parents, nanna, Uncle Alan and Aunty Elaine. While one of those—my nanna—has since passed on, it sure would feel like home to spend my Christmas among that company again.

And so, as I embark on my eleventh successive American Christmas, I can at least pause and find solace in the fact that mental planning is already underway for a festive holiday in Britain. After all, I now have something—this article—by which to hold myself accountable. And by that very token, there's hope yet that an article not yet written might one day recount my return home, providing detailed insight to those, like my wife's grandma, who would ask the question, "do you celebrate Christmas in England?"

Laurence is a British writer and humorist who lives in the United States. He also hosts the popular web series, "Lost in the Pond" on YouTube. He has an infuriating habit of taking America to task by pointing out how things are done in the UK. He really needs to stop this behavio(u)r. It's anti-American.

GREAT BRITONS: WILLIAM WALDORF ASTOR

The American Anglophle That Became a Lord

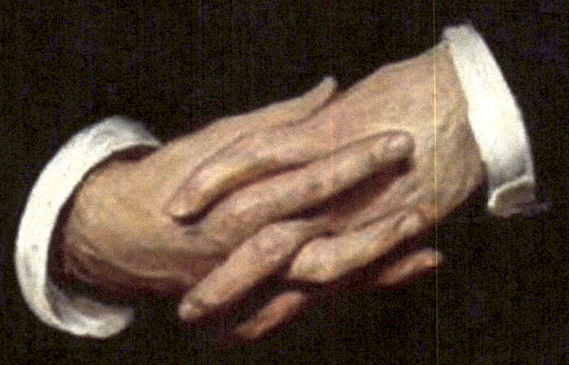

Inheriting the vast fortunes of the Astor family was just the beginning for William Waldorf Astor. Educated and raised in Europe, he found the rough-and-tumble of life in America too much, so he moved to England in 1893. He bought several properties, most notably Cliveden, from the Duke of Westminster, and Hever Castle, once the home of Ann Boleyn. He extensively renovated the houses and gardens, indulging his taste for the arts. By making lavish gifts to numerous hospitals, universities, the Red Cross, and countless other charities, he was able to obtain a peerage, becoming a Viscount, and establishing a heritable peerage that still exists. His success was not admired by the media or the public on either side of the Atlantic, and he was regularly criticized, leading him to live the life of a recluse.

In 2007, at the age of 105, Brook Astor died. Her final years were mired in scandal, with her son, Anthony Marshall, appealing at the time of her death his conviction for financially exploiting her, for which he was jailed in 2013. As they watched an iconic American family decline, with media coverage of crumbling mansions and lost fortunes, many may not have realized that there is a branch of the family across the Atlantic, which has fared much better and still wields considerable influence in Britain.

The Astor family had its roots in Europe, and Johann Jakob Astor arrived in Baltimore in 1783 from Germany, after a few years in England where he changed his name to John Jacob Astor. He became America's first multi-millionaire, and one of the top 10 wealthiest men in history. His wealth came from fur trading, opium smuggling and investment, leaving his eight children to found a dynasty powerful throughout the 18th and 19th centuries. One of John Jacob Astor's grandsons was John Jacob Astor III, born in 1822, who inherited half of the vast Astor estate. He lived in New York City with his wife, the Georgia-born Charlotte Augusta Gibbes. They had just one child, a boy, born in 1848. They named him William Waldorf.

The child grew up mostly with tutors, in Germany and Italy, and he had limited contact with his parents, who were cold and distant with him. His father wanted him to grow up and manage the family fortune, and with that in mind, he went to Columbia University, as his father had done before him, before taking the United States Bar in

KEY FACTS

- Born 1848 – died 1919
- Inherited the Astor family fortune
- Moved to England, becoming a citizen and a peer
- Renovated the stately homes of Cliveden and Hever Castle

1875. Wanting to make his mark on the world he decided to become a politician, using his family's connections with Roscoe Conkling, a powerful Republican from New York with considerable influence in the political machinery of the times. He was elected to the New York State Assembly, and then to the New York State Senate.

But when he made a run for the US Congress, he was twice defeated and retreated from politics. His shy manner and sensitivity to negative media attention proved too much for him. So wounded was he that he wanted to retreat to his childhood home of Italy, and he approached the President, Chester A. Arthur, who had cut his political teeth in the New York Republican machine. Arthur obliged by appointing him head of the US Legation in Rome, a post he held from 1881 to 1885. Clearly little was expected of him, and the President's parting words were, go and enjoy yourself, my dear boy. He did, indulging and developing his passion for the arts in what was surely the ideal environment.

In 1890 his father died, he inherited the family fortune and became the wealthiest man in America. He built the Waldorf Hotel on the site of a former home, and when his cousin and business rival John Jacob Astor IV built one next door, they joined forces, and the buildings became the Waldorf-Astoria Hotel. That did not, however, settle the rivalry, which descended into a dispute over which branch of the family was entitled to the official 'Mrs. Astor' title. William lost, and stormed off to England with his wife and children. There he rented Lansdowne House, in Berkeley Square, London for a few years, before buying Cliveden, the country estate of one of Britain's wealthiest men, Hugh Lupus Grosvenor, 1st Duke of Westminster.

He also purchased a London home, 2 Temple Place, on the Thames Embankment, which he spent

Hever Castle

$1.5 million renovating. Lavishly and eccentrically furnished with oak, mahogany, ebony, marble and semi-precious stones, it was the work of a collector for whom nothing was too pretentious to incorporate into the edifice. It became the nerve-center of his business empire.

William had many reasons to leave America, not least his fear that his children would be kidnapped. He went so far as to fake his death, having his American staff tell the press he had died of pneumonia. He was quickly found out of course, and his reputation reached a new low-point. Driven to withdraw even more from the public gaze, he retreated to Cliveden, where again he made grandiose changes to the interior of the vast house and re-modeled the gardens. Then tragedy struck, and his wife, Mary Dahlgren Paul, only 36 years old, died at Christmas, 1894. Left with their five children, William became a recluse.

Cliveden was perhaps too full of ghosts, or perhaps he was simply bored, but in 1903 he purchased Hever Castle, in Kent. The castle, dating from 1270, had been the childhood home of Anne Boleyn, and Henry VIII had given it to Anne of Cleves when he famously had their marriage annulled, leading to the foundation of the Church of England. William Astor set to work, renovating and building on the site. He added a 'Tudor Village' to house his guests, and built a yew maze in the gardens. He also added an Italian garden to display his collection of Italian sculpture. In 1906 he moved permanently from Cliveden to Hever Castle, giving the Cliveden estate to his son Waldorf, as a wedding present. Cliveden would become famous for the lavish parties of Nancy Astor between the wars, where the worst and best of the political and literary world gathered.

Along the way, he had picked up British citizenship in 1899, a move that further alienated him from the American press. Once a citizen he decided to rise through the social ranks via philanthropy and began to make generous donations to suitable organizations. A quarter-million dollars went to the Hospital for Sick Children, Great Ormond Street. Professorships were endowed at Oxford, Cambridge, and University College, London. The Red Cross, various soldiers' organizations – the list goes on and on, but it did the trick. There is a great British tradition that philanthropy deserves a reward, and Astor was duly rewarded in 1916 when he was offered a peerage and became Baron Astor of Hever Castle. The following year he was elevated to Viscount.

These rewards were not without their critics,

Cliveden House

and the idea of an American coming to England and buying a peerage was seen by many as less than acceptable. His support for peace during WWI, his leaving America, everything he did drew censure, and he was fired at from both sides of the Atlantic. He became sickly, and on the 18th of October 1919, he was found dead of a heart attack in a toilet of a home in Brighton. The American estate, worth $60 million, was heavily taxed because of his expat status. William Astor, the 4th Viscount Astor, and great-grandson of William Waldorf is the stepfather of Samantha Cameron, the wife of former Prime Minister David Cameron.

Sites to Visit

Most of Lansdowne House, which stood in the Southwest of Berkeley Square, London, was demolished, including its lavish 18th-century interiors. It was designed by the architect Robert Adam. The surviving part, which is the home of the Lansdowne Club, an exclusive private members club, is a Grade II listed building.

2, Temple Place, London WC2, near Somerset House, once known as Astor House, is today a gallery space, open from January to May each year for a significant exhibition taken from the collections of regional museums. The interior is largely intact.

Cliveden House, Cliveden Road, Taplow, Buckinghamshire, is today a luxury country hotel, leased from the National Trust. Non-residents can take tea in the Great Hall or dine in one of two restaurants.

Hever Castle, near Edenbridge, in Kent, is open all year round. The grounds open at 10:30, and the Castle at noon. Closing times vary with the seasons. It is also possible to stay in the castle.

Further Research

- The Astors, 1763-1992: Landscape with Millionaires, by Derek Wilson, 1993
- The Astors, by Virginia Cowles, 2017
- The Astors: The History and Legacy of One of the World's Wealthiest Families, by Charles River Editors, 2017

THIS ENGLISH LIFE

The Scoop on British Christmas
By Erin Moore

A few days before England's two-pronged poker of autumnal atmosphere, Halloween and Bonfire night, we celebrated my husband's 43rd birthday. My parents had brought Tom a mysterious velvet pouch. Inside was a little barrel-shaped implement with a long handle that I only recognized because its use had already been explained to me. Tom, however, knew what it was for right away, and he was thrilled. Whatever that silver stilton scoop was doing in a Florida estate sale, it's ours now—and not a moment too soon, because Christmas is coming.

Even though I really dislike blue cheese, Stilton is traditional at Christmas and at our house, we go big: 2.2 kilos of the stuff every year. I blame myself. Ten years ago, planning our first Christmas on our own in London, Tom and I were childless and looked for ways to make the holidays feel festive in a grown-up way. We had stocked a case of champagne, we'd planned our feast, and it was to include a sizeable wedge of moldy cheese. Although we were slightly constrained by having a refrigerator the size of a footlocker, we'd acquired a Coleman cooler to contain the overabundant blessings we were about to receive, in the form of poultry, pastry, and pudding.

A few days before Christmas, I stopped at La Fromagerie, with its damp and overwhelmingly redolent cheese room. This cheese room is probably sizeable, for a space dedicated to providing the perfect climate for cheese, but as a room let's just say it is not large. Some would call it cramped. And at this time of year, crowded would be an understatement. Out of the cheese room, through the small shop, and down the street, the line stretched. At least 50 people were waiting. I was coming from yoga class and feeling so chilled about it that I could have made my own little cheese-protecting microclimate. Here was a Christmas queue to reckon with, but I'd been in London for two years, and I was something of an expert, thank you very much.

Twenty minutes later, a frantic-looking cheese monitor broke free of the shop with a credit-card reader, asking whether anyone wished to buy only ONE cheese. I waved, handed over my card, stilton please, and five minutes later was practically assaulted by a bowling ball of a bag containing the biggest wheel of cheese I had ever purchased. Not a wedge, but a whole stilton. I looked at my receipt: £70! Friends, in pre-Brexit pounds that was about $125 worth of cheese.

I carried the cheese back home and up the four flights of stairs to our flat, wondering how on earth I was going to manage to eat half of it in the ten days before abstemious January began. The answer: I wasn't. We would have to recruit many friends. We were going to have to make new friends to get through our massive backlog of cheese. And that's precisely what happened in 2009, and every year since that we have lived in London. If we're home, you're invited. And this year we won't be hacking away at our outsized stilton with a cheese knife, no way. We will be scooping it out, scattering the crumbs over the floor and treading them into the carpets like royalty.

In the first week of November, the conversation around the school gates turns to Christmas plans (also,

Diwali). Most families are planning to go away as soon as school is out—visiting family, skiing, or sun-seeking. But we prefer to do those things in February. For most of the years since we moved here, we have not traveled at Christmas because the last two weeks in December are among the best of the year to be right here. The city empties out around the 20th. No one is working, at least not seriously. A Christmas party thrown on December 22nd, after seasonal obligations are complete, is a truly festive and joyful event. Everyone there knows what they are missing: weather delays, crowded stressful trains, planes, and traffic, inevitable flu.

But staying put requires planning. Because the same shops that have been bombarding us with their Christmas wares for the past four months will close for days on end, just when festive emergencies are at their height.

A friend of a friend once held the incredibly enviable job of "Head of Christmas" at the posh supermarket chain Waitrose. She got to eat/live/breathe Christmas all year long. Perhaps this is why she only stayed in the job for a few years. I suppose it could get monotonous trying to decide whether gingerbread fairy houses or gingerbread Georgians would be the more popular kit next year.

Just like at Waitrose, in every home you need someone to be the Head of Christmas. The emails begin arriving in August and, sitting on a beach in France; I ignore them at my peril. One of the first is from the company that delivers our groceries, letting me know that at midnight on Thursday, October 4th, Christmas delivery slots officially open for booking. I'm allowed up to two, with a rather large minimum order and an extra delivery charge. I dutifully set my iCal reminder and prepare to wake at midnight two months hence.

I am far from the only one sweating the festive season summer. The British calendar lacks the speed-bump that is Thanksgiving, so there is no barrier to department stores opening their Christmas departments in July. In the "High Street shopses," as A.A. Milne called them, festivity arrives reliably by late September. Christmas lights are installed throughout September and then lit in late October or early November.

If you wait for these early warning signs of Christmas, though, you've already missed out on some very important deadlines. Where we live, it is impossible to gain an audience with any department store Father Christmas, unless you've booked it by the end of September. My kids were already out of luck by the time I remembered to do this in October. Controversially, Harrods had opened Father Christmas bookings to preferred customers first, only to see every slot fill up with the children of their highest spenders, leaving no slots for anyone else.

We will be driving an hour south to what we hope will be a very atmospheric Christmas tree farm where the kids will hike through what we hope will be a non-sodden woodland to visit what we hope will be a sober and convincing Father C. My iCal reminder is already set for August 31st, 2019 so we can go back to Fortnum's next year. Excuse me while I pause in my typing to reserve slots for ice skating, the Nutcracker… Would tickets to a pantomime feel like overkill? Wait—hold the phone—has Fortnum and Mason's special mincemeat sold out already? (Haha! Not this year. My husband was over there in October and bought two jars.)

Next, it is time to decorate the house. In true American style, I am going for a big light display. The lighting store around the corner sells me their most prominent lights. I spend three hours painstakingly attaching them to the front of the house with cable ties. At dark thirty, I plug them in and, with a resounding plink we have the least overwhelming light display ever. There is nothing worse than going for gaudy and getting tasteful instead, or worse, looking like you made no effort at all. Effort at Christmas is practically a religion in itself. It is certainly mine.

Last year I decided to go for the largest possible Norwegian pine. A 6-foot tree would sit comfortably in our living room, but comfort is overrated, and an 8-foot tree seemed like a great idea at the time. The doorbell rang at the appointed time (booked it in August, natch) and four Polish guys dressed in kilts carried it upstairs in a neat net bag. When unsheathed, it dwarfed the room. A ladder proved pointless. While we were busy ascending to the apex of a conventional ladder, the tree was busy sloping in the opposite direction to its narrow topmost branches. But if we thought decorating that tree was a challenge, the greatest was yet to come. How would we (correction: I) ever get it out again?

Epiphany dawned with the cold realization that the tree couldn't go back down the stairs, leaving me no choice but to defenestrate it from the first floor. I succeeded in getting it out to the balcony, but it was too heavy to javelin-toss onto the front lawn, so it ended up plummeting to its death in the basement stairwell. My antics drew a large crowd of what I can only hope were well-wishers from the hotel and pub across the street, as well as neighbors waiting to see what the crazy lady at #73 was up to THIS time. We were all laughing, but Christmas is no joke, people. Hand me my stilton scoop; I'm going in.

Erin Moore is an American who has been living in London for 10 years. Her book, That's Not English: Britishisms, Americanisms and What Our English Says About Us, *is available on amazon.com.*

THE GREAT EXHIBITION

Showcasing Empire: The Great Exhibition of 1851

On 1 May 1851, the newly erected Crystal Palace flung open its doors for the very first time, revealing its casket of wonders to the 25,000 people that had gathered outside the doors. The Great Exhibition was an unprecedented event in British society, as for the first time in history Britain's treasures, from both home and abroad, were placed on display for all to see. The Crystal Palace was, for six months, home to a dazzling array of the world's raw materials and produce, the best of British technology, manufacturing and design, and a range of spectacular art and cultural heritage. The British writer Charlotte Bronte, on visiting the exhibition in the summer of 1851 wrote, "Its grandeur does not consist in one thing, but in the unique assemblage of all things."

The Great Exhibition was a masterstroke of imperial branding, showcasing Britain's role as a global leader, civilizing power, and technological force, and creating a sense of national unity and pride. In this respect, it was the materialization of British identity for the first time on the public stage, allowing people across all social classes to participate in the spectacle of British expansion.

The Age of Exhibitionism: Henry Cole and the Inspiration for the Exhibition

In many respects, the impetus for the Great Exhibition of 1851 was commercial. During the 1840s, a new phenomenon had emerged in British society, in which small-scale exhibitions of British manufactured goods were put on display, in order to educate the British public and develop their tastes. Domestic demand was a key driver of imperial trade, and the rise of forms of conspicuous middle-class consumption had fuelled demands for luxury and manufactured products in Britain. Public display was increasingly viewed as a way to stimulate growth, publicize British manufacturing, and changing public tastes. During the 1840s, the Royal Society for the Encouragement of Arts, Manufactures and Commerce (RSA), recently given a royal charter under the patronage of Prince Albert, put on a range of product showcases that gave much-needed publicity to British manufacturing and industry.

KEY DATES

- 1847 - RSA granted a royal charter
- 1 June 1849 - 11th Quinquennial Paris Exhibition
- 1850 - Royal Commission for the Exhibition of 1851 formed
- 1 May 1851 - The Great Exhibition opens to the public

KEY FIGURES

- Henry Cole - Exhibition organizer and civil servant
- Prince Albert - Prince Consort and Exhibition organizer and patron
- Queen Victoria - British Monarch 1837-1901
- Isambard Kingdom Brunel - British civil engineer, part of the Crystal Palace Commission
- Joseph Paxton - Architect of the Crystal Palace

In 1849, the British civil servant Henry Cole visited the 11th Quinquennial Paris Exhibition, where he was profoundly impressed by the grandeur of the event, and the range of products on display. However, the purpose of the Paris Exhibition was not merely a mechanism to support French production but was also a cultural event designed to send a message to the world. The previous year had witnessed considerable upheaval in France, including the deposition of the Bourbon monarch Louis-Philippe, and the proclamation of the Second Republic. The Exhibition was, therefore, a way to express French unity, stability, and vitality, to legitimize the new regime and importantly, to showcase France's newest colonial acquisition, Algeria. The event was a roaring success: not only was it well received in France, but it also attracted considerable attention throughout Europe.

The 1849 Paris Exhibition gave Henry Cole several ideas. He wanted to create a similar exhibition in Britain, on a lavish scale, which would not simply focus on British manufacturing, but that would highlight Britain's role as a global power. Such an event would be a powerful statement of Britain's place in the world, drawing together artifacts and products from across the British Empire, and demonstrating Britain's economic and political might. Furthermore, a forward-looking and progressive display of technology, industry, and manufacturing would prove to be the ideal antidote to two decades of social and political upheaval, both within Britain and across the continent. As Britain approached the mid-century, what better way to look to the future than through a display of Britain's cutting-edge technology?

Immediately on his return from France, he appealed to Prince Albert and the Queen Victoria for royal backing to establish a group that would investigate the possibility of such an event in Britain. In 1850, the Royal Commission for the Exhibition of 1851 was established, with Prince Albert as the founding president. Its members were given the gargantuan task of arranging the Exhibition within a year; no small feat, given the ambitious plans of Prince Albert and Henry Cole.

The Cave of Wonders: Building the Crystal Palace

The first major problem facing the organizers was the question of where, and in what building, would the Exhibition be held? As the intention of the Exhibition was to showcase British wealth, prosperity and technology, the structure in which these objects were housed and displayed also needed to represent a triumph of British design and engineering. In January 1850, a new commission was created in order to oversee the planning and construction of the Exhibition building, comprising a number of famous architects, engineers, and notables, including Isambard Kingdom Brunel. Calls went out for proposals for the building and attracted a significant amount of initial attention. However, the commission was unsatisfied with the results. They were initially even unable to agree on the proposed site for the Exhibition and debated at length between plots in Hyde Park, Regent's Park, Battersea, and even the Isle of Dogs.

Eventually, the commission decided on Hyde

Park as the most appropriate and central site for the Exhibition, much to the chagrin of local residents. To stand out in such a location, the Exhibition structure needed to be iconic, progressive, and a technical triumph, in addition to being temporary, quick to construct, and most importantly, cheap. The winning design ultimately came from Joseph Paxton, who had gained success and notoriety building greenhouses for the Duke of Devonshire. In his design, the Exhibition would be clothed in glass, creating an iconic building that would be seen from afar, glittering in the sunlight.

Paxton's design was a triumph of engineering and impressive design, creating a structure that would accommodate the local nature, provide sufficient space for all of the exhibits, and be quick and cheap to erect. Construction began in July 1850 and was completed within five months. In this period, 900,000 square feet of glass was installed in the cast iron frame. The Palace was 563m wide, 139m long, and 41m high, with enough space inside to even enclose two large elm trees that sat on the Exhibition site. The Crystal Palace was born.

Open Day: Showcasing Production

On 1 May 1851, Queen Victoria officially opened the Crystal Palace and the Great Exhibition of the Works of Industry of All Nations. The exhibits drew widespread awe and acclaim, as they showcased such a wide variety of traditions, technological processes, cultures and art forms. The total number of exhibits on display was in excess of 13,000, arranged in a chaotic and overwhelming manner throughout the building. The brightness of the building created a dazzling visual cacophony, and many visitors remarked upon the disorienting profusion of the Exhibition.

The organization of the displays followed particular themes, gently moving the visitor along a narrative of progress. The first section focused on raw materials and produce, most of which came from Britain's colonies. In this section, India took pride of place, as Britain's most significant colonial territory. In particular, one of the most impressive displays to come from India was the Koh-i-Noor, the world's largest known, cut diamond, which had been acquired as part of the Lahore Treaty the previous year. The Koh-i-Noor was a triumph and operated as a metaphor for the dazzling brilliance of the Crystal Palace, and the exhibition as a whole.

The Exhibition then focused on machinery and mechanical processes that showcased technology. In this section, for example, visitors could trace the production of cotton from the plant all the way to the finished product. Other exhibits included displays of steel manufacture. The third section centered on the manufactured goods produced in Britain, and across the Empire, including telescopes, kitchen appliances, and clothing, and finally, the fourth section displayed works of art and beauty: the pinnacle of human creative and technical achievement. This structural organization allowed the visitors to learn, sometimes for the first time, the processes that led to the construction of the objects they used in their everyday lives: clothes, china, shoes, paper, and tools. It also created a teleological narrative of progress, moving from the raw materials, through manufacture, to the sublime beauty of human creativity, technology, and artisanship.

The Exhibition was an unprecedented success. It is thought that in six months over the summer of 1851, one-third of the entire population of Britain attended the Exhibition, which recorded average daily visits of 42,830. Many visitors returned multiple times; such was the richness and diversity of the objects on display.

Public Education and Victorian Paternalism

One of the most striking features of the Great Exhibition of 1851 is its wide appeal across the social spectrum. The event proved to hold a powerful attraction for the working classes, who had, in most cases, never before had the opportunity to see such a rich and varied display of products and artifacts. The Crystal Palace alone, with its striking glasswork and unique features, created a spectacle that hundreds of thousands of working men, women and children flocked to witness. For these people, the Exhibition made British imperialism a visceral reality: for the first time they were able to see and share in the spoils of Empire and to observe the material consequences of British expansion for themselves.

For some of the Exhibition organizers, including

Prince Albert, this was an intentional consequence of the project. The Exhibition was designed to have an appeal that cut across class divisions, and Albert saw to it that affordable tickets were made available to poorer visitors on certain days. The introduction of tickets for just one shilling allowed almost anyone to visit the Exhibition and ensured that the event went beyond elite and middle-class circles. The Exhibition broke down the traditional class barriers that compartmentalized public space: in the Crystal Palace, working men rubbed shoulders with the aristocracy and the middle class, creating a sense of national unity that had not been allowed to occur in public space before. Over the course of the Exhibition's run, four and half million of the total six million tickets were sold in the cheapest category, demonstrating the degree to which the working classes were finally allowed to participate in what had hitherto been thought of as solely the preserve of elites.

However, this was not necessarily because Albert and the other Exhibition organizers wanted to create a more egalitarian society, or felt strongly about working-class rights. Rather, it stemmed from a belief in the educational power of material culture and technology. It was thought that, by educating working class people about British and imperial culture, art and technology, they would be 'raised up,' and improved, drawing them away from less genteel and 'uncivilized' working class forms of entertainment. Victorian sensibilities were suffused with Christian morality, and in this period there was a keen vocation to educate and 'civilize' the masses, both at home and in their colonial territories overseas. The developing museum culture proved a useful mechanism for the transmission of these Victorian moral values, of hard work, Christian goodness, industry, and progress.

Legacy

The Great Exhibition was a huge success, attracting over six million visitors and generating a significant amount of unexpected profit (£186,000). This money was put to use in creating three permanent museums not far from the original Crystal Palace site, that could be used to house come of the exhibits: the Museum of Manufactures (later the Victoria and Albert Museum), the Natural History Museum, and the Science Museum. Prince Albert became an influential patron of this burgeoning museum culture, and the museum quarter of South Kensington remains a major tourist attraction in London to the present day. Proceeds from the exhibition were also used to fund research in science and engineering, creating an educational trust that continues to operate today.

The Crystal Palace itself was only ever designed to be a temporary structure, but after the success of the Exhibition, it was felt that the building should be relocated to a permanent site. After much deliberation, a plot was chosen on Sydenham Hill, near Penge. Although many of the same materials were used, the building was completely redesigned in a Beaux-Arts style with a new vaulted roof. In its new home, the Crystal Palace was the site for exhibitions, events, concerts, and plays, and it successfully attracted large crowds in its early years. However, the upkeep of the building proved too costly to sustain, and gradually it fell into a state of disrepair. In the aftermath of World War One, the Crystal Palace was temporarily reopened as the Imperial War Museum and then underwent a considerable renovation. However, in 1936, disaster struck: a fire broke out inside and consumed the entire building in just a few hours. With the cost of rebuilding prohibitively expensive, the story of the Crystal Palace came to an end.

The Great Exhibition was not without its critics, and many members of British elite society felt that it was a travesty and a waste to allow working class people entry to such a lavish display of culture. Many thought that the event would descend into a mob, causing violence and damage to the precious artifacts. From another perspective, theorists such as Karl Marx criticized the Exhibition as a triumph of commercialism, encouraging forms of consumer culture that would only serve to oppress the working classes. While this may be true, the Exhibition was unprecedented in fostering public education for the working classes and creating a museum culture that was based on the principle of accessibility and shared cultural heritage.

Ultimately, the Great Exhibition allowed Britain the opportunity to look at itself in the mirror. By gathering such a diverse and rich display of British and imperial material culture together in one space, the Exhibition allowed visitors to see, for the first time, their own identity as an imperial nation.

This burgeoning sense of identity would fuel the Victorian age, creating a sense of national pride and unity, and cementing a belief in the civilizing power of empire.

Sites to Visit

The Victoria and Albert Museum, South Kensington, London. This iconic building was constructed, along with the nearby Science Museum and the Natural History Museum, in order to permanently house some of the exhibits put on show in 1851. Development on this site was funded by the profits made on the Great Exhibition and represents an extension of Prince Albert's convictions regarding public education and the display of the material culture of the British Empire.

The Tower of London, Tower Hamlets, London. The Tower of London is the current home of the fabulous Koh-i-Noor diamond, which was featured at the exhibition. It is currently laid into the Queen Mother's crown and remains in the Jewel House in the Tower of London.

Hyde Park, Kensington, London. Visit the original site of the exhibition and the Crystal Palace, close to the Albert Memorial and Royal Albert Hall in Hyde Park.

Film and TV

Victoria and Albert, a 2001 BBC miniseries based on Queen Victoria's early life and marriage to Prince Albert, deals with the Great Exhibition and Albert's increasingly public role.

Further Research

- John Davis, The Great Exhibition, (Sutton, 1999). A useful introduction to the exhibition, with rich descriptions of the major displays and artifacts.
- Jonathon Shears (ed.), The Great Exhibition, 1851: A Sourcebook, (Manchester University Press, 2017). A useful introductory work focusing our sources of information about the exhibition.
- Heritage Hunter and Andrew Chapman, The Great Exhibition in Colour, (Prepare to Publish, 2016). This beautiful volume brings together a number of color illustrations of the Great Exhibition made by Victorian artists.

THE FIVER: CHRISTMAS NOVELS
By John Rabon

Christmastime is a perfect season for reading. With the cold weather, a good fire, and a mug of cocoa (or warming beverage of your choice), you can just curl up with a blanket and a good book. Plenty of works have been written about the Christmas season, and while some of the most influential, such as 'Twas the Night Before Christmas and The Grinch, were written by Americans, British authors have also put their indelible stamp on the holiday. Charles Dickens, through five different works essentially brought the holiday back to life and turned it into the celebration we know today.

The Snowman – Raymond Briggs

Unusual amongst the other works on this list in that this book doesn't have any words, The Snowman was published in 1978 as an illustrated children's book about a Snowman that comes to life. The Snowman and the boy who built him then have a magical adventure through the countryside before the Snowman melts in the morning. It was adapted into a cartoon and the song "Walking in the Air" from the special is constantly on stores' Christmas playlists.

A Star Over Bethlehem – Agatha Christie

While largely known for her mysteries and characters such as Hercule Poirot and Miss Marple, Agatha Christie was also a very religious person. Her religious beliefs come out largely in this collection of poems and short stories published as Agatha Christie Mallowan (her title, Lady Mallowan, earned from her second husband). The short stories vary from a donkey that witnesses the birth of Jesus to a London widow who encounters Jesus on a water taxi and has a profound experience. It's certainly worth reading for a better understanding of her abilities as a writer.

Letters from Father Christmas – J.R.R. Tolkien

Another author essentially known for one genre is J.R.R. Tolkien. Very different from his stories involving elves and hobbits, Letters from Father Christmas takes a page from his contemporary C.S. Lewis and imagines letters written from the supernatural spirit himself. Tolkien actually wrote the letters for his children between 1920 and 1942 as if they were from Father Christmas (or his chief elf secretary) to add to the holiday magic for them by relating stories that happened to Father Christmas. The letters were amongst Tolkien's posthumous works and show not only the full range of his writing but also the lengths he would go to for his family.

The Adventure of the Blue Carbuncle – Arthur Conan Doyle

Not really about Christmas, this Sherlock Holmes story by Arthur Conan Doyle is the only one of the great detective's cases that takes place during the holiday. In the days following Christmas, Watson visits Holmes, and the two become embroiled in the search for a missing jewel. After catching the villain in the story's conclusion, Holmes indulges in the holiday spirit to grant mercy on the thief. As with many Holmes stories, it's been adapted multiple times and might even be shown on TV around the season.

Dickens at Christmas – Charles Dickens

We couldn't get through this list without including at least one Dickens work, and if you can find this edition in print or on an e-reader, Dickens at Christmas is the book you need. Containing all five of his Christmas novels from A Christmas Carol to The Cricket on the Hearth, it also features several short stories (including "The Story of the Goblins Who Stole a Sexton" from The Pickwick Papers) that have helped to define the holiday for every generation since. It really is the most comprehensive collection of Dickens Christmas stories around and totally worth your money whether you get it at discount or pay full price.

EDVARDVS

EDWARD II
THE KING BETRAYED BY HIS WIFE

Ultimately a failure as a king, Edward II spent the majority of his reign battling with the baronial lords of the time who constantly rebelled and sought to gain power over the king and control of the country. Edward II incurred large debts during his years as King and oversaw the Scots' famous victory at Bannockburn by Robert the Bruce. Criticized for his habit of taking close personal friends and lavishly bestowing them with titles and wealth, Edward was constantly at odds with his nobles. Betrayed by his wife, in politics and matrimony, Edward was forced to renounce his throne to his son before dying a sad death while held captive at Berkeley Castle.

The fourth son of King Edward I and his first wife Eleanor of Castile, Edward II endured a childhood marked by loss. Eleanor of Castile was separated from Edward through the majority of his childhood and died when he was just six years old following an extended illness. Edward I was fighting in three countries over the next few years of young Edward's life. When Edward I remarried he focussed his time on his new family and rarely saw his other sons.

Raised by a dedicated Royal Household, Edward was given a religious education by Dominican friars. Edward enjoyed horse-riding and music but was criticized for his regular association with laborers and other members of the lower-class. An image of Edward as a somewhat shallow and irresponsible person took seed during his childhood years and set him on a course of hostility with his court that he would struggle with for the rest of his life.

During 1297 and 1298, Edward II was left as the acting regent of England while his father fought a campaign in Flanders against the French King Philip IV. As part of a peace treaty, Edward was betrothed to Isabella, King Phillip's daughter who was then only seven years old. Edward was taken to Scotland with his father in 1300 to command a division and was declared the Prince of Wales in 1301. The young prince was being groomed for a future as King.

According to some historians, the single most significant person in Edward's life was not his father, his wife or his priest but his childhood playmate Piers Gaveston. Piers was the son of a noble knight from Gascony and was brought to Edward's household as a companion to for

KEY FACTS

- Edward II was born on the 25th of April 1284 at Caernarvon.
- He succeeded to the English throne on 7th July 1307, aged 23 and became the King of England, Overlord of Ireland and Scotland and Duke of Aquitaine.
- Edward II was married in 1308 to Isabella of France, daughter of King Philip IV. Isabella was nicknamed the She-Wolf and after 19 years of marriage was instrumental in having Edward deposed and killed.
- Following his abdication from the throne and ten months of imprisonment, Edward II was killed on 22nd September 1327.

the young prince. Edward's life was filled with Gaveston, and contemporary chroniclers of royal lives have launched in-depth investigations into whether or not the pair were intimate. The details of the relationship remain unclear but in 1306 Gaveston was knighted by King Edward I a few days after the Feast of Swans before being promptly exiled by him in 1307.

Just one month after his father's death the newly crowned Edward II brought Galveston back from exile and made him the Earl of Cornwall, a title generally reserved for the royal family and married him to the wealthiest lady in the land, Margaret de Clare. As if that wasn't enough, Edward appointed Gaveston regent of England while he went to France for his wedding to 16-year-old Isabella of France. None of this was well-received by the English aristocracy. In fact, the special treatment given to young Galveston was so badly received by the aristocracy that Edward's own Council launched a revolt.

Thomas of Lancaster, a Marcher Lord who was in the enviable position of being a cousin to both the King and his new queen as well as holding five powerful earldoms, led the revolt against Edward. Within a year of his accession, Edward was forced by his Council to take the Earldom of Cornwall back from Gaveston and again sent him into exile.

In response, Edward appointed Gaveston as his Lord Lieutenant of Ireland, a move that further enraged the Barons.

Within one year Gaveston had returned to Edward's court thanks to Edward's efforts that involved a complicated game of favors that involved the Pope and the monarchy of France. When Gaveston's influence over government and excessive spending of the country's revenue got too much for the Barons, they forced the appointing of 21 Lord Ordainers who took over the management of the economy.

Tensions between the unpopular king and the barons remained high, and the earls opposed to the king, led by the powerful and wealthy Earl of Lancaster, kept their personal armies mobilized. In 1312 the barons had Galveston excommunicated by the Archbishop of Canterbury and seized him following a short siege. Accused of being a traitor, Gaveston was executed.

The storm clouds parted for just a moment to welcome Edward and Isabella's first child into the world, a son who would go on to become Edward III, but soon things got even worse for the unhappy king. In 1314, seven years into his reign Edward came up against Robert the Bruce in the Battle of Bannockburn and suffered a defeat that gained Scotland its independence. It would take three centuries for the English to recover this loss and the huge debts left by Edward's Scottish campaign made him even more unpopular with the people.

In the tense time that followed the loss of Scotland, Lancaster was able to insert himself as the leader of the Lord Ordainers, effectively the leader of the formal government of England. Excluded and despised Edward turned to his friends, most notably the Lord le Depenser and his son, who he pampered with favors and titles, just as he had pampered Gaveston.

The Earl of Lancaster and Roger de Mortimer, Earl of March formed a powerful enough alliance to wage war with the king and a civil war ensued. The le Depensers were banished, but Edward managed to capture both Lancaster and Mortimer. Lancaster was executed, and Mortimer was held in the Tower of London. By now it was known to all that Edward's wife Isabella was having an affair with Mortimer. In 1323, Isabella took matters into her own hands, contriving Mortimer's escape from the Tower into France and following with her son Edward III, heir to the English throne.

In September 1326, the ambitious trio landed in Suffolk with an army and declared the young prince-governor of the country. With no army and no support from his people Edward II was easily captured, his companions the le Depensers were hanged, and he was imprisoned in Kenilworth to await his fate. After being forced to abdicate by a representative delegation of barons, clergy and knights who agreed that Edward II was unfit to lead the country, his son Edward III was proclaimed King of England at Westminster Abbey on 20 January 1327.

Conveniently, Edward II died in custody on 21st September. Little is known about the circumstances of his death, but it is thought that Mortimer likely arranged for his murder. Mortimer's dominance did not last long, however. He and Isabella soon fell out of favor with the populace as they amassed and spent a huge fortune and in 1330, King Edward III initiated a coup d'etat, arresting and executing Mortimer on charges of treason. But that's the story of a different king.

Legacy

King Edward II's legacy is not a particularly glorious one. Unpopular with his baronial lords, his court and his people, Edward's reign was primarily spent avoiding his duties and king and buying the affection of his so-called 'favourites.' A dismal reign, Edward's time on the throne saw English defeat at the Battle of Bannockburn. Much writing on Edward II following his death has focussed on his relationship with Piers Gaveston and alluding to his possible homosexuality. An unpopular and inadequate king, Edward II was nonetheless a source of fascination, particularly to the Victorians who learned about his life from the likes of Charles Dickens and Charles Knight.

Film and TV

- Braveheart (1995)
- Marlowe (1991)
- Edward II (1991)
- Edward II (1970) (TV Movie)
- Edward II (1982) (TV Movie)

Warwick Castle

Further Research

- Mortimer, Ian, and Warner, Kathryn (2015) Edward II: The Unconventional King
- Jones, Dan (2013) The Plantagenets
- Phillips, Seymour (2011) Edward II (The English Monarchs Series)
- Doherty, Paul (2004). Isabella and the Strange Death of Edward II
- Haines, Roy Martin (2003). King Edward II: His Life, his Reign, and its Aftermath
- Merritt, Stephanie (2002) Gaveston (fiction)
- Hunt, Chris (1992) Gaveston (fiction)
- Pentford, John (1984) The Gascon (fiction)

Locations to Visit

- Caerphilly Castle, the place Edward II spent his last weeks in hiding.
- Warwick Castle, the location where Piers Gaveston was tried and killed.
- Bannockburn, the place England was defeated by the Scots under Robert the Bruce during Edward II's reign.
- Edward II's place of death, Berkeley Castle in Gloucestershire, UK
- Edward II's place of burial, Gloucester Cathedral in Gloucestershire, UK.

Top 10 British Christmas Carols

By John Rabon

One of the best parts of the holiday season (or the worst, depending on your perspective), is the singing of Christmas carols. Carols have a very specific definition of being a song or hymn that related to Christmas, and there are many out there both religious and secular. Their themes range from retelling the story of the nativity to espousing the goodwill of the season. Chances are if you sing Christmas carols, you'll recognize one of the ten below, all of British origin.

I Saw Three Ships (Come Sailing In)

A traditional English carol, "I Saw Three Ships" reportedly dates back to 17th-Century Derbyshire when it was first printed, though it wasn't published officially until 1833 by a solicitor named William Sandys. One of the interesting aspects of the song is that it talks about the ships sailing into Bethlehem, which is many miles from any body of water.

God Rest You, Merry Gentlemen

Dating back to the 16th Century (and possibly earlier), the song is one of the oldest carols around, and the earliest printed edition was done in 1760. In the carol, the singer reminds the listener that there is no reason for despair because the birth of Christ means the triumph of good over evil. The song gets a reference in Charles Dickens's A Christmas Carol as Ebenezer Scrooge chases off a caroler singing it in front of his counting house.

The Holly and the Ivy

Greenery in Christmas decorations was inherited from Pagan celebrations, and for Christmas, the evergreens came to symbolize the eternal life offered by Jesus Christ. A traditional Christmas hymn, "The Holly and the Ivy" is replete with similar symbolism, describing the holly as bearing the crown and the berry as red as Christ's blood.

Sans Day Carol

A traditional Cornish piece, "Sans Day Carol" (or "Saint Day Carol") was written in the 19th Century. Like many, it describes the birth of Jesus and also incorporates the symbolism of the holly. The lyrics specifically compare holly berries at their various stages of life to Jesus at his birth, during his life, and his death on the cross.

O Come, All Ye Faithful

There seems to be some speculation on who this hymn's original author was (including King John IV of Portugal), but at least two of the supposed authors, John Reading and John Francis Wade, are English. The hymn was originally four verses, but later expanded to six, and exalts the virtues of Christ while also describing the Wise Men's journey to visit the young Jesus.

Good King Wenceslas

"Good King Wenceslas" is one of those great carols that describes the spirit of Christmas, and in this case, specifically charity to the poor. In it, lyricist John Mason Neale retells the story of the Bohemian King Wenceslas who goes out on the Feast of St. Stephen (December 25, the Second Day of Christmas) to give alms to the poor. Wenceslaus, in reality, was a 10th Century Duke whose martyrdom gave birth to a Cult of Wenceslaus in Bohemia and England. He was later venerated and posthumously made a king.

Here We Come A-wassailing

"Wassailing" is actually the action of going door-to-door singing carols wishing good health. It doubles as both a Christmas and New Year's song as the lyrics make reference to both holidays. In the past, it also referred to a drink made of ale, apples, spices, and mead that the house would offer to the carolers to help them keep warm.

The First Noel

Also known as "The First Nowell," is another Cornish hymn, this one published in 1823 as another edited work of William Sandys. The song's lyrics describe the Annunciation to the Shepherds and the Adoration of the Shepherds as well as the journey of the Magi. The hymn has an unusual melody amongst English folk songs in that it repeats a musical phrase and is followed by a musical refrain that varies the phrase.

Deck the Halls

One of the most festive holiday songs, the melody for "Deck the Halls" dates back to 16th Century Wales while the lyrics were written by Scotsman Thomas Oliphant in 1862. There are a few variants of the lyrics, and the one known to most Americans is quite different than the original, which describes the merry drinking that goes on during the holiday as decorations are hung.

Hark, the Herald Angels Sing

While the original tune was by German composer Felix Mendelssohn, everything else about this song is decidedly English. Charles Wesley wrote the lyrics in 1739 and originally intended for his words to be married to slow and solemn music, but musician William H. Cummings had other ideas. Cummings adapted Mendelsshon's "Festgesang" to Wesley's lyrics and gave birth to a Christmas classic that is a favorite of choirs all over the United Kingdom.

CHRISTMAS SHOPPING IN LONDONTOWN

By John Rabon

Covent Garden

Shopping can be a wonderful and hectic activity during Christmastime even in London. Of course, the city's shopping centers, markets, and high streets offer plenty of options for Christmas gifts along with decorations galore. If you happen to be in London during the holiday season, we hope you'll consider one of these ten shopping destinations that are full of Christmas cheer and presents for your friends and family.

Westfield London

Americans in London might find some home comforts in Westfield London shopping center, a destination similar to many American shopping malls. Westfield does it up during the holidays not only with decorations but craft-making events such as Christmas paper and wreath making worships and Santa's Snowflake Grotto. There is also an ice skating rink on site and plenty of places to eat and shop to get into the holiday spirit.

Spirit of Christmas Fair

A great place for Christmas gifts, the Spirit of Christmas Fair in Olympia features of host of independent boutiques and craft makers selling unique holiday items. The food hall and foot court also have an array of food and drink of the season, while the Home & Garden workshops give you a chance to make some of your own special Christmas presents.

Christmas by the River

Hosted each year at London City Bridge, Christmas by the River is one of London's top Christmas markets. Little wooden cabins sell anything from bespoke Christmas gifts to food and drink of many countries' Christmas celebrations. The market goes along the Queen's Walk from Hay's Galleria to The Scoop at More London. With stunning views of Tower Bridge in the distance, it's definitely a place to visit during the holidays.

Bond Street

Full of high-end designer shops, Bond Street is a top shopping area of London. And while it didn't make our list of some of the top places for Christmas Decorations in London, it still has a dazzling display of holiday lights that you'll want to visit. Last year's display featured peacock lights, and it remains to be seen what spectacular decorations are in store for this year.

Southbank Centre's Wintertime Market

Another riverside Christmas market, the Wintertime Market at Southbank Centre is part of the area's winter festival. As with Christmas by the River, Wintertime Market features a number of chalet-like retailer booths selling Christmas goodies and food and drink, such as mulled wine. The Bar Under the Bridge is a great spot to visit, featuring a menu full of cheese-themed dishes.

Covent Garden

Variety is the Christmas spice of life at Covent Garden. Unlike the more high-end retail of Bond Street, Covent Garden features a mix of shops that cater to all tastes along with dining establishments and three pop-up markets that offer everything from antiques to hand-made items. If you do read our article about Christmas decorations, you'll know it's also one of the best places to take in the holiday lights.

Selfridges

One of London's best department stores, Selfridges is the place that coined the phrase "the customer is always right." As such, in addition to the numerous items you can find throughout the year to satisfy your loved ones' desires, Selfridges also opens up its Christmas shop for the holiday featuring personalized items and Christmas decorations galore. The store doesn't skimp on its own decorations either, so be sure t take a look at the ornamentation inside the shop as well as its display windows.

Clockwise: Harrods, Winter Wonderland, Southbank Centre, Selfridges

Angel's Market at Winter Wonderland

Winter Wonderland is a wonderful carnival that takes place every year in Hyde Park, and the Angel's Market is a magical shopping experience in the middle of all the rides, food, and performances. The market shops focus heavily on English and German crafts and gifts while offering a great number of crafts from artisans. It's also one of the largest Christmas markets in the city, so it's a definite must visit when you consider everything else Winter Wonderland has to offer.

Oxford Street

Perhaps the best shopping street in London, it's also one of the busiest at any given time of year and definitely is at Christmas. It has over 300 shops, outlets, and stores (including the previously mentioned Selfridges). It's also got one of the best Christmas lights displays in the entire city, which are bound to put you in the holiday spirit as you look for presents.

Harrods

With the motto "All things for all people, everywhere," Harrods is a number one shopping destination year-round. This goes double for the holiday season, with decorations that will make you think Harrods is secretly Santa's workshop. Harrods hosts its own Christmas shop, and there's a Christmas Grotto where kids can visit Father Christmas. Beyond the dazzling selection of gifts, the store's Christmas window displays are a highlight of the city's holiday decorations. Needless to say, whatever you need for your Christmas experience, you're bound to find it at Harrods.

THE AA
Britain's Automobile Association

AA Service Box in Loch Ness

With their distinctive patrol vehicles and motoring guides, the Automobile Association is a British institution dating back to the earliest days of motor cars in the UK. Early drivers faced many hazards – uncertain mechanical reliability, a lack of road signs, poorly built roads, and police eager to catch speeding drivers for the revenue it brought in to their town. Beginning as a bicycle patrol to warn drivers of speed-traps, in the more than 100 years since it was formed the AA has evolved as motors cars and driving have evolved. What began with three men on bicycles grew into a full emergency service for drivers, with mobile mechanics, guides to repair shops, hotels, and overseas travel. It also offers insurance and financial services. The yellow vans and motorbikes remain a feature of driving the roads of Britain, and its distinctive 'AA approved' logo is seen everywhere.

Since people first began to drive motor cars, they have taken a unique view of traffic regulations. Otherwise, law-abiding citizens often consider them nothing more than a nuisance and attempt to avoid penalties where ever possible. It was out of that attitude that the Automobile Association was formed in 1905. Just a few years earlier, in 1896, speed limits on cars had been raised to 14 mph, from the earlier 2 or 4 mph limits. Car manufacturing in the UK was still in its infancy, but Herbert Austin had just recently opened the first factory of Wolseley Motors Limited in Birmingham.

A new Traffic Act came into force in 1903, establishing vehicle registration; drivers licenses (although no test was required); braking ability requirements; the new crime of reckless driving; and a new speed limit of 20 mph. The imposition of a speed limit caused bitter debates in Parliament, with many groups and individuals opposed to any limit at all. Considerable hostility built up, well summarized by Lord Montagu of Beaulieu, when, in 1907, he addressed the House of Lords:

"Policemen are not stationed in the villages where there are people about who might be in danger, but are hidden in hedges or ditches by the side of the most open roads in the country In my opinion ..speed traps.. are manifestly absurd as a protection to the public, and they are used in many counties merely as a means of extracting money from the passing traveler in a way which reminds one of the highwaymen of the Middle Ages."

KEY FACTS

- Began in 1905 with three bicycle patrolmen warning of speed traps
- Today has 10 million members across the UK
- Mobile mechanics in distinctive yellow vans help motorists who have broken down
- Publishes definitive guides to hotels, restaurants, car repair and travel

So it was perhaps not surprising that in June 1905, Charles Jarrott, a car dealer, organized a meeting at the Lyons' Trocadero Restaurant on Shaftesbury Avenue, London, to plan an escape from the oppression of police speed-traps. Initially calling themselves 'The Motorists' Mutual Association', but almost immediately changing their name to the Automobile Association, this new group began by recruiting a motorcyclist and three pedal cyclists to ride the roads and warn motorists of speed-traps they were approaching. At first, they only worked on weekends, without a uniform, and patrolled the roads to Brighton and Portsmouth. The cyclists, skilled at judging speeds, waved red flags at drivers they judged to be driving over the speed limit. The service proved popular with motorists, and from an initial membership of 100, the Association had 14,000 members by 1914, supported by a thousand cycle patrolmen, who were issued with uniforms in 1909. Their official duties were described as indicating dangers on the road and helping motorists who have broken down.

In 1906 the AA set up a legal defense fund for its members and a year later partnered with Lloyds of London to offer vehicle insurance, at no profit to the AA. With the rapid growth of car ownership, touring by car had become a widespread habit, so a process for approving repair businesses was developed. 1908 saw the publication of the first AA Members' Special Handbook, which listed agents and car repairers, who in turn were able to display the distinctive AA logo.

The following year hotels began to be listed in the handbook. The first AA Secretary, Stenson Cooke, had previously been a wine and spirit salesman, so in devising a system to classify hotels, he turned to the 'star' method used for brandy and started issuing stars to hotels based on their quality and facilities. To ensure independence, and to give confidence in the system to their members, all hotel inspectors paid for their rooms, and they were never allowed to accept any favors from hoteliers.

In 1911 the patrolmen changed from directly warning drivers of speed traps to a more subtle approach, to avoid accusations of interfering with the execution of Police duties. From now on the patrolman would always salute when passing a car bearing an AA badge – except when they knew there was a speed trap. The member's handbook advised drivers to 'stop and ask the reason' why they had not been saluted. Road traffic legislation in 1929 and 1930 eventually removed the 20 mph speed limit, but the practice of saluting continued until 1962, when patrolmen moved from motorcycles to driving Minivans.

With motoring still in its infancy, local village and town councils did not consider road signs their responsibility, so the AA began putting up road signs of their own, indicating places, mileages and road hazards. This continued until 1939 when it became the legal responsibility of local authorities. During these early years, there was also an interest in touring the Continent and items on conditions in the countries immediately across the Channel appeared in the handbooks as early as 1908. Today the AA runs a full travel service.

Copying the recently introduced Police telephone boxes, the AA began to install their own phone boxes, for use by their patrolmen, in 1912. Over time almost 1,000 boxes were installed, of which just 19 remain today.

During WWI AA members were actively encouraged to donate their cars for war service, and a number were converted into field ambulances and used on the Western Front, in France. The 8th (Cyclist) Battalion of the Essex Regiment was formed, with over 100 members drawn for the AA bicycle patrolmen.

By 1920 membership had reached 100,000, and in the hard economic times following the war years, the government encouraged motorists to use benzole manufactured from British coal tar to replace the more expensive imported petrol. However the distribution of this material was very poor, so the AA stepped in and opened fuel stations stocking benzole. It was 1932 before petrol distributors copied them, at which point the AA closed their stations. In the 1920's patrolmen began to use a combination motorbike with a side-car, equipped with tools and spare parts for repairs and by 1938 there were 1,500 on the road, as well as 850 bicycle patrols. By the outbreak of WWII, there were 2 million cars on the roads, and 750,000 of them were members of the AA.

Following WWII there was petrol rationing, which the AA campaigned to have lifted, succeeding by 1950 – three years before the end of sugar rationing. Using war-time developments in two-way radios, a night-time emergency call service was introduced in 1949. With Prince Philip now the patron of the Association, they were charged with organizing signage, parking and traffic control for the coronation of Queen Elizabeth in 1953. In 1967 they AA returned to the insurance business, following the collapse of several low-priced car insurance businesses – insurance remains a significant AA function, as does banking, with AA Savings being a significant presence in the financial services industry.

There are today over 10 million members in the AA, and the road-side repair service uses GPS positioning and computerized diagnostics to help motorists who have broken down. Cell phone apps keep a driver in touch with AA patrols. In recent years the association has branched out into a home emergency service, with a list of approved plumbers, heating engineers and other household services. It also engages in political campaigning for the rights of motorists and for road safety, through its independent charity called the AA Charitable Trust.

Sites to Visit

Unfortunately, the collection of about 30 vintage AA vehicles and bikes still in existence is in the hands of private and AA-associated collectors. Although sometimes shown at various events around the country, there is no central display of them that can be easily visited.

Of the 19 AA phone boxes still existing, eight

Old AA Road Map

are listed buildings, protected from removal. They are scattered across England, Scotland and Wales, but the closest to London is perhaps the 530 Brancaster, Norfolk box, which can be found on the A149 (running between Hunstanton-Wells), around 300 meters west of the junction with Common Lane, in Brancaster Staithe, Norfolk.

GREAT BRITISH ICONS: BRITISH RAIL

By David Goodfellow

Gloucestershire Warwickshire Steam Railway

The early history of rail transport in Britain was one of private enterprise. Using a network largely created during the stock-market bubble of railway companies in the 1840s, many private lines developed. By the 1920s these were merged into the Big Four – regional networks that monopolized the railways. At the end of WWII, a socialist government under Clement Attlee brought the system under central government control. After some initial success British Rail, as it was called, came into competition with road transport, and consistently lost money. British Rail moved rail transport from the age of steam into the age of electricity and diesel, but in 1962 the network was gutted, when thousands of miles of track and thousands of small stations were closed by a government hostile to both rail transport and nationalized industry. After the Thatcher years of privatization, British Rail was returned to private hands in 1993. The result has been a broken system, with high fares, bad service, and continuing losses.

British Rail was born on the 1st of January 1948, and it had been a long and difficult birth. The railway network had been the creation of many private companies, starting with the first passenger-carrying public railway, which used horse-drawn carriages, and opened at Oystermouth in 1807. The invention of the steam engine led to more and more lines being built, culminating in the 1840's with Railway Mania, a speculative share bubble of hundreds of companies promising to build railways. The bubble burst, as they all do, but it left a legacy of over six thousand miles of track, the backbone for a viable railway network. Without it, the development of the subsequent private railway system would probably have been impossible, since most economists consider railways a natural monopoly, where the cost of the supporting system – the track - precludes its duplication by a rival firm.

In the system that did develop, each company owned a fragment of the network, but this made profit-making difficult, and the companies were constantly failing. During WWI the government took control of the total system, for the war effort. Immediate improvements and efficiencies were seen, and in an attempt to preserve them, the post-war government passed the Railways Act of 1921, commonly called the Grouping Act. The 120 companies in existence at the time were grouped into four regional behemoths – Great Western

KEY FACTS

- Created in 1948 by the nationalization of private operators
- Privatized in 1993, returning to a network of private companies
- Controversial and politically-charged history
- Strong public support in the UK for re-nationalization

Railway; London and North Eastern Railway; Southern Railway; and the London, Midland and Scottish Railway. Some small lines were excluded, and so was the London Underground, which was already in public hands.

In theory, these companies should have been successful – they had a monopoly in their region and could charge fares that would return a profit. But that didn't happen. Road transport was growing fast, and the government built roads for lorries but didn't pay for the long-overdue improvements to the railway tracks. The Big Four, as the railways were known, complained of unfair competition, and the result was increased taxation of road vehicles. Still, the system and the railways entered a slow decline.

There were ideological factors at play too. The 19th and early-20th centuries were a time of social upheaval, as working people struggled for a larger share of the productivity of the nation. Trade Unions and political parties supporting the ideals of socialism grew steadily, and in 1900 the 'broad church' of the Labour Party united many smaller socialist movements under one roof. By the 1920s it had become the main opposition party, overtaking the older Liberal Party and challenging the Tory conservatives for power. Nationalization – the taking under government control of private businesses, especially natural monopolies – was a cornerstone of socialist thinking and official Labour Party policy.

Many outsiders were surprised to see Winston Churchill, the charismatic leader of the British people against Nazi Germany, thrown out of government even before the barrels of the guns had cooled. Germany officially surrendered on May 8, 1945, and a General Election was held on

July 5. Clement Attlee, leader of the Labour Party and deputy prime minister during the war, saw an unprecedented 12% swing to his party, and Labour formed the first post-war government. High on their radical, socialist agenda, alongside the creation of a free-to-user public health system (the NHS), was the complete nationalization of all transport, from railways and trucking to ports, shipping, and buses. There was a staunch determination from the returning soldiers and their families that the fruits of victory should fall to them, and not to the Conservative Party, whose main goal was to restore the status quo.

Attlee's government soon lived up to its pledges, and the Transport Act of 1947 included the complete take-over by the government of the Big Four – who had effectively already been united under wartime controls. The new entity was christened British Rail. The system was divided into six geographic regions, and its first priority was to restore the rail network itself – badly damaged by bombing – and to improve and extend the rolling stock. By the early 1950s, British Rail was making a small profit.

A new challenge faced the system when the Conservatives were returned to power in 1951. They promptly privatized road transport, which soon became a significant rival for rail, with its ability to deliver door to door. Another new development, air transport operating with the many surplus planes left from the war, competed for speed, and British Rail's newly-won profits evaporated. European railways had modernized in the post-war years, converting from coal-powered steam to electric and diesel. Attlee, as well as British Rail's Chief Engineer, wanted to continue with coal and steam, mainly because the country had no money to import oil, and the coal miners were a key element of the support for Labour. Almost 1,500 new steam locomotives had been ordered by 1953. At the end of 1954 the government published a report – Modernisation and Re-Equipment of the British Railways – to bring the system up to date, and to make it profitable again.

The plan had good intentions, but only limited success. Some lines were electrified, and there was a major conversion from steam to diesel, but a diversity of locomotives was bought, which raised maintenance costs. There was a focus on single-car freight hauling, at a time when this was shifting to roads. Worse, BR was trapped in a legal requirement to carry any and all goods, at standard published rates, so they often carried cargo at a loss. Road haulers were not bound by this, and they could refuse unprofitable loads. Although this issue had been identified by the Big Four in the 1930s, it was 1962 before the law was changed to allow BR freedom of contract, so that they could refuse unprofitable work.

By 1962 BR was losing more and more money – its loss that year was equivalent to £2 billion today. The Conservative government of the day appointed a businessman, not a railwayman, to cut costs. This was Richard Beeching, controversially paid a high salary to do the job, he produced the Beeching Report in 1963. His plan was to cut 5,000 miles of track and close 2,363 small stations. Most of this was done, without regard to the societal impact on small communities, which was severe. The Transport Minister at the time, Ernest Marples, was closely involved in road transport and owned 80% of a road construction business, so the belief continues that he was not impartial in his handling of railway transport. Less controversially, this period also saw the formal branding of the railway as 'British Rail,' the adoption of the blue color for trains, and the use of the 'double-arrow' logo.

The 1970s saw the arrival of high-speed diesel, with the InterCity 125 High-Speed Train (HST). What would have been the world's first tilting train – able to lean around bends, and so travel faster; the Advanced Passenger Train (APT) – was thwarted by politics and a premature release, and never came to pass.

By the 1980s the rolling stock was aging, and again the replacement was a mixture of successes and failures. British Rail abolished the regional sections, and instead separated passenger service from freight, creating several specialized areas. Costs were still high, and fares rose much faster than general prices during this period, pushing more passengers onto the roads and to bus transport. The nationalized service remained a battleground of conflicting politics, but surprisingly Prime Minister Thatcher gave limited support to expansion and improvements. She did, however, carry out some privatization, peeling off the Railway Hotels, and handing them to private owners. She was certainly not shy in other areas, and her period in power saw most of Britain's nationalized industries handed over to private ownership.

It was up to her successor, John Major, to end the railway nationalization of the post-war socialists. With the Railway Act of 1993, this was achieved. But how should it be done? BR wanted to remain a single unit, others wanted a return to the Big Four, and the Treasury proposed reverting back even earlier, creating 25 passenger railway franchises. This was the decision taken, and over 100 separate companies emerged from British Rail.

Most agree that the privatization has not been a success. Government subsidies in one form or another continue to prop up the private owners, most noticeably Virgin Rail, owned by Richard Branson. The service is plagued by breakdowns and poor-quality carriages, and the fares are 5 to 6 times those of nationalized railways in Europe. Temporary re-nationalization has been done with some failed private lines by the current Conservative government, and complete re-nationalization remains official Labour Party policy. Under Labour's present leadership it could well come to pass if Labour returns to power. Nationalization remains the preference of a large majority of the public.

Sites to Visit

- The National Railway Museum is on Leeman Road, York, North Yorkshire.
- Shildon Locomotion Museum is in Shildon, County Durham.
- Numerous other local museums across the country preserve local stations, facilities, locomotives, and rolling stock. https://en.wikipedia.org/wiki/List_of_railway_museums_in_the_United_Kingdom

Further Research

- British Rail: The Nation's Railway, by Tanya Jackson
- Inside British Rail: Challenges and Progress on the Nationalised Railway, 1970s-1990s, by Stephen Poole
- British Rail Designed 1948-1997, by David Lawrence
- The Times History of Britain's Railways: From 1603 to the Present Day, by Julian Holland
- Railway Day Trips: 160 classic train journeys around Britain, by Julian Holland

THE SLANG PAGE
British Medical Terms

A&E - *n* - Accident and Emergency, what Americans would call the Emergency Room.

Antenatal - *adj* - Prenatal care.

Anti-Histamines - *n* - Allergy/hayfever medication.

Bairn - *n* - Another word for baby, usually used in Scotland, but also common in the north of England – particularly in Newcastle.

British Medical Association (The BMA) - *abbr* - The main association and trade union representing Doctor's in the United Kingdom. They also publish the British Medical Journal, the main publication for new medical research in Britain.

Boss Eyed – *adj* – Crossed Eyed.

Care Home – *n* – Nursing home.

Casualty Department – *n* – The emergency room or the A&E.

Chemist - *n* - Pharmacist but it should be noted they can also provide simple medical advice without having to go to a doctor.

Chunder - *v* - To vomit.

Fit - *v* - A seizure of epileptic fit.

GP - *n* - General Practitioner - your regular family doctor.

Harley St – *n* – Street in London where private Doctors practice – usually expensive and exclusive, not part of the NHS.

National Insurance – *n* – Government mandated insurance system, equivalent would be Social Security in the USA. Also pays for the National Health Service.

NHS – *abbr* – National Health Service. Britain's nationalized health system.

Paracetamol - *n* - The British equivalent to Tylenol.

Plaster - *n* - A band-aid.

PMT – *abbr* - How British women refer to PMS - short acronym for Premenstrual tension.

Poorly - *n*- A way to describe someone not feeling well.

Sectioned - *v* - To be committed to a mental health facility against your will.

Sick - *n* - The standard term for vomit or to throw up. "Oh man, I'm covered in sick."

Sickie - *n* - To take a day off of work or school but not actually be sick.

Social Care - *n* - Official term that covers the old age care of the elderly in Britain, covers care homes and the funding needed to care for Britain's older population.

Spastic - *n* - A very insulting and derogatory term for someone who is mentally challenged.

Sticking plaster - *n* - A band-aid.

STI - *abbr* - Sexually Transmitted Infections, the British use this instead of STD.

Struck off – *v* – To be disbarred or lose a professional license. Do not see a Doctor who has been struck off!

Surgery – *n* - 1. Doctor's or Dentist's office. 2. When an MP meets with his/her constituents.

Ulcer – *n* - Canker sore.

www.ingramcontent.com/pod-product-compliance
Lightning Source LLC
Chambersburg PA
CBHW061118010526
44112CB00024B/2902